2022 edition

THE REAL SKINNY GUIDE TO

THE TOP 22 COUNTRIES TO RETIRE TO

CONTENTS

INTRODUCTION / ABOUT THIS BOOK iii

ASIA
Cambodia 3
Indonesia 17
Malaysia 31
Philippines 45
Thailand 61
Vietnam 75

CENTRAL AND SOUTH AMERICA
Belize 91
Colombia 105
Costa Rica 119
Ecuador 133
Mexico 147
Panama 161
Peru 175
Puerto Rico 189

EUROPE
Croatia 205
France 219
Italy 233
Malta 249
Portugal 263
Spain 277

MIDDLE EAST AND AFRICA
South Africa 293
Turkey 307

Index 324
About the Real Skinny Guides 328
The Authors 328
Credits and Acknowledgements 329

ABOUT THIS BOOK

Why write a book about the top countries in the world to retire to? Why publish during a global pandemic and why publish it specifically for the Australian market?

Consider these facts:

- ★ According to the Australian Bureau of Statistics, as at May 2020, there were 3.9 million retirees in Australia, 55% of people over 55 were retired, and half a million people intend to retire within 5 years.

- ★ The average age Australians intend to retire is 65.5 years, with about 4.2 million of us intending to retire in the next 15 years.

- ★ According to studies, for a comfortable retirement, single people need $545,000 in retirement savings and couples will need $640,000. These figures presuppose that the retirees own their homes outright.

- ★ Australia's skyrocketing house prices, however, mean that home ownership is next to impossible for anyone under 35.

- ★ It is clear that many Australians will still be paying a mortgage by the time they retire and will not have saved the required amounts to ensure a comfortable retirement.

- ★ According to several media reports, the majority of Australians are worried about retirement.

Yes, Australia is still a wealthy country and it is still a great country to live in. And for the most part, it is still a good country to retire in – *if you can afford it.* But many Australians will find that by the time they decide to retire at age 65, they will either have not saved enough to fund their retirement or not own their home outright. And the aged pension they will receive is hardly enough to allow them to sustain the comfortable lifestyle that they have been accustomed to during their working years.

This is why, for more and more Australians, retiring abroad has become a desirable option. And thanks to the availability of information through the internet, advances in mobile communication and logistics, retiring abroad has become a *feasible* option.

Consider these other facts:

- ★ English is widely spoken and understood by almost everyone throughout the Philippines (see page 47) and in Cambodia, English is actually the second language of the country (see page 4). So communicating with the locals here is a breeze!

- ★ Thailand has top-notch, accessible and reasonably priced health care: for example you can get a full dental cleaning done here for only AUD $45 and while a complete health check-up only costs AUD 151 (see page 64).

- ★ Belize, a lush, tropical Caribbean paradise nation, has the best retiree program – you only need to be at least 45 years old (not 65 like in other countries) to obtain permanent residency status there (see page 95).

- ★ Croatia is one of the safest countries in the world to live in and life here moves at a relaxed pace (see page 206).

- ★ If you think retiring in France is out of your budget, think again: cheap real estate is sprouting everywhere, and you can buy retirement villas in rural areas for as low as AUD$164,000 (see page 221).

- ★ Retiring in Italy is both feasible and desirable: healthcare here is excellent and cheap, its regional cities are among the most beautiful in the world, and it has, quite simply, the finest cuisine in the world (see page 234).

- ★ Portugal is blessed with 300 days of sunshine every year, has some of the best beaches in Europe and vibrant cities packed with restaurants, cafes and museums, and has some of the kindest and most compassionate people you'll be fortunate to mee (see page 264).

Each country mentioned in the list above, and indeed, every country that is featured in this book, has attributes – its culture, low cost of living, climate, food, level of English spoken by its population, and so on – that make it a good option to consider for overseas retirement for Australians.

Retiring overseas can be an exciting, fulfilling and richly rewarding experience. We hope this book helps you make that happen.

ASIA

Phnom Penh, Cambodia

Retire in Cambodia

Reasons to Retire in Cambodia

If living better for less is your idea of retirement, then Cambodia is one of your top choices in Asia. It has been a popular tourist destination because of the world-famous Angkor Wat. At the same time, the country's recent development efforts have made it one of the best places for foreign retirees to thrive in.

Cambodia has different kinds of settings and atmospheres – from colonial cities to ancient temple grounds and pristine islands. If you are a history lover, the country offers up its traditions and traditional architecture. Foreigners enjoy the laid-back tropical lifestyle while others choose to relocate here for professional and business reasons.

With English as its second language, it will not be difficult to navigate around the major cities. Plus, the locals have that friendly "Khmer smile" that will make your stay worthwhile. Over the years, there have been around 100,000 expatriates who became permanent residents in the country. This explains the variety of international restaurants sprouting throughout the major cities. Another reason why people choose to retire in Cambodia is its most flexible and accessible long-term residence visa. The country recently launched the ER visa, which is the stepping stone to a 12-month multiple entry visa.

Using USD as the de facto currency has made the economy more stable over the past years. In fact, it is one of the fastest-growing economies in the world because there have been a lot of foreign investments in the country, covering all major industries from agriculture to tourism.

Why Retire in Cambodia:

★ A country rich in history, traditions, and culture.
★ English is the second language of the country.
★ Despite using USD as the de facto currency, the cost of living remains low.
★ Tropical, laidback lifestyle.

Cambodia has some similarities with its neighbouring countries Laos, Thailand and Vietnam when it comes to culture and tradition. The majority practice Buddhism, with a good number of Christian and Muslim minorities harmoniously residing here.

Cambodians are known for their positive attitude despite the tumultuous history they bear. Life is also centred on family and food. You will find big families sticking together with great respect for their elderly. During festivities, everyone gathers, even if it means cramped quarters.

It may not be necessary to learn the local language as the locals can speak English, especially in the big cities where tourists frequent. However, in retiring here, you will need to know at least the sompiah, or the traditional Cambodian greeting that involves pressing the hands together like in a prayer, followed by a bow. To show more respect, put your hands a little higher and bow a little lower.

Climate

With its location overlooking the Gulf of Thailand, Cambodia enjoys a tropical climate. It is hot all year round, with the rainy season to watch out for from June to October. The cool-dry season starts from the end of November to February while the hot-dry season covers March to May.

The regional monsoon season helps cool things down with rainfall tending to arrive in the afternoon, then continuing for a couple of hours. This helps in making sure that the country's rice fields are fertile and forests lush. The best time for travellers is from November to February, when it is possible to walk around leisurely and enjoy what Cambodia has to offer.

Cambodia is rarely hit by typhoons because those would usually veer north, hitting Vietnam and Laos first. Upon hitting Cambodia, a storm would eventually weaken. The tropical cyclones will still bring heavy rains that would cause flooding between October and November.

Cost of Living

A dollar goes a long way in Cambodia, making the country affordable for many foreign retirees. One can get high quality service for less. For example, a tailored shirt and pants will not cost more than AUD 47.30.

The cost of living per couple can start from AUD 1,351 per month. That price can increase to AUD 2,703, if you prefer to live more comfortably by eating every day at restaurants and travelling around the country.

Expenses	Prices
Rent (two-bedroom apartment in Phnom Penh)	AUD 676
High-speed internet	AUD 27
Electricity and water	AUD 135
Phone with basic data plan	AUD 13.50
Loaf of white bread	AUD 2
A dozen eggs	AUD 2.15
Local beer	AUD 1.35
Tuk tuk cost	AUD 2.70 - 4.05

Housing

Rent is cheap in Cambodia. It is possible to rent an apartment in the capital Phnom Penh with only AUD 411 per month. If you prefer to live in a serviced apartment, you can find a one-

bedroom with access to the pool, gym and cleaning service at AUD 676 per month.

It is also good to keep in mind that foreigners cannot own land in Cambodia. There are other possibilities, such as buying the land through a local company or acquiring Cambodian citizenship instead. If you successfully get through, then expect to pay AUD 270,270 for a two-bedroom apartment or a villa.

There are no trends of retirement villages in Cambodia. Who would prefer to retire in a retirement village if there are plenty of home choices? Getting a helper does not cost a lot of money as well.

There are expat districts in Phnom Penh, Siem Reap or Sihanoukville. For example, in Phnom Penh BKK1, BKK2, BKK3, Toul Tum Poung 1 (Russian Market) and Tonle Bassac are popular areas. In Siem Reap, it will be best to live around Wat Bo and Sala Kamreuk where most of the tourist facilities are, while Victory Beach is the place to be in Sihanoukville.

Healthcare in Cambodia

For the past decades, government efforts have significantly improved the healthcare system in Cambodia. However, it still ranks as one of the poorest in Southeast Asia with half of Cambodians relying on traditional medicine.

With a dysfunctional healthcare system, public hospitals are below standards and underequipped. Private hospitals can offer better quality healthcare at a reasonable cost, but they may still lack the specialist or the equipment on-site to treat serious medical conditions.

It will be best to fly to Bangkok or Ho Chi Minh if there are any complicated medical conditions. Because of the risks involved, make sure you have international travel insurance whose coverage includes evacuation and repatriation.

It is also recommended that you get the necessary vaccinations before traveling to Cambodia especially against dengue, tetanus, and hepatitis.

How to Retire in Cambodia (Retirement Visa)

The Cambodia Retirement visa or ER is a straightforward process. You may apply for a regular E class visa on arrival, and then extend via the ER extensions with the following conditions:

★ You must be 55 years old or older.

★ You must prove that you are retired. That means you need to have proof of pension or social security and have enough funds in the bank that can support you while in the country.

This extension is valid with various lengths, with an approximate cost of AUD 392 for the whole year. The ER visa also allows you to have multiple entry to the country. Getting an ER visa extension with an agency will save you a lot of time and trouble.

Just keep in mind that with the ER visa, you are not permitted to work in the country. Otherwise, you will be fined AUD 135 and you'll have to leave the country within a week.

Work

You cannot work, study, or start a business with a retirement visa in Cambodia. They have other visa categories to choose from instead.

If you are keen to work while you are in Cambodia, then better be equipped with a work permit and an employment card through the Ministry of Labor and Vocational Training. This is after obtaining an E-class visa that is valid for 30 days.

If you intend to start a business or work as a freelancer, you may get the EB visa, while if you prefer to study in your retirement days, there is the ES visa to take care of that.

Tax*

With a retirement visa on hand and proof that you are receiving retirement pensions, you don't have to pay any taxes in Cambodia. You will only be charged with Cambodia-sourced income progressively. See the table below:

Taxable Income	Tax Rate
KHR 0 – 500,000	Exempted
KHR 500,001 – 1,250,000	5%
KHR 1,250,001 – 8,500,000	10%
KHR 8,500,001 – 12,500,000	15%
KHR 12,500,001 and above	20%

Meanwhile, if you become a resident of Cambodia, all earnings worldwide will be taxed. There is also Value Added Tax (VAT) at 10%.

*KHR has been retained as default currency for all tax and immigration investment figures in this article. Currency exchange rate KHR1 = AUD0.00033

Food in Cambodia

Cambodian food isn't as popular as that of its neighbouring countries Thailand and Vietnam, but it can be good. With its diverse range of influences, from Chinese and Thai, Khmer cuisine offers a range of flavours without the heavy spices.

Local food in Cambodia often features coriander, lemongrass and other aromatic herbs. There is less use of coconut milk and chili. Cambodians put big importance on their rice culture so you can find rice in much of their daily cuisine. Here is a list of Khmer food that should not be missed:

- **Fish amok** is Cambodia's most famous dish. It is a slightly sweet curry with slok ngor, or a local herb that is subtly bitter. It is made with fresh coconut milk and kroeung, served in banana leaf.

- **Kuy teav** is a famous street food dish that is usually served during breakfast. This is noodle soup made from pork or beef producing a delicious broth. It is topped with fried shallots, bean sprouts, garlic and other aromatic herbs. There is an option to include sides such as chilli paste, lime and hoisin sauce.

- **Beef loc lac** refers to stir-fried tender beef strips served with sliced cucumbers, tomatoes and onions. Sometimes, it comes with an egg on top, and is dipped in lime juice and pepper.

- **Khmer curry** is a milder and sweeter version of curry compared to what you can find in India and Thailand. Its ingredients include chicken, coconut cream, fish sauce, milk, turmeric, ginger, diced sweet potatoes and herbs. Serving Khmer curry with hot steamed rice or a

baguette will absolutely satisfy all your senses.

- **Nom banh chok** or Khmer noodles are popular during breakfast. It consists of thin noodles made from rice topped with green fish curry. You will find these sold in the streets by ladies carrying baskets hanging from a pole.

- **Bai sach chrouk** (pork and rice) may sound like a simple dish, but it is very tasty. The pork is sliced thinly, marinated in palm sugar and fish sauce, followed by a slow grilling over warm coal, leaving a sweet smoke smell over it.

- *Sngor chruak sach trei* (sour fish soup) is essential in every meal. It is easy to make with just a fresh fish from Tonle Sap, seasoned with Asian basil and coriander.

- **Nhoam krauch thlong** (pomelo salad) is refreshing and best eaten during lunch when the sun is at an all-time high. Cambodian salads are usually associated with sour fruits instead of vegetables, mixed with pork belly, toasted coconut, and dried shrimp. It is completed with mint and fried shallots garnishes.

- **Prahok** is usually added to the local dishes or served with rice. It refers to crushed and fermented fish paste, making it salty and a little smelly. You either love it or hate it.

- **Green mango salad** is known for the refreshing feel. It is crunchy and zesty with its fresh ingredients from chilli, fish sauce to sliced green mango, tomatoes, cucumber, onion, pepper and fresh basil or mint.

There is a sufficient option of international cuisine in Cambodia from Japanese, American and French restaurants. There are also international hotel brands that serve international cuisine.

Recommended Cities in Cambodia

Siem Reap

If you are looking for the real heart of Cambodia, that's where Siem Reap comes in. Who can say no to the world-famous Angkor Wat Temple complex composed of hundreds of unique temples? After all, it is the pride of all Cambodians.

That makes living around here charming. You can spend hours wandering around and down the river. The old French Quarter also showcases a beautiful blend of French and Sino-Khmer architecture, filled with artisans, silk weavers, sculptors and many other talented artists.

Pub Street is another area frequented by expatriates for its booming nightlife, with all types of restaurants, bars and pubs. Otherwise, you can also travel across town to the lovely riverside where you can enjoy your cocktails surrounded by a lush garden. If this isn't enough, there is a golfing scene here too, with three eighteen-hole golf courses.

Essentials in Siem Reap:

* **Healthcare:** Not all hospitals in Siem Reap have staff who can speak English. Like the rest of the cities in the country, Siem Reap still has a long way to go. Here is a list of hospitals favoured by local expatriates:
  * Royal Angkor International Hospital
  * Neak Tep Clinic
  * Angkor F Clinic
  * Khemarak Angkor Polyclinic

* **Accessibility:** With Siem Reap a popular tourist destination, the new international airport can connect with major cities in Asia from Singapore, Hong Kong, Seoul, and a lot of Chinese cities. To access the rest of the world, travellers need to transit via the nearest Bangkok.

Things You Can Do in Siem Reap

Because Siem Reap is a green city, it will be nice to walk around as long as you can bear the hot and humid temperatures. Aside from exploring the Angkor Wat complex, there are also mountains to hike as well as the Tonle Sap Lake. Massage places are plenty. Here's what you can see and do while in Siem Reap for entertainment:

* Phare Circus
* Cambodian Landmine Museum
* Night markets
* Old market
* Angkor National Museum
* Floating Village
* Pub Street
* Cooking classes
* Go cycling in the villages
* Pottery class
* Artisans Angkor
* Golf courses

Phnom Penh

The capital city of Cambodia is also the largest city in the country. Here you can find a great mix of cultural landmarks, colonial buildings, markets, pagodas and palaces. Tourists usually skip the capital and only cover Siem Reap, but retiring in Phnom Penh is another story.

There is a growing local coffee culture, an array of choices for restaurants (from street food to fine dining) and shopping malls. Phnom Penh offers convenience with personal services and healthcare, including gym memberships, golf courses, and spas. Places for socializing, such as AmCham and Rotary, never come short.

Essentials in Phnom Penh

* **Healthcare:** The best medical care in the country is located in Phnom Penh. It has reputable hospitals, doctors and clinics, as well as a good number of pharmacies. However, we strongly recommend that if you have any underlying conditions, it will be best for you to fly to Bangkok. If it's nothing serious, you may consider the following hospitals:
  * Royal Phnom Penh Hospital
  * Sen Sok International University Hospital
  * Khema Clinic and Maternity
  * Embassy Medical Center

* **Accessibility to major airports:** Phnom Penh International Airport is adequately connected to major parts of East Asia such as Kuala Lumpur, Beijing, Tokyo, Bangkok, Seoul, Jakarta, Taipei,

Singapore, Hong Kong and Hanoi. To get to other parts of the world like the Middle East, USA or Australia, travelers can conveniently connect via Bangkok.

Things You Can Do in Phnom Penh

There are so many things you can do as a retiree in Phnom Penh, from taking a crash course in meditation in Wat Langka for free, to learning the Khmer language. If that's not enough for you, you can also give Khmer boxing a try. Otherwise, here is a list of things you can see:

- ★ Tuol Sleng Genocide Museum
- ★ Royal Palace
- ★ Mekong River
- ★ Wat Phnom
- ★ Silver Pagoda
- ★ National Museum
- ★ Central Market
- ★ Wat Langka
- ★ Russian Market
- ★ Aeon Mall
- ★ Tonle Bati
- ★ Din Art Gallery
- ★ Samai Distillery

Kampot

If you prefer an exotic, laidback and affordable area in Cambodia, Kampot may be for you. It is also called the 'Lost Riviera', and is located only a mile away from the ocean and three hours away from Phnom Penh. Here, you'll find a relaxing riverside retreat surrounded by forests, fertile fields and mountains. Fruit farms and plantations are common sights.

Tourists don't usually visit this area so you can rest assured you'll be away from the main route. Although it is the largest city in Cambodia, retirees can find a charming blend of old-world architecture, colonial buildings and traditional landmarks. It has also caught up with international banks and businesses opening up in recent years.

What makes Kampot appealing is the riverside, where locals and foreigners soak up in its relaxing ambiance. The city centre is also manageable to navigate around because the major places are located by the river or near it. There is also a good number of western-style grocery shops where imported products are available.

Essentials in Kampot

- ★ **Healthcare:** There are still a few hospital options in Kampot. Here are some of the ones you may consider:
  - ★ Kampot Referral Hospital
  - ★ Kampot Khemra Clinic
  - ★ Sonja Kill Memorial Hospital

- ★ **Accessibility:** The nearest airport is Sihanouk International Airport, a two-hour drive away. Or you can simply drive three hours to Phnom Penh.

Things You Can Do in Kampot

The stunning natural environment of Kampot attracts all kinds of travellers, thus the continuous expansion and other developments in the town. Imagine wide riverside boulevards and colonial buildings, giving out an old-world charm.

If you are looking for the best bars and restaurants, head no further – most of them are near the promenade. Here, you'll find French, Italian, Spanish and American cuisine owned by expatriates. Although there are no major landmarks, it does not mean there is a shortage of things to do. Here are some of them:

- ★ Kayaking, paddle boarding and kiteboarding in the river
- ★ Cardamom mountains
- ★ Rural railways
- ★ Pepper plantations

Sihanoukville

Without a doubt, the top coastal resort in Cambodia is Sihanoukville, also known as the Saint Tropez of Southeast Asia. This is where undeveloped coastline can be found, as well as ten white-sand beaches and more than twenty undeveloped islands for both tourists and locals to enjoy. If you are looking for fresh ocean breeze, a tropical climate and affordability, then Sihanoukville is the perfect place for you. The daily living cost here is considered the lowest available out of the major cities. A monthly budget of AUD 1,644 for a couple can go a long way. It is also good to know that the real estate industry here has been growing with many landlords offering fully furnished apartments for at least AUD 274 a month – still half the cost of that in the capital city. If you prefer to live in a villa, then make sure to allocate AUD 685 a month for that.

Sihanoukville is a beach town that has something to offer to everyone, no matter what their budget range may be. Despite its distance to Siem Reap and Phnom Penh, English is still the second language here and is widely spoken. The basics are also well-covered from banks, ATMs, internet and an airport too!

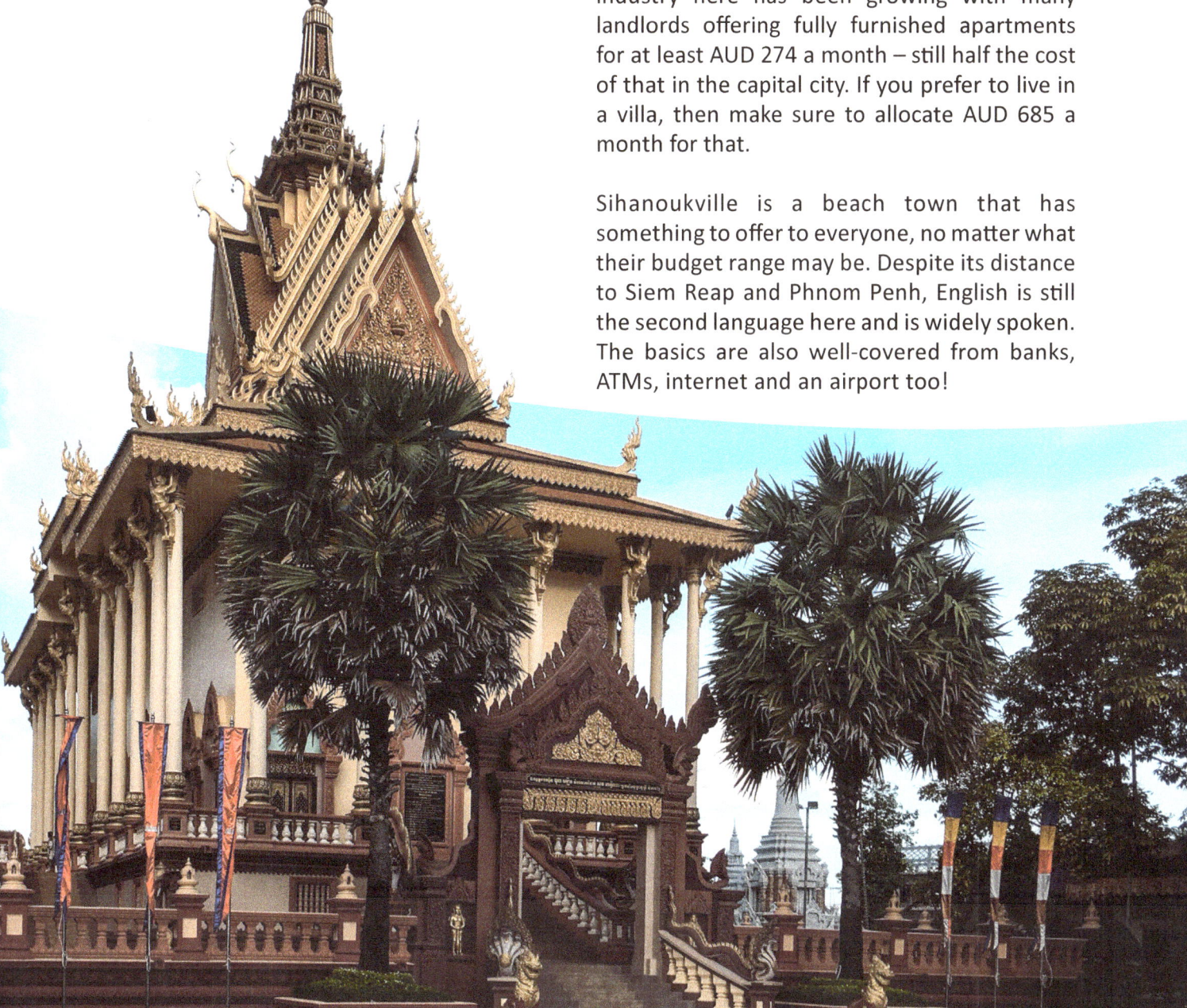

Essentials in Sihanoukville:

- **Healthcare:** Sihanoukville may not have the best medical care in Cambodia, but it has improved a lot in the past few years. For something not-so-serious such as immunisations, scrapes, sore throats and cuts, here are some options you may go for:
    - Sihanoukville International Clinic
    - CT Clinic
    - Sihanoukville Referral Hospital
    - Sonja Kill Memorial Hospital

- **Accessibility:** You may either drive for 5 hours to Phnom Penh or take the plane to Sihanouk International Airport, which is the country's largest international airport. It serves a variety of airlines that connect the city to Phnom Penh and Siem Reap, as well as to Beijing, Bangkok, Macau and Manila.

Things You Can Do in Sihanoukville

The lifestyle enjoyed in Sihanoukville range from café hopping by the beach, rest and relaxation, enjoying freshly caught seafood to snorkelling, scuba diving and kayaking. One of the recommended things to do is taking a trip to the beach town of Kep where you will find a fresh crab market. Here are the top things you may see and do here:

- Serendipity Beach
- Independence Beach
- Otres Beach
- Kbal Chhay Waterfall
- The Led Zephyr
- Queenco Fitness Club and Spa
- Top Cat Cinema
- Phsar Leu Market

Is Cambodia LGBT-friendly?

Cambodia is a gay-friendly country – maybe not as gay-friendly as Thailand, but the locals respect and accept them. Members of the LGBT community will feel welcome and safe traveling in the major cities.

Retiring here as a gay person, it will be comforting to know that since 2003, the country has held Pride celebrations every year. Phnom Penh also has a growing gay scene, from bars to spa-boutique hotels. Keep in mind that Cambodia is still a conservative country so locals who are gay may still struggle in coming out. Public displays of affection are not welcome anywhere.

Senior Discounts

Cambodians have huge respect for their elders, but there are not many discounts or benefits offered to seniors. With the cost of living in Cambodia, you may not need the discount. Even the locals contribute for twenty years to get a lifetime pension when they retire.

Living in Cambodia: What to watch out for

Cambodia is a paradise but has its own struggles that you need to be prepared for if you see it as your future retirement home. Here's what you need to watch out for:

- ★ **There is limited healthcare in Cambodia.**
  As we have covered in the health section, if you have serious medical issues, Cambodia may not be the best place for you to retire. We may have to wait for a few years for the country to catch up with fully equipped hospitals and specialists.

- ★ **Watch out for your bag.**
  Cambodia is a safe place to retire, but it does not mean that you can let your guard down. In the big cities, petty crimes such as theft are common. Exercise caution and don't carry a lot of money in your bag.

- ★ **There are limited direct flights to Cambodia.**
  Flight-wise, you may have to fly via Asia's major cities such as Bangkok, Singapore, Tokyo or Hong Kong to reach either Phnom Penh or Siem Reap. It does not have any flights to further places like Sydney or Dubai.

- ★ **Infrastructure is still not well-developed.**
  While everything is still basically cheap in the country, you can't expect to get a five-star infrastructure. While traffic gets worse each year, there is still no mass transit system that can support the population. Also be prepared to face power outages in the neighbourhood that lasts 3 – 5 hours a day. Cambodia still has a lot to catch up on compared to its neighbouring countries such as Vietnam and Thailand.

- ★ **Big cities tend to be dirty.**
  Throughout the city of Phnom Penh, it is apparent that caring for the environment is the main priority, yet the locals tend to throw stuff anywhere they like while waiting for someone else to clean it up. Residents and businesses take their garbage bags out to public streets waiting for garbage collectors that don't come often. This creates a stench of spoil and rot in the streets.

Summary

Cambodia's continuous development brings a lot of future potential for all stakeholders: residents, tourists, investors and foreign retirees. It is not a perfect country (yet) but it remains to be among our top choices for the low cost of living, the scenery and the promises it holds.

Healthcare: ★★
Culture: ★★★★★
Cost of Living: ★★★★★
Housing: ★★★★
Accessibility: ★★★
Safety: ★★★★

TOTAL STARS: 23 ★

The Lawn in Canggu, Canggu, Bali, Indonesia

Reasons to Retire in Indonesia

Countless travelers visit Indonesia, and some choose not to leave — and we can't blame them! Who wouldn't be enamored by the warm hospitality of its people, the ideal climate, and the amazing natural landscape of the country? With its 17,000 unique islands to choose from, you will never run out of things to see and do. Each island offers a rich and varied lifestyle for foreign retirees. Each island has its own story to tell.

The lifestyle in Indonesia includes a vibrant nightlife and entertainment. It features a thriving music scene that runs almost every evening. There are also regular art shows, music and film festivals that will surely satisfy your senses. Even if alcohol is expensive, it is not prohibited in the bars, restaurants and clubs.

Indonesia's expats also have a well-established organization that hosts weekly meetings and various events. Whether you prefer to volunteer or support charities, or travel together in a group, all you need to do is reach out to them.

To retire is to enjoy a good quality life, but in Indonesia, you can enjoy it for a lot less. There are affordable modes of transportation, cheap food, rent, and household help. Eating out is very affordable, as long as alcohol is not included. You can purchase the freshest produce in the markets too at the most reasonable price. Healthcare is still pretty decent in Indonesia. Anyhow, shall you suffer from something serious, Singapore is only a two-hour flight away.

Its close proximity to Australia has been one of its advantages, that when Australians think of a place to retire, Indonesia just easily comes up in one's mind. Indonesia is also a good base to explore the rest of Asia for its accessibility with Malaysia, Vietnam and Philippines.

Why Retire in Indonesia:

★ Get more for less with the low cost of living.
★ You can choose between living in the city, by the beach, or in the country.
★ People are friendly and it is not necessary to learn the local language.
★ Indonesia is well-connected to major parts of the world.

Culture

Indonesia has some of the friendliest people in the world, that you will immediately feel at home once you arrive. They are respectful whatever your religion or race is. 86% of the population are Muslim while the remaining are either Catholic, Protestant, Buddhist or Hindu. Nevertheless, the locals accept and respect you for who you are. Because they are gentle people, they also expect you to be the same. Thus, there is no room for loudness and aggressiveness in the country.

In fact, Indonesians don't prefer conflict and would avoid it as much as possible to save face. They easily get embarrassed so it is considered rude to even try to. Try not to raise your voice or make accusations. Always solve issues in private and not on the streets.

Language-wise, you don't have to worry about studying their language if you choose to live in cities frequented by tourists. Equipping yourself with English is enough for survival. However, if you decide to live in the rural areas, it will be helpful to know the basic things such as greetings, food, and directions.

Knowing the local language can gain their trust and encourage locals to open their doors for you. If you are keen to learn, there are millions of capable teachers willing to help you.

Climate

Indonesia's location at the equator gives the country a tropical climate, with temperatures ranging from 23 – 28 degrees Celsius. Humidity is quite high with extreme variations in rainfall. The dry season runs from June to September and the rainy season from December to March.

The western and northern parts of Indonesia have more precipitation due to the north and westward monsoon. The areas with most rainfall include Bali, Java, and West Sumatra. Typhoons often hit between September and December that bring rainstorms and heavy winds.

Cost of Living

The cost of living in Indonesia depends on where you live. For instance, the most expensive city is Jakarta, where one meal will cost you IDR 40,000 or AUD 3.75 in an inexpensive restaurant, which will be IDR 25,000 or AUD 2.35 in Bali.

The Indonesian Rupiah is affected by inflation, which is bad news for the locals. About 10% of the locals can't afford the standard cost of living which is AUD 13.50 per person per month. However, if you are bringing in dollars, you might not feel the cost that much. Relatively, Indonesia remains to be one of the attractive countries to retire in because of the low cost of living.

To live comfortably, AUD 1,216 per person per month will be enough to cover housing, food, transportation, and utilities. Here is a reference on the usual expenses in Indonesia:

Expenses	Prices
Rent (one-bedroom apartment in the city centre)	AUD 676
High-speed internet	AUD 41
Electricity and water	AUD 135
Phone with basic data plan	AUD 13.50
Loaf of white bread	AUD 1.60
A dozen of eggs	AUD 2.30
Local beer	AUD 4.05
Taxi per kilometer	AUD 0.47

Housing

A luxurious house in Indonesia can cost you AUD 1,351 a month, otherwise, you get something decent at AUD 541.

Keep in mind that foreigners can't buy houses or land in the country. What is possible is getting long leases. For instance, expatriates can obtain a 70-year lease on land. This is quite risky because foreigners may not get the same legal protections as the locals do. If you are keen, an apartment will cost at least AUD 4,460 per square meter in Jakarta.

There are retirement villages available in Indonesia. One example is The Bali Villages that starts at AUD 175,676 with monthly maintenance fee of AUD 269. Retirement homes are not yet adequate in the country. Given the risks and options above, the best alternative you may have is renting an apartment that costs a lot less. It will also give you the flexibility in case you want to move to another location in Indonesia or another country altogether.

Healthcare in Indonesia

There are both public and private healthcare options in Indonesia. The standard of public healthcare facilities is limited, and does not guarantee a doctor can speak in English. Private hospitals can be expensive, but boast better amenities with English-speaking staff.

Since expatriates are not covered under the country's universal healthcare scheme, it is best to make use of health insurance to have access to private healthcare. It is also good to know that wealthy Indonesians often go to Singapore to access the best healthcare, so shall you decide to live here, and if ever you need serious surgery, be prepared to fly and make sure your health insurance has international coverage.

How to Retire in Indonesia (Retirement Visa)*

The easier procedure of getting an Indonesian retirement visa has made the country a popular destination for retirees. With this type of visa, you can open an Indonesian bank account, get a driver's license, buy and register a car under your name and have access to local prices and discounts. You can also receive a multiple exit re-permit (MERP) that allows you to leave and come back as many times as you need.

Here are the requirements to get an Indonesian retirement visa:

- ★ You are 55 years old and above
- ★ Health insurance from Indonesia
- ★ A rental agreement for at least a year
- ★ Hiring a maid or domestic helper or a driver while in Indonesia
- ★ You have to be from one of the following countries: Argentina

Australia	Canada
Austria	Cyprus
Bahrain	Denmark
Belgium	Egypt
Brazil	Estonia
Brunei	Finland
Darussalam	France
Bulgaria	Germany

Greece	Norway
Hungary	Oman
India	Philippines
Iran	Poland
Ireland	Portugal
Iceland	Qatar
Italy	Russia
Japan	Saudi Arabia
Kuwait	Singapore
Liechtenstein	South Africa
Luxembourg	South Korea
Malaysia	Switzerland
Maldives	Taiwan
Malta	Thailand
Monaco	UAE
The Netherlands	United Kingdom
New Zealand	USA

You also need to have proof of sufficient funds, at least USD 1,500 per month or a total of USD 18,000 a year.

A retirement visa has a one-year validity, which you can renew annually for up to five years. Afterwards, you are eligible to apply for a permanent residence known as KITAP, which has a validity of five years. You may renew this indefinitely every five years.

* USD has been retained as default currency for all immigration investment figures. Currency exchange rate USD1 = AUD1.36.

Work

You cannot work or volunteer in Indonesia with a retirement visa, otherwise you have to apply for a work permit issued by the Ministry of Manpower instead.

Optionally, if you don't intend to lounge around the whole day, and rather start a business in the country, keep in mind that only the local residents in Indonesia can act as founders of the business. That way, that company can "hire" you and you will be eligible for a work permit.

Starting a business in Indonesia will involve a lot of paperwork written in the local language. The best option is contacting an agent who can help with the bureaucracy.

Tax*

Expatriates are considered as residents who spend 183 days in the country and therefore, need to pay a flat rate of 20% tax on all income earned in Indonesia. Capital gain tax is also charged for expats who make capital gains on assets in the country.

For retirees, since they are not working in the country, the pension they get from outside the country will not be taxed. If ever this pension accumulated interest, it will then be taxed 20%. Fortunately, there is also no VAT in Indonesia so you can consume guiltlessly. Meanwhile, shall you manage to still get a job in the country, here's a quick look on the progressive income tax rate in Indonesia:

Taxable Income	Tax Rate
0 – IDR 50 million	5%
Over IDR 50 million – IDR 250 million	15%
Over IDR 250 million – IDR 500 million	25%
Over IDR 500 million	30%

* IDR has been retained as default currency for all tax figures in this article. Currency exchange rate IDR 1 = AUD 0.000094.

Food

There are 1,300 ethnic groups living in the largest archipelago in the world. That's 17,508 islands bringing in 5,350 traditional recipes. The most common cuisine includes rice, noodles, and soup which you can often find in street eateries.

Indonesian cuisine is also influenced by the Middle East, India, and China, perhaps because the country has been involved in trade with these parts of the world throughout history. Indonesian cuisine is also getting more popular in Singapore and Malaysia, from its beef rendang to sambal. Here is a list of the most common food you'll find on an Indonesian table:

- **Nasi Goreng** is the most famous fried rice in the country. You will find them in both street eateries and high-end restaurants. What makes it a distinctive meal is the combination of sweetness and spiciness. The main ingredients are palm sweet soy and white rice plus any kind of meat and vegetables.

- **Rawon** refers to the thick beef stew from East Java. It has a strong flavor from kluwak or black nuts combined with various herbs and spices.

- **Satay** is any kind of skewered meat from chicken, mutton, beef, fish, and pork. The juiciness of the skewers comes from the marinade of soy sauce and spices, followed by grilling over charcoal. Topped with peanut sauce and chopped chili, it has an even more mouth-watering aroma.

- **Rendang** is the fork-tender, juicy beef with special gravy sauce made with coconut and herbs. It is served along with rice, vegetables, and green chili.

- **Bakso** is an Indonesian meatball made from beef and tapioca. It is served with a bowl of rice or noodles, vegetables, and warm broth. Optionally, you can add soy sauce and vinegar.

- **Indomie** is one of Indonesia's sinful products. The instant noodle brand is so cheap which can be made into a satisfying snack. Plus, there are many flavors to choose from.

- **Nasi Udok** is an aromatic dish that includes rice cooked in coconut milk, fried chicken, tempe, shredded omelet, and fried onion. It is then topped with sambal and emping.

With Indonesia's rich cuisine, your taste buds will never get bored. Every day can be filled with a new type of local food. In case you miss home, there are always plenty of international restaurants serving American, Chinese, Japanese, and Italian cuisine.

Recommended Cities in Indonesia

Lombok

Snuggling between Bali to its East and Sumbawa to its West, Lombok sits at 4,725 sq kms, which is not that much smaller than Bali. It has a population of over 3.1 million who enjoy a laid-back life. You can feel people's warmth because of the absence of the crowds and the overdevelopment of its neighbor.

Lombok has a thriving expat community, with foreigners coming from the USA, Australia, UK, New Zealand, Germany, Korea, Italy, and many other European countries. Despite this, the community remains small and everybody knows pretty much everybody.

There is also a growing range of cafes and restaurants, golf courses, as well as shopping options in Mataram, Cakranegara, and Sweta. Living here also provides an opportunity to have an amazing outdoor lifestyle. You can explore the area around the volcano, which is a designated national park that's perfect for trekking and exploring mountain villages.

Lombok is also home to the world-famous Gili Trawangan, Gili Meno, and Gili Air. It is an untouched paradise, located far away from the busy cities. Living here is perfect for those who wish to have a peaceful retirement with an affordable way of living. A single person is expected to spend AUD 608 – AUD 2,027 a month, while a couple can still be living under AUD 2,703 a month.

Essentials in Lombok:

- **Healthcare:** There are a few hospitals in Lombok but in case of serious problems, it is always advisable to fly to Bali, Jakarta, or to Singapore. Here are two hospitals in the area:
    - RS Harapan Keluarga
    - Rumah Sakit Risa Klinic
- **Accessibility:** When the new international airport on the island at Praya was built in 2011, accessibility has improved significantly in Lombok. A lot of foreigners still go via Bali where there are daily direct flights via Garuda and Lion Air which take about 40 mins, or by ferry from Padang Bai. The Lombok International Airport also operates regular flights to Jakarta, Kuala Lumpur, and Singapore.

Things You Can Do in Lombok

Lombok and its surroundings offer amazing beaches and historic sites, attracting more and more people into skipping Bali in exchange for Lombok's unspoiled nature. It has become a popular destination for diving, snorkeling, and surfing. For instance, Bangko Bangko in the southwest is the best place for surfers, while the Gilis Islands are famous for diving and snorkeling. If you prefer to party, then Gili Trawangan is the party island. Its beaches are perfect for family activities, picnics, and a romantic sunset drink.

In Lombok, visitors and retirees experience a genuine opportunity to enjoy its treasures at their own pace. Here are the points of interest you must add to your bucket list:

- Mount Rinjani
- Gili Trawangan Island
- Tanjung Aan Beach
- Surf Point Bongkas
- Gili Islands
- Kuta Beach
- Sembalun Village
- Gili Air Island
- Sudirman Antiques Shop
- Kondo Island
- Gili Meno Beach
- Merese Hill
- Kerandangan Beach
- Sendang Gile and Tiu Kelep Waterfall
- Tetebatu Waterfall
- Mawun Beach
- Batu Bolong Temple
- Mount Rinjani National Park

Bali

Our list of reasons to retire in Bali is long. Firstly, the Balinese are very warm people, and their culture never ceases to amaze. Bali's population is mostly Hindu so the way of life and their openness is so refreshing especially for retirees. It is easy to adjust around them because almost everyone speaks English so you no longer have to learn the local language. They are also known to be proud of their traditions so try to learn a word or two, and it will be appreciated by the locals.

At your doorstep, you can find beautiful beaches, sumptuous food for a fraction of the cost, and excellent shopping. Despite being one of the top destinations in Asia, the cost of living is still relatively low. For example, you can rent a two-bedroom villa with a pool for only AUD 946 a month. If you prefer to hire a maid, it will only cost you AUD 101 a month. There are areas in the region that can fit your taste. Do you prefer the beaches, nightlife, and shopping? Then Seminyak is the place to be. If you would rather meditate and learn Indonesia's arts and crafts, then head to Ubud. If you love surfing, then better base yourself in Uluwatu where the waves can get intense.

Essentials in Bali:

- **Healthcare:** The healthcare in Bali is good enough, although it is still not up to standards compared to other countries. There are small specialized clinics with doctors and nurses who can speak English. Here are two hospitals we recommend – both located in Kuta:
    - International SOS Clinic
    - BIMC Hospital
- **Accessibility:** The Ngurah Rai International Airport is the second busiest airport in the country. The international terminal opened in 2013, providing 62 check-in counters. It connects the island to all parts of the world including Moscow, Kuala Lumpur, Hong Kong, Manila, Beijing, Melbourne, and Doha.

Things You Can Do in Bali

There are more things to do in Bali beyond its turquoise waters and exotic temples. After all, with its location about eight degrees south of the equator, you can expect a tropical, warm climate all year round. Getting around is not hard either, with taxis all over the region available at your disposal.

A retirement day may include off-the-beaten-path experiences. You can walk, cycle, or quad bike around the local villages and admire the rice terraces, bamboo forests, and jungles. You can follow this up with an exhilarating white water rafting at the Ayung River, and when exhaustion arises, you can always head to the beach and witness the relaxing sunset. Here are other places you can fill your time with while in Bali:

- ★ Sacred Monkey Forest Sanctuary
- ★ Mount Agung
- ★ Waterbom Bali
- ★ Double Six Beach
- ★ Seminyak Beach
- ★ Bali Wake Park
- ★ Nyaman Gallery
- ★ Sindhu Market
- ★ Nusa Dua Beach
- ★ Kelingking Beach
- ★ Canggu Beach
- ★ Sanur Beach
- ★ Devil's Tears
- ★ Samasta Lifestyle Village
- ★ Uluwatu Temple
- ★ Jatiluwih Green Land
- ★ Mount Batur
- ★ Bali Bird Park
- ★ Thomas Beach
- ★ Batu Bolong Beach

Yogyakarta

Also known as Jogjakarta, Yogyakarta has been a popular sanctuary for foreigners from countries such as Japan and Australia. There is also a community of expatriates – mostly artists and entrepreneurs who want to experience a very culture-steeped life. It is a bustling town on the island of Java and is considered an important center of culture and Javanese arts. This includes ballet, batik textiles, literature, drama, music, poetry, silversmithing, and wayang puppetry.

It is also home to a huge student population with more than 90 universities to choose from. And because you can find almost all kinds of ethnicities here, the city is also called Little Indonesia. The low cost of living compared to Jakarta and Bali is another reason that it continues to attract foreigners who want to have a good stretch to their dollar while enjoying a quality life. You can have access to good healthcare, property and food prices are lower, and you have a variety of things to explore.

However, keep in mind that not everyone can speak English so for a foreigner to adapt, it is essential to spend time studying the language so you can communicate more effectively.

Essentials in Yogyakarta

- ★ **Healthcare:** Yogyakarta has several hospitals that offer any kind of medical treatment. Some hospitals even provide private nurses and home visits. Here are some of the good hospitals in the city:
    - ★ Jogja International Hospital
    - ★ Sardjito Hospital
    - ★ Panti Rapih Hospital

- ★ **Accessibility:** To reach Yogyakarta from outside Indonesia, there are three

options for transit: Jakarta, Singapore, and Bali will connect you to New Yogyakarta International Airport. There is also a train that connects the city to Java Island.

Things You Can Do in Yogyakarta

Yogyakarta boasts a myriad of heritage buildings and important monuments, from the famous Borobudur and Prambanan temples, to the Malioboro street which is a popular shopping and culinary area. The natural attractions are of abundance. Aside from the Merapi volcano, the city is also close to the beaches such as Ngobaran and Baron. There are also lakes, caves, and gardens to explore. Retiring here means doing what the locals do. You may support a community of artists and participate in art festivals. Alternatively, many retirement clubs are also available offering activities from archery, horse riding, yoga, and martial arts. Here are other things you may see:

- Merapi Volcano
- Ullen Sentalu Museum
- Malioboro Road
- Pinus Pengger Nature Tourism
- Sewu Temple
- Taman Pintar Science Park
- Ganjuran Church
- Yogyakarta Palace
- Yogyakarta Monument
- Plaosan Temple
- Wisata Seribu Batu Songgo Langit
- Bukit Panguk Kediwung
- Jogokariyan Mosque
- UGM Campus Mosque
- Jogja Bay Waterpark
- Pule Payung
- Affandi Museum
- Sosrowijayan Street
- Warung Bato

Is Indonesia LGBT-friendly?

Indonesia is a Muslim country so keep this in mind whether you're only staying here for a short time or staying here for good. The country is conservative and LGBT rights have been deteriorating. There are already movements criminalizing gay sex. For instance, the city of Palembang in South Sumatra has already passed a bill doing so.

This means same-sex marriage and even civil partnerships are illegal in the country. Because of this, there have been attacks on the LGBT community that may go unpunished. Therefore, if you're a gay couple, find another country that will be more comfortable and more open to your relationship—otherwise expect to live in fear.

Senior Discounts

There are various benefits as a senior in Indonesia. Therefore, upon purchasing any product or services such as transportation, it is best to ask the vendor beforehand.

Living in Indonesia: What to Watch Out For

As exciting as it might be to live in Indonesia, there are still downsides to be aware of before leaving everything behind and moving here. Here are some of them:

- ### Beware of malaria in Indonesia
  With Indonesia's tropical climate, malaria can be a problem in the villages. The urban areas of Jakarta and Bali will be safe from it, but if you choose to live in the rural areas such as Sumatra, Sulawesi, and Kalimantan, you will need to take extra precautions such as anti-malaria vaccination.

- ### Air pollution in the big cities is problematic.
  Air quality in the big cities, especially Jakarta, suffers from seasonal haze from the forest fires of Malaysia. It may cause respiratory problems, especially if you have asthma. Make sure to have the necessary medication on hand.

- ### People tend to overcharge foreigners.
  If you look western, the locals may assume that you have a lot of money and will tend to charge you a higher price. It may be useful if you have an Indonesian friend who can go with you to bargain if you need to go shopping.

- ### Terrible traffic is common.
  The traffic can be terrible in the big cities. Even the island of Bali experiences traffic jams that can spoil your day. The pollution generated by the fumes hangs like an umbrella over the city.

- ### Indonesia's culture is conservative.
  The country, first and foremost, does not have a drinking culture. Thus, you may find alcohol prices to be inflated. Be careful with carrying alcohol around as there is a chance that police might stop to question you. Also, Indonesia is still a Muslim country that you need to adjust the way you dress. Women need to wear skirts that go below their knees.

Summary

Indonesia has a long legacy of being the best destination for travelers around the world. Its beauty also attracts foreigners who prefer to call it their home. Give it a few more years and it will surely improve for the better, and perhaps more cities will be more desirable for those willing to stay forever.

Healthcare: ★ ★ ★
Culture: ★ ★ ★ ★
Cost of Living: ★ ★ ★ ★ ★
Housing: ★ ★ ★ ★
Accessibility: ★ ★ ★ ★
Safety: ★ ★ ★ ★

TOTAL STARS: 24 ★

Regalia suites, Jalan Sultan Ismail, Chow Kit, Kuala Kumpur, federal territory of Kuala Lumpur, Malaysia

Reasons to Retire in Malaysia

Malaysia is a diverse country, with Malay, Chinese, Indian and European ethnicities blending together in a unique fashion. The nation celebrates 300 festivals every year and has more public holidays than any other country in Southeast Asia.

Malaysia is one of the top countries in which to retire. Firstly, there's the tropical climate with two seasons a year. The first half is hot and humid associated with the rainy and dry season, and the other half is more humid with more rain. Secondly, you will not have trouble adjusting to the language because everyone speaks in English. It is also used in business and road signs.

Its cuisine also deserves a special place. Its food comes from the best food influences – China, India, Indonesia – giving it a distinctive taste. All you have to do is explore its street food scene and coffee culture to get the perfect treat at a reasonable cost.

As for cost of living, Malaysia is in our top spot for how it stretches your dollar while still providing you with great quality of life. Malaysia is home to Mount Kinabalu, which stands at 13,435 feet and is one of the most prominent mountain parks in the world. You can also snorkel and dive as marine parks are scattered throughout the country. Whatever lifestyle you prefer to live, Malaysia can offer, from bustling cities to beach towns and everything in between.

Why Retire in Malaysia:

★ It is an amazing country for adventure lovers
★ You'll get warm weather all-year round
★ Malaysia offers variety from its culture, cities and towns to fit your preferred lifestyle
★ It offers delectable cuisine you won't find anywhere else
★ Top notch healthcare? Look no further. Malaysia has it!

Culture

Making friends in Malaysia is easy. Since everybody speaks English, foreigners from an English-speaking country do not have to spend time learning to be fluent in the language to communicate with the locals. The locals are also very nice people who are curious about the expatriates who choose their country to which to retire. Food is a major part of the culture so if you want to connect with anyone, food is a good topic to start with.

One of Malaysia's core concepts is 'budi', meaning politeness and respect are essentials to human interaction. This reflects in the behaviour of people from most backgrounds. It is no wonder you'll find Malaysians to be gracious, good-natured, calm and polite.

As much as possible, Malaysians will do everything not to 'lose face', a concept embedded in most Asian cultures. This refers to a person's honour and reputation. They don't want to risk losing face so conservative conduct is the way to go.

Islam remains to be the official religion of Malaysia and has the largest following in the country. This is because of its geographic position on the main historical shipping routes between Arab, Indian and European regions. The rest of the population practices Hinduism, Sikhism, Confucianism and Taoism. Many Muslims pray five times a day so don't be surprised if it suddenly interrupts your time with a Malaysian.

Climate

Malaysia has two distinct geographical parts: Peninsular Malaysia or the mainland, which shares borders with Thailand and Singapore; and Malaysian Borneo which refers to the East Malaysian border with Indonesia. These two areas experience different climates.

East Peninsular Malaysia, with its large hills separating east and west, experiences turbulent weather during its monsoon season which is from mid-October to the end of March. The West Peninsular Malaysia experiences the southwest monsoon from May to October. There are cooler places as well such as the Penang Hill and Cameron Highlands. These places are popular on the weekends for those looking for a quick fix.

With a tropical climate, with wet and dry seasons every year, you may expect it to rain almost every day but, most of the time, rainfall tends to be just a quick shower. Being prepared and bringing an umbrella with you everywhere you go, though, will be a wise thing to do. Temperatures range from 20 to 30 degrees Celsius throughout the year.

Cost of Living

If you don't intend to eat in mid-range restaurants every day, a couple can cover their general living expenses and rent in the major city of Kuala Lumpur with AUD 2,200. It will be cheaper in other places like Penang, where rent is half the price.

With AUD 3,200, a couple can live large. Here are some other costs for reference:

Expenses	Prices
Large bag of local fruits	AUD 11
Whole steamed fish	AUD 13
Plate of noodles with chicken and vegetables	AUD 3
Massage	AUD 20
Cleaning lady-per hour	AUD 7

Housing

A one-bedroom flat in Kuala Lumpur costs AUD 800 monthly, while a three-bedroom condo at 2,300 square feet, with access to a pool and a small gym, costs AUD 1,200. However, if you decide to own a home, a foreign retiree can buy properties in Malaysia. Just take note that you will incur a capital gains tax.

Alternatively, if you prefer assisted living, there are also well-developed retirement villages with great amenities and facilities to choose from.

- ★ GreenAcres Retirement Village
- ★ Sri Seronok Retirement Village
- ★ The Green Leaf
- ★ De Luxe Retirement Home
- ★ Eden-on-the-Park Seniors Lifestyle Resort
- ★ Eden-on-the-Park Nursing Care Residen

Healthcare in Malaysia

The country is ranked among the world's top health tourism destinations, and that's because healthcare in the country is top-notch and at a low cost. A general check-up costs AUD 18, overall health screening at AUD 80, and dental cleaning at AUD 33.

Most doctors are trained in the US, UK, and Australia and speak excellent English. We recommend getting health insurance so you can have access quicker.

How to Retire in Malaysia (Retirement Visa)*

Malaysia has made it easy to retire in the country. Its retirement visa option is considered to be one of the best in the world.

"Malaysia My Second Home" or MM2H grants expatriates a multiple-entry visa valid for ten years. It can be automatically renewed upon its expiration.

The main requirement to get an MM2H visa is RM 150,000 (AUD 48,036) deposited in the bank of your choice, which will not be necessary if you have a pension. Otherwise, you have to prove a monthly income of RM 10,000 (AUD 3,202). Any money you bring in the country is exempt from tax.

Other requirements include not having a criminal record and being in good health. Take note that you have to pass a medical examination when you arrive.

* RM has been retained as default currency for all immigration investment figures in this article. Currency exchange rateRM1 = AUD 0.32.

Work

With the MM2H visa, you can work up to twenty hours a week, but only if you have specialized skills applied within certain approved sectors. The decision will be based on a committee, on whether a Malaysian could do the job instead.

Otherwise, you are permitted to set up and invest in businesses in Malaysia where you don't have to be actively involved in the daily operations. If you want to be more involved in the business, you will have to switch to a working permit.

Tax

You will only get taxed for your Malaysian-sourced income. All kinds of funds remitted into the country are tax-free – including pension and investment income coming from overseas. Foreign-sourced income is not taxed. From April 2015, the government introduced a 6% consumption tax, which is not so bad.

Food

Because of its multi-ethnic (Malays, Chinese and Indians) composition, Malaysia offers a rich variety of cuisine, with wide-ranging and diverse flavours. Its fusion cuisine, in particular, blends the unique characteristics of Malaysian dishes, giving you the best of the best.

You can taste this in their rendang, which combines meat with many regional spices and coconut milk; or in their laksa, a spicy noodle with a curry-like base, topped with fish cake, bean curd and prawn. Mentioning all the food you can eat here won't do Malaysia justice. You just have to go there and try it. Here are some of the local foods you will have more chances to indulge in while in Malaysia:

- ★ **Nasi Lemak** is loved in every household in Malaysia. It has a few variations but the basic consists of rice cooked in coconut milk, topped with spicy sambal chili sauce. You will often find fried egg on the side, and on top can either be pork, beef, sambal squids, sambal fish, or chicken.

- ★ **Ikan Bakar** literally means grilled fish. It is marinated and spiced up with chili paste and grilled to perfection, then served with hot rice, side vegetables and curries on the side.

- ★ **Nasi Kandar** refers to rice and Indian style curry, usually mutton curry. Its name comes from Malaysian villages with mobile vendors carrying a kandar as they sell these curries.

- ★ **Roti Canai** is a dough that is firstly stretched out and folded into small squares. Afterward, it is fried in oil making is crispy and then served with a curry dipping sauce.

- ★ **Curry Laksa** and **Asam Laksa** are two kinds of laksa in Malaysian cuisine. Laksa refers to the famous spicy noodle soup with thick wheat noodles. While coconut laksa has a coconut milk-based curry soup, the latter has a tangy, spicy sour soup that uses tamarind, onion, red chillies and pineapple.

- ★ **Char Kway Teow** is a dish that includes stir-fried wide rice noodles with bean sprouts, chives, shrimp and egg.

- ★ **Hokkien Me**e is a dish that comes from Fujian, China. It is dark colored prawn noodles usually fried in lard on high heat resulting in something amazing.

- ★ **Nasi Campur** refers to a plate filled with rice and an assortment of dishes such as fish curry, omelettes and cutlets.

- ★ **Bak Kut Teh**, which literally means 'meat bone tea' features slow-cooked pork with herbs and other spices. It is usually eaten during breakfast and is one of the popular meals in the country.

- **Ais Kachang** is a shaved ice dessert. It is basically ice with beans drenched in syrup and served with condensed milk, gula melaka and creamed corn.

Travelers come to Malaysia only to try its food, while being a retiree means you will have a wide selection to choose from every day. The good news is, if you ever find yourself missing international food, Malaysia has international restaurants, too, that serve Japanese, American and European dishes.

Recommended Cities in Malaysia

Kuala Lumpur

Here is the main city and the hub with all the conveniences that you need, from malls at every corner, universities, to the main hospitals. This is where embassies and high commission offices are located, too.

Its international airport is well-connected to all the major parts of the world. With most of the population in the country residing here, you are promised a vibrant city, spread over 200 square kilometres.

What's great about living in the capital city is the large open-plan living areas. You will find newly constructed condos and bungalows built every year. Even in the suburbs, you can find modern living spaces associated with floor-to-ceiling windows that allow natural light to come in.

Cultural expression here has more variety and freedom. This means, even if you are not practicing Islam, the people living in the city allow you to practice your own religion.

Essentials in Kuala Lumpur:

- **Healthcare:** The government is investing more and more in marketing the country as a global medical tourism destination, and Malaysia's great healthcare system has earned this designation. Retiring in Kuala Lumpur means you can benefit from easy access to inexpensive healthcare, well-trained medical staff and updated facilities. There are also tons of pharmacies found in the malls or in the city. Here are some of the recommended hospitals in the city:
    - Assunta Hospital
    - Beacon Hospital
    - Cardiac Vascular Sentral Kuala Lumpur
    - Sunway Medical Centre

- **Accessibility:** The Kuala Lumpur airport, also the largest and busiest airport in the country, has been ranked as one of the world's top airports. A lot of airlines operate in the airport. connecting Malaysia directly to the US, Europe, Middle East and Australia. Kuala Lumpur is only an 8.5-hour flight away from Sydney.

Things You Can Do in Kuala Lumpur

The location of the capital also makes it the perfect base for day trips to Malacca, Penang and Ipoh. Tourism is the main focus in the city, thus, the list of things to do can be very long. From traditional to contemporary, you'll find something suitable for your taste. A day of a retiree's life in Kuala Lumpur can include a morning walk in one of the parks, shopping in the afternoon, and dining in one of the skyscrapers overlooking the city. Here are the must-see things to see and visit:

- Petronas Towers
- Sri Mahamariamman Temple
- Kuala Lumpur Bird Park
- National Museum
- Sunway Lagoon Theme Park
- Aquaria KLCC
- Central Market
- Hutong
- Royal Selangor Visitor Centre
- Kuala Lumpur Tower
- Kuala Lumpur Butterfly Park
- Alor Street
- Jamek Mosque
- National Zoo of Malaysia
- China Town
- Istana Negara
- Maybank Numismatic Museum
- National Mosque
- Batu Caves

Kota Kinabalu

Malaysia is often advertised around the world using images from Kota Kinabalu. Imagine dense jungles and roaring rivers! If you are a nature lover, either for beaches or lush rainforests, then retiring to the eastern part of the country might be for you. Kota Kinabalu is the capital state of Sabah, Borneo, which has been a growing resort destination because of its proximity to five tropical islands – only fifteen minutes by boat.

Home to a million people, Kota Kinabalu also has a rich history. While under British colonial rule, it was known as Jesselton, until it became fully part of Malaysia. And like most Malaysian cities, it is a melting pot of various cultures.

Even if it is a part of Malaysia, many locals believe that it is a very different place. The people who live in Sabah are made up of indigenous people and the rest are either Filipino or Indonesian. You will find more Chinese-owned shops. The cost of living in this island is also relatively low, but also beware that job prospects here are low.

Essentials in Kota Kinabalu

- **Healthcare:** There are several hospitals on the island of Sabah to choose from.
    - Duchess of Kent Hospital
    - Gleneagles Kota Kinabalu
    - KPJ Sabah Specialist Hospital
    - Queen Elizabeth Hospital
    - Hospital Tuaran
- Accessibility to the major airport: Kota Kinabalu Airport is Malaysia's second busiest airport and the main gateway to Sabah. Located 8 km from the city centre, it connects the island to other East Asian cities such as Tokyo and Shanghai, and also Perth in Australia.

Things You Can Do in Kota Kinabalu

Activities will never come short. Whether on land (like Mt. Kinabalu, Malaysia's highest mountain at 13,435 feet) or at sea (like Tunku Abdul Rahman National Marine Park), there are plenty of places to visit. Here are places of interest on the island:

- Atkinson Clock Tower
- Signal Hill Observatory
- The Green Connection Aquarium
- Tanjung Aru Beach
- Likas Bay Beach
- Tunku Abdul Rahman Marine Park
- Double Six Monument
- Northern Coast
- City Park
- Kokol Hills
- Lok Kawi Wildlife Park
- Inobong Visitor and Research Center
- Kinarut
- Tambalang Racecourse
- Chinatown
- Tun Fuad Park
- Perdana Park
- Petagas War Memorial
- Kota Kinabalu Wetland Centre
- Sembulan Riverfront
- Sabah State Museum
- Islamic Civilization Museum
- Science and Technology Museum
- Sabah Art Gallery
- Borneo Art Gallery
- Sabah State Library
- Sacred Heart Cathedral
- Sabah State Mosque
- Pu Tuo Si Chinese Temple
- Kota Kinabalu City Mosque
- Sri Pasupathinath Alayam Hindu Temple
- Sri Subramaniar Hindu Temple
- Che Sui Khor Chinese Temple
- Gurdwara Sahib Sikh Temple
- St. Michael's Church
- Tzer Ying Buddhist Temple

Penang

Thousands of expats have long been enjoying all this small island off the west coast of the Malaysian peninsula. There's plenty to enjoy — from its tropical weather and the beaches, the shopping hubs and the restaurants, to the low cost of living. Rents in spacious apartments are half the price of those in Kuala Lumpur.

International high-end brands are available when you go shopping at Gurney Plaza or Queensbay Mall. But just a few kilometres away, you can explore jungles and secluded beaches, where you can take a food tour, cooking class or visit an orangutan shelter.

With an area of 293 square kilometres, there is no shortage of culture and arts. George Town, a bustling UNESCO World Heritage City, is a well-preserved town filled with colonial buildings and Chinese clan houses. Get lost in the maze of streets bursting with multicultural heritage. The town celebrates festivals of all kinds, from celebrating jazz to international film festivals, not to mention the religious and cultural festivities you get to experience.

Essentials in Penang

- **Healthcare:** Health tourism in Malaysia is booming, especially in Penang. Eleven member hospitals and thirteen associate members are spread throughout the island. There is no doubt that you will be cared for well here, given the wide range of specialist medical services.

- ★ Public hospitals in Penang:
  - Balik Pulau Hospital
  - Penang General Hospital
  - Bukit Mertajam Hospital
  - Kepala Batas Hospital
  - Seberang Jaya Hospital
  - Sungai Bakap Hospital
- ★ Private hospitals in Penang:
  - Bagan Specialist Centre
  - Georgetown Specialist Hospital
  - Gleneagles Penang
  - Island Hospital
  - KPJ Penang Specialist Hospital
  - Lam Wah Ee Hospital
  - Loh Guan Lye Specialists Centre
  - Mount Miriam Cancer Hospital
  - Pantai Hospital Penang
  - Penang Adventist Hospital

★ **Accessibility:** Penang Airport is one of the country's better-equipped airports. It services major airlines connecting to major cities in Malaysia, while direct flights to major East Asia countries such as Hong Kong, Taipei and Singapore are available.

Things You Can Do in Penang

Penang is a popular tourist destination, with countless things to do and see. A typical day can be trying out cafes in the morning, followed by a visit to the museum, and then a walk to the Botanical Gardens. The evenings can be spent walking around George Town. Here's a list of recommended things to visit:

- ★ UNESCO World Heritage Zone and Armenian Street
- ★ Penang Street
- ★ Penang Hill
- ★ Penang Botanic Gardens
- ★ Kek Lok Si-Temple of Supreme Bliss
- ★ Tropical Spice Garden
- ★ Entopia Penang
- ★ Pulau Jerejak Resort
- ★ Tropical Fruit Farm
- ★ Bao Sheng Durian Farm
- ★ Snake Temple
- ★ War Museum
- ★ Toy Museum
- ★ Penang Bird Park
- ★ Amazing Nibong Tebal
- ★ Penang Peranakan Heritage
- ★ Teluk Duyung Beaches
- ★ Penang National Park
- ★ Golfing at Bukit Jambul

Ipoh

Ipoh is known to offer a high standard of living at a much lower cost. Located between Kuala Lumpur and Penang, Ipoh's vast greenery and sunny climate have long attracted active retirees.

Compared to other major Malaysian cities, it has a quaint and rustic feel to it. If you prefer a slower pace of living, consider Ipoh's laid-back culture and note that it does not compromise on convenience.

What draws retirees here are the many golf courses around the city, where you don't have to spend a hefty membership and initiation fee. Also, outside Penang, Ipoh has Malaysia's best food scene. Local restaurants, food courts, hawker stalls – you name it!

If you love golf, Ipoh is just the place for you. While you need to pay a big amount for membership in most places, you can get an all-year-round membership at a much cheaper cost.

Ipoh also prides itself for the good water quality that comes from the limestone hills surrounding the Kinta valley. There is an abundance of water here resulting in big and crunchy bean sprouts.

Essentials in Ipoh

- **Healthcare:** Like any other Malaysian city, Ipoh boasts a number of hospitals. Both private and public hospitals are well-equipped with professional doctors, more than adequate facilities and advanced technology. Here are our recommended hospitals in Ipoh:
    - Fatimah Hospital
    - Hospital Pantai Ipoh
    - KPJ – IPOH Specialist Hospital
    - Kinta Medical Center
- **Accessibility:** Ipoh is located only a couple of hours drive north of Kuala Lumpur. Its small airport only operates flights into Singapore. It is accessible by train, bus and taxis, so you will not have problems getting around.

Things to do in Ipoh

Ipoh is the gateway to the Cameron Highlands Hill Station, where you can enjoy a refreshing mountain climate and scenic landscape. Its natural attractions include plenty of parks, lakes, forests and limestone hills.

If you are a tea lover, you are just in the right place, as the Cameron Highlands is the perfect place to grow tea. Entertainment wise, there are lots of sports and leisure activities in the region. If you prefer to learn tai chi or want to spend your time making arts and crafts, exploring culinary arts, swimming, dancing or simply play mahjong, Ipoh is very much for you. Here are other relaxing things you can do:

- Gua Tambun Cave Paintings
- Birch Memorial Clocktower
- Ipoh Railway Station
- Ipoh Town Hall
- Muzium Darul Ridzuan
- Padang Ipoh
- Kong Heng Square
- Concubine Lane
- Han Chin Pet Soo
- Ipoh Wall Art Murals at Ipoh Old Town and Ipoh New Town

Is Malaysia LGBT-friendly?

The country is still sensitive regarding the LGBT community. Generally speaking, being LGBT in the country means you must avoid public displays of affection with a same-sex partner. There are spots in Malaysia that are marginally more tolerant, especially in Kuala Lumpur, where gay bars and discreet hotels are available — but the country's overall attitude towards other genders and non-heterosexual relationships is something you might need to consider.

Senior Discounts

Seniors can enjoy a lot of perks from both the public and private sectors. For public transportation, a 50% discount is offered to those 60 years old and above. There are also cafes, restaurants and theatres that offer up to a 10% discount, while theme parks and cinemas offer 50% off.

Living in Malaysia: What to Watch Out For

Like any other country in the world, there are things to watch out for while you decide to retire in Malaysia. Here is a list of things you have to be beware of:

★ **Crime Rate in Malaysia.**
Malaysia's crime rate of 58.55% can be a little concerning. You have to watch out for snatch thefts and sexual assaults, crimes which seem to be reported more in the media. Relatively, however, Malaysia is still a safe country with low violent crimes. What you may likely encounter are taxis refusing to use meters and dishonest people pretending to be deaf. You just have to watch out for your bag and make sure you are living in a secure place.

★ **There's terrible traffic, especially in the big cities.**
In bigger cities with their traffic congestion, driving can be a pain. Navigation will be easier though, as signs are written in English.

★ **Don't drink the tap water.**
Like many countries, it is not advisable to drink tap water. This is because it is heavily chlorinated. Locals would either boil and filter the water before using or buy bottled water.

★ **Beware of the Malaysian rules.**
This includes public drunkenness, which is illegal in Malaysia. Shall you decide to drink, do it responsibly inside a bar or at home. If you are drunk, better get a taxi to take you home.

Summary

Malaysia is one of our favourite choices for countries to which to retire because it ticks all the major factors that make it the perfect place to spend the rest of your retirement days.

Healthcare: ★★★★★
Culture: ★★★★★
Cost of Living: ★★★★★
Housing: ★★★★
Accessibility: ★★★★★
Safety: ★★★

TOTAL STARS: 27 ★

Boracay, Philippines

Retire in the Philippines

Reasons to Retire in the Philippines

The Lonely Planet describes the Philippines as a land apart from Southeast Asia, and this rings true geographically, spiritually and culturally. The Philippines is the only country in Asia that had been colonised by Spain for three hundred years, followed by the Americans for fifty years. That means a lot of its cultural influences, like in architecture and in food, came from these countries.

Whether you prefer to have an active or relaxed lifestyle, in the bustle of a city or in a quiet seaside town, you can find something that will suit your taste from amongst its over 7,000 islands.

Why Retire in Philippines:

- ★ English is widely spoken throughout the country
- ★ Cost of living is relatively low
- ★ There is lots of rich history and culture to discover
- ★ There are more than 7,000 islands to explore
- ★ The country offers an easy retirement visa scheme

Culture

English is the second language in the Philippines, so you won't have any problem navigating around knowing only English. If you choose to learn the official language, Filipino, you will find it surprisingly easy, too, as a lot of its vocabulary is borrowed from English, Chinese, Spanish, Malay, and Arabic — plus the pronunciation tends to be phonetic.

Eighty-six percent of its population is Roman Catholic — and it's the only country in the world, aside from Vatican City, that still prohibits divorce.

Filipinos are warm people. They also love karaoke, with at least one member of the household who can sing and hit a note. If you love Christmas, then living in the Philippines will be perfect for you, as Filipinos are known to celebrate the longest Christmas ever, with preparations starting in September.

Climate

The tropical country has two major seasons: the rainy season that comes from June to November and the dry season from December to May. The dry season can be further subdivided, with December to February as the cool – dry season and March – May as the hot- dry season. There are southwest and northeast monsoons to watch out for. Excluding Baguio, the average annual temperature is 26 degrees Celsius.

The Philippines experiences a great amount of rainfall from July to November. Rainfall distribution depends on the region, with southwest and northeast monsoons affecting the islands year-round. This means wherever you go, you have to keep an umbrella handy with you at all times whether it's to shield yourself from the sun or from any sudden rain. Every year, typhoons batter the Pacific eastern coastline of Luzon, Samar and Leyte.

Cost of Living

Retirees can stretch their dollar here. The cost of living in the Philippines is significantly lower compared to the USA and Australia. As this edition goes to print, currently, AUD 1 is equivalent to PHP 37.21, which can afford you a good value meal.

The basic salary in the country is AUD 378 per month, while the median salary of Filipinos is about AUD 676 per month. The latter can cater to those who are living in Manila, but unfortunately, those who earn the basic salary may find it difficult to adapt.

If you want to live a decent lifestyle, AUD 2,027 is a good amount to start with. Here are the monthly expenses it can cover:

Expenses	Prices
A villa outside Manila	AUD 541
Utilities (water, garbage collection, electricity)	AUD 135
Internet	AUD 27
Toiletries	AUD 13.50
1-hour massage	AUD 6.75
Haircut	AUD 4.05
Groceries	AUD 135
Eat-out at local restaurants	AUD 13.50
Rideshare or taxi ride	AUD 6.75

Housing

With an SRRV visa, foreign retirees can only purchase a condominium or a townhouse. It will not be possible for a foreigner to own a fully detached home. The good news, however, is you may use your deposited amount of USD 10,000 (AUD 13,700) to secure a home.

It is best to research the location suitable for you, as some parts of the country don't have sufficient infrastructure. Make sure to choose an area that is not prone to flooding or power outages. The price of a one-bedroom apartment in the city centre costs about AUD 81,081. A town house in the suburbs outside Manila will cost the same.

Residential villages in the country are well-developed and are a more expensive option. Some examples are Amongsana Retirement Village and Forbes Hill. A good option for assisted living is Dona Rosario Residence located in Muntinlupa, with prices starting AUD 2,027 per month.

Healthcare in the Philippines

Filipino nurses and doctors are well known internationally, which means the country offers excellent healthcare. Whether you choose to go to public or private hospitals, you will find the staff to speak well in English.

40% of the hospitals in the country are public. Even in public healthcare, you can count that the doctors and nursing staff are highly proficient. Keep in mind, however, that there are still some limitations. Because public healthcare is relied upon by a huge number of Filipinos, public hospitals are often understaffed and patients may experience delays in treatment.

Middle-class Filipinos would prefer private hospitals because they are more equipped and efficient. The services in private hospitals are much faster too. Private hospitals can be a little expensive, but compared to what foreigners are paying abroad, it is still relatively cheaper. Whatever you prefer, we recommend having health insurance. The general consultations cost about AUD 8, while consultations with specialists cost around AUD 13.50. Also note that before you get admitted to the hospital, you need to make a down payment.

Pharmacies never come short. Most medicine is available in the country, although some prescription medications may not be available. It is always best to bring the necessary medication with you, prescribed in your home country.

How to Retire in the Philippines (Retirement Visa)*

The Philippines offers a straightforward procedure for retirees called Special Resident Retiree's Visa (SRRV). It is a lifetime visa with multiple entry and exit privileges. To be approved, you need to meet the following criteria:

★ You have to be at least fifty years old

★ Have USD 10,000 deposited into a bank account in the Philippines; if you do not have a guaranteed monthly income, you'll need to deposit USD 20,000 instead

- ★ You need to provide a pension of at least USD 800 per month or if you're a couple, USD 1,000 a month

Upon approval, you will be entitled to the government health care program, and exemption from certain taxes. If you don't meet the age requirement, the Philippines is also offering retirement for people 35–49 years old but they must have at least USD 50,000 deposited in the bank.

* USD has been retained as default currency for all immigration investment figures in this article. Currency exchange rate USD1 = AUD1.36.

Work

The good news about having an SRRV visa is that you are permitted to work, study, or invest in the Philippines. With the start-up scene in the Philippines booming in recent years, you can also start your own business here. The industries that are thriving in the country are F&B, tourism, BPO and retail.

Tax

The Philippines has a friendly tax code for expatriates. Foreigners will only be taxed on income earned in the country, with charges not more than 35%. Meanwhile, if you plan to take a full retirement, the government won't tax your pension or any kind of retirement plan.

It is also good to know that 12% of value-added tax applies to all kinds of sales, barter, exchange, or lease of goods and services. This is usually integrated or added to the bill that you need to pay.

Food

Filipino cuisine has been influenced by China, India, Arabia, Spain and the United States. Slowly, the country's cuisine is gaining popularity around the world – partly thanks to Jollibee, that little bee that wins over McDonald's here. The locals value strong flavour so you might find the food in the Philippines to be too sweet, too salty or too heavy.

Filipinos love to eat rice with every meal. They eat rice for breakfast, lunch, and dinner, and sometimes, even during snack time. Here are the must-haves of Filipino cuisine:

- ★ **Lechon** refers to the fully roasted suckling pig, which Filipinos rave for because of its juicy meat and crunchy skin. It is always present in all kinds of Filipino festivals. After the sinigang, it is considered the national food of the country.

- ★ **Sinigang** is a sour soup with pork as the main ingredient, tossed in with a variety of vegetables. The meat is sometimes beef, shrimp or fish. It is enjoyed by every household whether it's the dry or the wet season.

- ★ **Kare-kare** is a thick and rich stew made from crushed peanuts, beef and oxtail, and vegetables. It is the Philippine version of curry, minus the spiciness. It is often served with shrimp paste and rice.

- ★ **Fried lumpia** is a Chinese-influenced version of spring rolls. It is deep-fried rolls with minced meat, onion and carrots.

- ★ **Bicol express** is a stew that features meat, coconut milk and long chili peppers – a dish that traditionally came from Bicol.

- **Pancit palabok** is a noodle dish layered with rich orange sauce made from shrimp broth, pork shrimps, and pork rinds.

- **Bulalo** is a broth rich with beef flavour, a result of boiling for hours. And yes, Filipinos love to sip their hot soup despite the scorching weather.

- **Adobo** is meat cooked with vinegar, garlic, salt, pepper and soy sauce. It is perhaps every Filipino's favourite dish!

- **Halo-halo** or literally "mix-mix" is a unique dessert filled with crushed ice, milk, and various ingredients, such as ube, coconut strips, sago, fruit slices, flan and a scoop of ice cream. Filipinos love their halo-halo, especially in summer.

This list is just for starters. There is more to try and taste when you decide to go in depth in the regional cuisine. International restaurants are available in the major cities of the Philippines such as Manila, Cebu and Davao in case you crave other types of cuisine.

Recommended Cities in the Philippines

Cebu

The number of foreigners choosing Cebu is increasing, as its retirement features have been growing every year. It has anything a retiree could ask for, from top hospitals to the various entertainment options, and an international airport that connects to cities such as Dubai and Los Angeles.

The city has been growing as a business hub, with facilities on par with that of the capital, Manila. Malls have international and even luxury brands available, so you can easily find western restaurants and products. Plus, you will have access to countless beaches and nature parks.

Essentials in Cebu:

- **Healthcare:** Like Manila, Cebu hospitals and healthcare offer high-quality service and facilities. Living here means you will have access to some of the top hospitals in the country that can deliver in the field of surgery and other medical services. Public and private hospitals, specialty clinics and other health facilities are available here.
    - Cebu Doctors University (CDU) Hospital
    - Perpetual Succor Hospital
    - Cebu City Medical Center
    - Cebu (Velez) General Hospital
    - Chong Hua Hospital

- **Accessibility:** Cebu International Airport is the second-busiest airport in the country. It is well-connected to the rest of the country as well and operates direct flights to major cities in Asia. The recently constructed world-class airport is an hour's drive away from Cebu City.

Things You Can Do in Cebu

The province is hailed as the Queen City of the South for a reason. From the festivals it celebrates each year and the historical sites to the food and the energy of the people, there will never be a dull retirement day. Here is a quick list of things you can see and do while retired in Cebu:

- ★ Cebu Heritage Monument
- ★ Colon Street
- ★ 1730 Jesuit House
- ★ Oslob for the Whale Sharks
- ★ Cebu Metropolitan Cathedral
- ★ Basilica del Santo Nino
- ★ Tops Lookout
- ★ Fort San Pedro
- ★ Terrazas De Flores Botanical Garden
- ★ Cebu Ocean Park
- ★ Anjo World Theme Park
- ★ Waterworld Cebu
- ★ Temple of Leah
- ★ Buwakan ni Alejandra
- ★ Moalboal
- ★ Pescador Island
- ★ Osmena Peak Dalaguete
- ★ Simala Shrine
- ★ Bantayan Island
- ★ Virgin Island
- ★ Camotes Island
- ★ Malapascua Island

Laguna

If you prefer to live in the countryside with a plethora of waterfalls, springs, rivers and lakes, consider Laguna as your retirement destination in the Philippines. One of the towns, Los Baños, has numerous hot and cold springs in the resort town of Mount Makiling. On the mountain's slopes, you can find a botanical park and the National Arts Center. Another town to consider is the historical Calamba, where the ancestral house of the country's national hero Jose Rizal can be found.

One of the most convenient, self-sustained suburban communities in Laguna is Brentville International Community, a 54-hectare village in Biñan, Laguna, offering a diversity of living options.

Essentials in Laguna

- ★ **Healthcare:** There is a long list of hospitals in Laguna, ensuring that whatever health issues you have, you will be well taken care of. Here are some of them:
  - ★ Balibago Polyclinic & Hospital, Inc
  - ★ Calamba Doctors Hospital
  - ★ Community General Hospital of San Pablo City
  - ★ Family Care Hospital
  - ★ Gamez Hospital
  - ★ Healthserv Los Banos Medical Center
  - ★ Laguna Doctors Hospital
  - ★ Los Baños Doctors Hospital & Medical Center, Laguna
  - ★ Pamana Medical Center

- ★ **Accessibility:** There is no airport in Laguna. The nearest airport is in Manila, around 2.5 hours' drive away.

Things You Can Do in Laguna

You never have to get out of Laguna to experience both the beach and the countryside. Locals living near Laguna often visit nearby coastal provinces on the weekend, visiting the many tourist spots it has to offer. A normal retiree day will probably include a soak in one of the hundred springs in the Laguna, followed by a walk in the botanical garden. There is no shortage of things you can do. Here, we've listed down a few:

- Pagsanjan Falls
- Rizal Shrine
- Lake Pandin
- Enchanted Kingdom
- Sampaloc Lake
- Nuvali
- Hidden Valley Springs
- Seven Lakes of San Pablo City
- Lake Caliraya
- Laguna Bay
- Bato Springs Resort
- Taytay Falls
- Hulugan Falls
- Dalitiwan River
- Mt. Makiling
- Mt. Banahaw
- Paete Town

Pampanga

The former U.S. base has been developing, with the economy steadily increasing day by day. There are newly built malls, a few more hotels, and condominium units. With the Subic-Clark-Tarlac Expressway newly opened, one can travel to Manila in about 2.5 hours.

The Clark Freeport and Special Economic Zone is an area in Angeles City transformed into a modern industrial estate. It now serves as the centre for leisure, fitness, and entertainment in Central Luzon. The area is also predicted to be the next sanctuary for the business process outsourcing industry.

The Philippines has started building a green, disaster-resilient city called New Clark City. It is an ambitious goal, but when that time comes – possibly around 2022, more people will move to Pampanga.

Essentials in Clark

- **Healthcare:** Like other major parts of the Philippines, there are excellent hospitals in Pampanga. They are often sufficient with good facilities, otherwise, Manila being 2.5 hours' driving distance away is also another option. Here are hospitals you may consider in Pampanga:
    - Angeles University Medical Center
    - Clark Central Medical Hospital Inc.
    - Dee Hwa Liong Foundation Medical Center
    - Manabat Maternity & General Hospital
    - Our Mother of Perpetual Help Hospital
    - Pampanga International Hospital

- **Accessibility:** Clark International Airport serves Central Luzon, Northern Luzon, and even Metro Manila. It has been expanded and can accommodate a million passengers. However, most of its destinations are only cities in Asia, such as Seoul and Singapore. Locals still travel to Manila to connect to other faraway places.

Things You Can Do in Pampanga

Pampanga is also well known as the culinary capital of the Philippines. It is the home of sisig (chopped pig's head parts, grilled and mixed with chicken liver) and morcon. A retiree's life can be spent on food tripping, then burning the calories by going around these places in Pampanga:

- ★ Hydro sports in Pradera
- ★ Nayong Pilipino Clark
- ★ Bacolor and San Fernando
- ★ Puning Hot Springs
- ★ Sky Ranch
- ★ Arzobispado De Pampanga Church
- ★ Mt. Pinatubo
- ★ Sandbox
- ★ Mt. Arayat National Park
- ★ Aqua Planet
- ★ Museo Ning Angeles
- ★ Pamintuan Mansion
- ★ Miyamit Falls
- ★ Candaba Swamp
- ★ San Fernando Train Station
- ★ Holy Rosary Parish Church

Manila

If you are keen to spend the rest of your life in the concrete jungle with a lower cost of living, Manila can offer that to you. The capital offers a rich nightlife scene and an array of international and local restaurants. You will have all the conveniences, as well as easy escape routes to nature parks and beaches such as Puerto Galera and Laguna.

Compared to its Southeast Asian neighbours, Manila has a high population density, with people from the provinces drawn to Manila to make a living. Manila is usually skipped by tourists who directly fly to other famous islands to explore and relax, but it is a vibrant city where you can learn a lot about the country's rich history.

Essentials in Manila

- **Healthcare:** Manila is where you will find the best healthcare options in the country. After all, it is home to three Joint Commission International-accredited hospitals. The skill and competency of the medical staff in the capital are excellent. Here is a list of hospitals in Manila you may consider:
    - Makati Medical Center
    - St. Luke's Hospital
    - Asian Hospital
    - Capitol Medical Center
    - Manila Doctors Hospital
    - Medical Center Manila
    - Philippine General Hospital

- **Accessibility:** Manila is served by two international airports that connect the country to all parts of the world. It is only a 16-hour flight to New York and 10 hours from Sydney. Manila is also well-connected to all domestic airports from the northernmost in Batanes to the southernmost, in Sulu.

Things You Can Do in Manila

Manila can be chaotic, but it has its own charms that work well for both locals and foreign retirees. It has the country's top universities, high-end malls, five-star hotels, budget markets, old churches, and museums and parks. Here are the places that will either take you back in time or immerse you in the current culture:

- Fort Santiago
- National Museum
- Intramuros
- San Agustin Church and Museum
- Manila Cathedral
- National Museum of Natural History
- Rizal Park
- Manila Ocean Park
- Manila Bay
- University of Santo Tomas
- Quiapo Church
- Divisoria Market
- Chinatown
- San Sebastian Church
- SM Mall of Asia
- Malacanang Palace
- Metropolitan Museum of Art

Palawan

The geographical location of Palawan makes it one of the safest islands in the country against natural disasters. There is no volcano, you don't have to worry about earthquakes and it is also rarely hit by typhoons.

It has an amazing ecologically balanced environment, rich in biodiversity and teeming with protected areas. With cleaner surroundings, safe neighbourhoods, and a competitive cost of living, all while offering a good mix of urban and rural lifestyles, both locals and foreigners are attracted to retire here.

Essentials in Palawan

- **Healthcare:** The healthcare services on this big island are sufficient enough that residents and travellers have nothing to worry about when it comes to medical emergencies. There is a good number of affordable healthcare institutions that provide high-quality services. Here are some of the best hospitals in Palawan:
  - Palawan Adventist Hospital and RTN
  - Rizal Rural Health Unity and Narra Municipal Hospital
  - Aborlan Medicare and Roxas Medicare
  - Brooke's Point District Hospital

- **Accessibility:** There are four major airports in Palawan that connect to Manila and Cebu. Puerto Princesa International Airport is the main gateway that serves major airlines in the country. The airport is conveniently located half an hour away from the city centre and includes an ample number of facilities.

Things You Can Do in Palawan

Palawan is one of the most visited places in the Philippines. Imagine retiring to the best island in the world, a citation awarded by the Travel + Leisure in July 2020. Wake up with the foggy mountain view, spend the morning with a walk on the shore or a swim by the beach, and the rest of the day exploring the many hiking trails and

waterfalls the island has to offer. Here are the things you can do more than once in Palawan:

- ★ Island hopping in Honda Bay
- ★ Scuba diving in El Nido
- ★ El Nido beaches
- ★ Port Barton
- ★ Tabon Caves
- ★ Baker's Hill
- ★ Palawan Wildlife Rescue and Conservation Center
- ★ Underground River
- ★ Tubbataha Reef National Marine Park
- ★ Starfish Island
- ★ Estrella Falls
- ★ Bakbakan Falls
- ★ Tay Tay
- ★ Nagkalit-kalit Waterfall
- ★ Iwahig River Firefly
- ★ Simizu Island
- ★ Busuanga Island
- ★ Mitra Ranch Horses

Is the Philippines LGBT-friendly?

The Philippines has been highly ranked as one of the most gay-friendly countries. Filipinos have, for example, developed rich gay lingo that is derived from Taglish (Tagalog–English) and is widely used in the country, even by non-lesbian, gay, bisexual and transgender (LGBT) folks. If you are a gay couple, you will feel very welcome here.

Last September 2017, the House of Representatives approved sweeping LGBT rights in the country. The bill prohibits discriminatory acts against the LGBT community, such as gender profiling, denying access to any public or medical health service. That being said, same-sex marriage is still prohibited in the Philippines.

Senior Discounts

Senior citizens in the Philippines are entitled to a 20% discount on local transportation fares, purchases of medicine, diagnostics and hospital laboratory fees in hospitals, as well as in the cinemas and concert halls. Seniors can also get a 5% discount on water and electricity bills and are also exempt from paying the value-added tax.

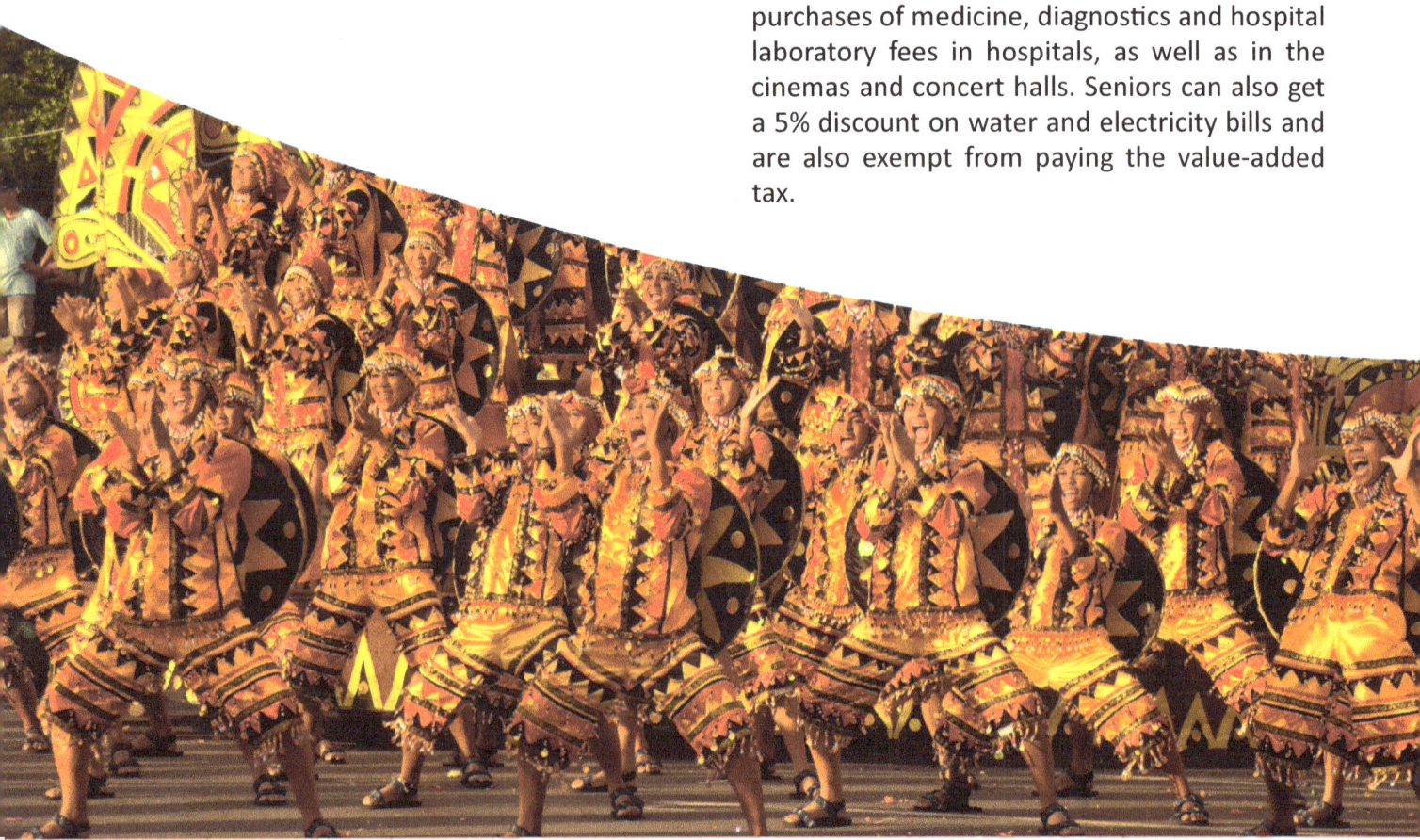

Living in the Philippines: What to Watch Out For

★ ### Foreign property ownership is not allowed.
Foreigners are only permitted to purchase condominiums and townhouses, while land ownership is limited to Filipino citizens only. If you want to own a house in the country, you need to have a long-term lease agreement with a Filipino landowner. Otherwise, you may also consider purchasing through a corporation as long as it is 60% owned by Filipinos.

★ ### Safety can be a concern.
While living in the Philippines, you should be aware of the possibilities of theft, robbery, mugging and other petty crimes. Poverty is still one of the challenges the country is facing. Although most retirement communities are located far from dangerous areas, it is best to avoid walking late at night, alone, while flaunting jewellery.

★ ### Power outages are part of daily life.
Infrastructure is not very dependable in the country. Internet service can be slow and power outages are common.

★ ### Deal with terrible traffic.
Unfortunately, the Philippines has the worst traffic in Southeast Asia. In the capital, Manila, the traffic congestion is probably the second-worst in the world. If you plan to meet friends outside, you may want to avoid the rush hour or allocate enough time to get you from point A to point B.

★ ### The country is prone to natural disasters.
With the country's geographic circumstances, it is highly prone to earthquakes, typhoons, volcanic eruptions and flooding. That said, there are areas in the Philippines that have been safe from typhoons and earthquakes, such as Palawan.

Summary

Having lived in the Philippines for some time in my life, we try not to be biased in our rankings. All that was mentioned here has been well-researched and confirmed with respected institutions. In summary, the country has a lot to offer retirees and, although it might not be perfect, it will always be a home we'll keep on coming back to.

Healthcare: ★ ★ ★ ★ ★
Culture: ★ ★ ★ ★ ★
Cost of Living: ★ ★ ★ ★
Housing: ★ ★ ★ ★
Accessibility: ★ ★ ★ ★
Safety: ★ ★ ★

TOTAL STARS: 25 ★

Bangkok, Thailand

Retire in Thailand

Reasons to Retire in Thailand

For decades, Thailand has been one of the top destinations not only for short visits but also for retirement. If you are visiting Thailand for the first time, be warned that it is hard not to fall in love with the country, with its rich culture to its out of this world cuisine, the perfect warm weather to the beaches you can easily access, from the temples you can explore to the smiles of strangers you meet.

It can be a bit of a surprise, but the growing expatriate community can also make you feel at home. In fact, Thailand issued 80,000 retirement visas in 2018, a figure that continues to grow every year. It is also accessible through flights from all major cities that you can easily go back home if you prefer, or travel to neighbouring countries. Applying for a retirement visa is made easy and simple if you are at least 50 years old.

The cost of living is also reasonable compared to the quality of life that you can experience. And if you need any more convincing, Thailand has top-notch healthcare, an important factor in retirement. Hospitals are inexpensive as long as you have the necessary insurance. Whatever lifestyle you are aiming for, whether you want to be surrounded by buildings and action in the middle of a cosmopolitan city or live right in front of a white sand beach, the land of smiles has got it covered for you.

Why Retire in Thailand:

- ★ You can have the best of everything at a low cost
- ★ Top-notch and accessible healthcare at a reasonable price
- ★ International airports in major cities link the country to most parts of the world
- ★ Amazing history, culture, nature, people and food!

Culture

Do you know that Thailand is one of the few countries in Asia that have not been colonized by European powers? Thailand boasts and sustains a rich history and culture. About 95% of the population is Buddhist and believes in karma, compassion and calmness.

The government is a constitutional monarchy, and the residents have a high level of respect for the royal family. The country has a reputation for being the land of smiles, so living here and adapting to the lifestyle would lend a lot to a calmer, more peaceful mindset. This is probably one of the reasons why expat communities continue to thrive in the country.

Despite the news that Thailand's proficiency in English has been dropping, you don't necessarily have to learn Thai if you decide to retire in Thailand. Many Thais speak basic English in the areas where a large number of tourists visit. Going off the beaten path may require you to speak a little Thai to get by, but Thais are helpful people so you can easily get around.

Climate

Foreign retirees enjoy the tropical climate in Thailand. But keep in mind, while choosing the area to live in, that the country has different climate zones based on their rain pattern. In the northern inland plain, along with the north-western hilly area, it is hot for most of the year, except in winter when the night-time temperature drops to 15 degrees.

In Bangkok, the climate is hot all year round, and before the monsoon comes, the heat intensifies, so people can only take refuge in air-conditioned rooms. The same thing goes with Thailand's peninsula (Phuket, Koh Samui).

The monsoon season rain can be felt from mid-May to October throughout Thailand except in the peninsula, which experiences an abundance of rain from October to December.

Cost of Living

The basic cost for retirees is AUD 1,622 per month, which can go up depending on the place that you live. It can cover the cost of a two-bedroom apartment, eating out a few times a week, groceries and healthcare. Here are some basic expenses for reference:

Expenses	Prices
Inexpensive restaurant meal	AUD 2.70
Three-course meal at a mid-range restaurant	AUD 30
Local beer	AUD 2.40
One-bedroom apartment in the city centre	AUD 811

Bangkok remains to be the most expensive city, but if you prefer to live somewhere cheaper, then Chiang Mai is also a good option.

Housing

To help prevent foreigners from increasing the price of land and apartments, Thailand implements property ownership laws. It means that foreigners can buy a property like a condo or a villa, but they are not allowed to own the land. In this case, it might be easier to purchase a condominium. There is a possibility to extend the leasehold of the land, but the landowner is not obliged to do so.

Real estate agents are easy to find in Thailand and they speak English, too. The cost of a nice villa in Chiang Mai is AUD 337,838, while a

one-bedroom apartment will be around AUD 189,189.

Retirement homes are not very common options in Thailand, because it is normally the eldest daughter who looks after the parents when they get old. Here are a few options:

- ★ Thailand Retirement and Long-Term Care Communities in Pattaya
- ★ Golden Years Hospital, Bangkok
- ★ McKean Rehabilitation Center, Chiang Mai

Healthcare in Thailand

You can never go wrong with healthcare in Thailand. Ranked as the sixth-best in the world, the country is known in the medical tourism industry, offering world-class, inexpensive healthcare. Thailand is not one of the world's richest economies, but it succeeded in offering an affordable system to its people.

Healthcare is funded through taxation, and this allows hospitals to offer excellent quality. English-speaking practitioners are available, with most major provinces having one private hospital. Thailand's expatriates opt for private hospitals because they are still inexpensive. A dental cleaning costs AUD 45, while a complete health check-up is AUD 151.

How to Retire in Thailand (Retirement Visa)*

Thailand offers specific visa classifications for those who want to retire in the country: The non-immigrant O visa and the retirement visa.

There are two basic requirements to qualify for a retirement visa:

- ★ You must be at least 50 years old.
- ★ You have proof that you can financially support yourself. Either you have a monthly income, pension or passive income of THB 65,000 / USD 2,100, or you must have at least THB 800,000 / USD 25,500 deposited in a Thai bank account. The latter option must prove that the money has been in your account for at least two months before you can apply for a visa. And once you get the visa, THB 400,000 / USD 12,750 must remain in your account in the next three months. This means you cannot just borrow the money for a few days to meet the requirements.

The retirement visa needs to be renewed annually, with the same requirements each time. You also need to report to an immigration office every three months, and the process can be completed online once registered. You will also need comprehensive health insurance upon application.

There will be plenty of paperwork involved and most of them are in the Thai language. It will be best to get yourself an agent to help you through the processes and documentation.

* USD and THB have been retained as default currency for all immigration investment figures in this article. Currency exchange rate USD1 = AUD1.36; THB 1 = AUD 0.041.

Work

You are not allowed to work in Thailand with a retirement visa. However, you may consider investing in Thai companies. Foreigners can receive profits but cannot be involved in the daily operations. If you intend to work in Thailand, then you're better off getting a work permit.

Running a business online? That is possible for foreigners living in Thailand as long as it is a non-Thai website hosting. There are many cases when a foreigner marries a local who will become a business partner. In this case, the partner can front the business and will then prevent some bureaucratic knots.

However, if you don't have any success in building a business anywhere else, don't try it in Thailand for the first time. A big percentage of entrepreneurs end up losing all their money.

Volunteering also counts as work, so this is also not allowed with a retirement visa.

Tax*

If you live in Thailand, whether you are earning the money domestically or internationally, you will be required to pay taxes. Yes, even if you don't have a work permit. The tax rate varies and will depend on how much your personal income is.

Taxable Income	Tax Rate
0 – THB 150,000	Exempted
Between THB 150,000 – THB 300,000	5%
Between THB 300,000 – THB 500,000	10%
Between THB 500 – THB 750,000	15%
Between THB 750,000 – THB 1,000,000	20%
Between THB 1,000,000 – 2,000,000	25%
Between 2,000,000 – 4,000,000	30%
Over 4,000,000	35%

* THB has been retained as default currency for all tax figures in this article. Currency exchange rate THB 1 = AUD 0.041.

Food

Thailand's cuisine is so world famous that every major city in the world has access to Thai curry and Tom Yum soup. The first thing you'll notice is the distinctive, strong aromatic and spicy edge, then there's the attention to detail down to the very small ingredients. Its texture, colour and taste are well-thought out and so unique that you will keep on coming back for more. It's No wonder that seven Thai dishes appeared on the list of the World's 50 Best Foods.

There are four categories in Thai cuisine – *tom* which means boiled dishes, *tam* or pounded foods, *gaeng* which refers to curries and the *yam* or spicy salads. Although its historical influences come from neighbouring India, Malaysia and Indonesia, there are regional variations too. For instance, Northern Thai cuisine is similar to Myanmar's Shan State, Laos and the Yunnan province of China. While if you look at the southern part of Thailand, there are more cuisines that include the use of coconut milk and fresh turmeric.

You also have to watch out for the Royal cuisine, which traces its history back to 1351–1767, that uses a great deal of refinement, presentation and cooking technique. Here are the top dishes you will encounter every day should you choose to retire in Thailand:

★ **Guay teow** or noodle soup can be made with pork, chicken or beef, and rice or egg noodles. This tasty broth is complimented with a selection of condiments including sugar, dried chilli peppers, fish sauce and lime juice.

★ **Tom yum goong** or spicy shrimp soup is probably one of the most famous soups from Thailand. It's a sour soup flavoured with kaffir lime leaf, galangal root and

fragrant lemon grass. The dish also makes use of shrimp, chicken or mushroom.

★ **Tom Kha Gai**, or chicken in coconut soup, is a relative of tom yum soup but it is less spicy. Instead, it comes with creamy coconut milk producing a rich, sweet flavour.

★ **Som tam**, or spicy green papaya salad, comes from the north-eastern part of the country. It consists of shredded papaya, tomatoes, carrots, dried shrimp, peanuts, runner beans, palm sugar, tamarind pulp, lime juice, fish sauce and a lot of chillies! All these ingredients mixed together produces a legendary dish that will keep your senses awake.

★ **Pad Thai**, or Thai-style fried noodles, is usually the first cuisine tourists would try because it can be found in every street corner. It is a fried-noodle fish dish with shrimp or chicken and vegetables, with a splash of lime, making it perfect for its warm weather.

★ **Khao pad** or fried rice is similar to pad Thai but with rice instead of noodles. The dish often comes with cucumber and garnish.

★ **Panang** or Thai curry is the beginner's curry because of its level of spiciness. It is served with shrimp or vegetables.

★ **Gaeng keow wan** or green curry is the spiciest of all the curries, but sweet too. It is difficult to resist especially with fresh green chillies, ginger, eggplant and lots of coconut milk. Pair it with steamed rice to balance the spice level.

★ **Pad phak**, or fried vegetables, is a combination of many flavours – a blend of sugar, salt and spices, making it the perfect dish for vegetarians!

★ **Kao Niew Ma Muang** or mango and sticky rice is made of fresh mango slices and sticky rice lashed with sweet condensed milk. You can find this famous dessert in restaurants, grocery shops and street stalls.

There is no shortage of international cuisine in Thailand. With tourists coming from all parts of the world, every major city in the country has access to Western, Middle Eastern and other Asian cuisine.

Recommended Cities in Thailand

Bangkok

The capital of Thailand is huge and cosmopolitan. If you are looking for true urban living, Bangkok is the place to live. It is the regional centre for all things art, fashion and entertainment. Compared to other flourishing modern cities around the world with efficient and world-class transportation options, it is one of the most affordable.

You can get a bowl of noodles in the best street food stalls for only AUD 2.70. If you love shopping, Bangkok has a multitude of markets, from western-style malls to boutique shopping centres.

Majority of expats live in Bangkok, particularly in Sukhumvit Road because of its proximity to the Sky Train and the underground MRT. If you need more room, then going for Bangkok's suburbs, such as Bang Na and Nonthaburi, is a good idea.

Essentials in Bangkok:

- **Healthcare:** Private hospitals here are considered first rate. They often hire staff who are educated in the West. Plus, many doctors and specialists in the city speak English. Here are our recommended hospitals in the capital:
    - BNH Hospital
    - Bumrungrad International Hospital;
    - Samitivej Sukhumvit Hospital
    - Bangkok International Hospital
    - The Bangkok Christian Hospital
    - Saint Louis Hospital

- **Accessibility:** The Suvarnabhumi (pronounced as Suwannaphum) is the main hub for Bangkok Airways, Thai Airways International and Smile Airways. These airlines connect the country to Asia, Oceania, Europe and Africa, making the airport the seventeenth busiest in the world. The airport also connects the city to all other parts of Thailand.

Things You Can Do in Bangkok

The capital is where the temples and towering skyscrapers blend naturally. Thailand's stable economy is well reflected in its vibrant culture. With so many places to see and return to, a usual day can start in the busy maze of the floating market, then a relaxing lunch in one of the restaurants at Siam Paragon and, finally, exploring the night market. Here are some of the places in Bangkok that you'll keep coming back to:

- Floating Market in Bangkok
- Siam Ocean World
- Grand Palace
- Safari World Bangkok
- Wat Arun
- China Town
- Chatuchak Weekend Market
- Jim Thompson House
- Khao San Road
- Vertigo Rooftop Bar
- Asiatique Sky
- Calypso Theatre
- Khao Yai National Park
- Koh Kret Island
- Lumpini Park
- Sathorn Unique Tower
- Erawan Shrine
- Dusit Palace
- Wat Traimit
- Siam Paragon

Chiang Mai

Modern city life also exists here, for only a fraction of the cost compared to Bangkok. Located in northern Thailand, Chiang Mai is best for those seeking a calmer way of life. After all, it is home to hundreds of Buddhist temples, some dating back over 700 years.

Chiang Mai is also known as a university town, which means you'll find many arts and cultural displays in the local galleries and yearly festivals.

If there's one thing that's lacking here, it is the beach. The nearest beach is a plane ride away for less than a hundred dollars, in case you feel the need.

If you're up for an adventure, several national parks are within driving distance. You can access the highest mountain in the country from here. The rental cost is relatively cheap and you'll find most of the condos have access to swimming pools and gyms.

Essentials in Chiang Mai

- **Healthcare:** Many doctors and nurses in public and private hospitals are trained in western countries. Like Bangkok, Chiang Mai also enjoys excellent quality healthcare, plus, it's affordable too. Expats often feel that the healthcare they receive here is a lot better than what they receive at home. It is also good to know that hospitals in the city can perform heart operations and cosmetic surgery. Here are hospitals to consider while you live here:
    - Chiang Mai Ram Hospital
    - Lanna Hospital
    - Rajavej Chiang Mai Hospital
    - McCormick Hospital
    - Chiang Mai Neurological Hospital
    - Feung Fah Clinic

- **Accessibility:** Chiang Mai International Airport is the gateway to the northern part of Thailand. As one of the bucket-list spots of the country, the airport is currently the fourth-busiest and connects Chiang Mai to major Asian cities such as Kuala Lumpur, Beijing, Taipei, Phnom Penh, Seoul, Luang Prabang and Bangkok.

Things You Can Do in Chiang Mai

Chiang Mai remains to be a favourite spot for expatriates. If you love culture and history, Chiang Mai offers hundreds of temples, a variety of restaurants, countless outdoor activities and the surrounding countryside, which fits perfectly well with the modern amenities at reasonable prices. You can walk around the city and easily find fresh markets scattered throughout with products sold for bargain prices.

This is also a city where you can wear your shorts and shirt every day because of its warm climate. During winter, however, be prepared to wear sweaters as it can get pretty chilly. It is easy to feel at home with over 30,000 expatriates living here, organising weekly activities. Here are some other places you may consider in your list for further exploration:

- Doi Suthep
- San Kamphaeng Road
- Doi Inthanon National Park
- Warorot Market
- Mae Ping River
- Wat Phra Singh
- Wat Chedi Luang
- Jungle Temple
- Elephant Nature Park
- Huay Kaew Waterfall
- Wat Phra That Doi Suthep
- Wat Suan Dok Temple
- Wat Pha Lat
- Monkchat
- Thai Farm Cooking School

Phuket

The beach town of Phuket offers an easy lifestyle for retirees. Just because it has been welcoming tourists for years, does not mean it can't offer you your own paradise. With a little bit of research, you can find a two-bedroom apartment, walking distance to the beach, at $700 a month. If you prefer to have a bigger home that comes with a communal pool, be prepared to stretch your home budget to $1,000 a month.

Driving around is pretty straightforward and offers a great opportunity to find near-empty beaches. Going for the touristy beach is not a bad idea either because it means you can find restaurants serving your favourite cocktails.

It may not be the cheapest option in the country, with luxury hotels sprouting like mushrooms, but there are inexpensive ways to get the most out of your dollars while living here. For example, a general doctor still costs under AUD 13.70 per visit and a Thai massage will cost you AUD 10.95 per hour.

One benefit of living in Phuket is its offering of tropical and exotic life. Imagine the turquoise waters of the Andaman Sea along with the astonishing coastline, a few steps away, there's the jungle-topped mountains greeting you. With all these elements coming together, it is easy to overlook the monsoon weather, expensive taxis and the overdevelopment in the island. Somehow, all these became a part of Phuket's charm.

Essentials in Phuket

- **Healthcare:** Like the rest of the country, Phuket is never short of hospital choices. The city has more than enough hospitals and here are some of our recommendations:
  - Bangkok Hospital Siriroj
  - Bangkok Hospital Phuket
  - Vachira Phuket Hospital
  - Dibuk Hospital

- **Accessibility:** Phuket plays a major role in the country's tourism, which clearly explains how its airport is the third busiest in the country. The airport connects the area to the capital with an hour flight, as well as to major cities around the world that includes Hong Kong, Moscow, Tel Aviv and Sydney.

Things You Can Do in Phuket

If you love club hopping, being in the centre of the action, and an easy-going lifestyle, Phuket is the place for you. A day can start with a swim, followed by a relaxing brunch on a quiet beach. In the afternoon, you may continue your active lifestyle hiking the jungles, ending the day with the view of the sunset. If you need a little privacy, why not hire your own boat and go island-hopping? The evening can be spent in one of the bars in the Patong area. Need to go beyond the touristy sites? Here are some more of the best places to see and go to:

- Phang Nga Bay
- Phi Phi Islands
- Big Buddha of Phuket
- Bangla Road
- Chalong Temple
- Old Phuket Town
- Similan Islands
- Samet Nanshe viewpoint
- Karon viewpoint
- Mai Khao Beach
- Promthep Cape

- Koh Panyi
- James Bond Island
- Black Rock Viewpoint
- Siam Niramit
- Phuket Aquaria
- Rang Hill

Is Thailand LGBT-friendly?

Thailand is considered the most accepting country for the LGBT community in Southeast Asia. Visiting the streets of Bangkok can tell you that the country has a thriving LGBT scene. Their society is very LGBT-friendly — they even host Miss International Queen pageant yearly, the largest transgender pageant in the world.

When it comes to public displays of affection, you will not encounter any issues in the major cities. Gay-friendly hotels, nightclubs and resorts exist in Thailand. Just be careful and be discreet, if possible, when traveling outside of urban areas. If there is one thing to watch out for, it's their HIV rate, which is the highest in the world.

Senior Discounts

Senior citizens are well-respected in Thailand, however, discounts are not offered as much, even for transportation and admission fees. It does not mean you can't ask. Thais are hospitable so chances are they will accommodate your wishes. For the locals, there are senior benefits available monthly amounting to at least 600 baht.

Living in Thailand: What to Watch Out For

This paradise has a downside too and you have to be aware of these before deciding that Thailand is the place for you. Here are things that you should watch out for:

- ★ **Safety in Thailand.**
  It is relatively safe to live in Thailand, but keep in mind that violence can strike in the country every now and then. Physical attacks and theft may not be common, but it's still possible. Elements of organised crime will try to sell your drugs. If you're caught, the country has the right to give you a death sentence.

- ★ **Language Barrier is an issue.**
  Even in urban areas, you will still find the locals do not speak the English language very well so you may want to hire an interpreter. Even government officials and businesses communicate in Thai, so that it can be a struggle living in the country without knowing the basics. Knowing the local language can get you more benefits from haggling to not getting taken advantage of.

- ★ **Prostitution in the country**
  Prostitution is a serious cultural issue in Thailand. Young girls are often seen with older men who pay for services. Thailand may have a stable economy, but it does not mean that money reaches the poor. Some families tolerate and rely on the sex trade just to put food on the table.

- ★ **Corruption by police officers**
  It is common for police officers to squeeze out some funding from both tourists and expatriates. You may get charged with a crime or become a victim of false allegations so be careful with every action you may take. If you have done something wrong, police officers will be taking advantage of the situation. One solution is agreeing to go to the station or try offering THB 200 and see what happens.

Summary

Thailand remains to be on the top of everyone's retirement list. After all, Thailand is another term for paradise. Here's our final rating:

Healthcare: ★★★★★
Culture: ★★★★★
Cost of Living: ★★★★
Housing: ★★★★
Accessibility: ★★★★★
Safety: ★★★

TOTAL STARS: 26 ★

Hanoi train street, Trần Phú, Hàng Bông, Hoàn Kiếm, Hanoi, Vietnam

Retire in Vietnam

Reasons to Retire in Vietnam

Vietnam has long been one of the top choices of countries to retire to within Southeast Asia, and why not? From its progressive cities, ancient sites, uncrowded beaches, amazing food and welcoming people, it is hard not to consider the opportunity to stay. All these factors make it easy for expats and retirees to adjust to the local lifestyle.

The country also has one of the richest cultures in the region. If you are a lover of history, you will find a good number of UNESCO sites to discover and study. Travel to the urban areas and you'll notice the skyscrapers next to thousand-year-old temples or an ornate century-old mansion. The ambiance from the north, central and the south offer a variety of adventures. If you love to travel and explore while retired, Vietnam is also a great base for you.

There are plenty of nature reserves too, if you intend to live a more active lifestyle. With its outstanding scenery and gorgeous beaches, living in Vietnam guarantees lots of exploration and adventure. Vietnamese people are also welcoming and generous, so it is easy to make local friends.

With its rapid development, Vietnam is considered to be one of the strongest economies in Asia. This is apparent in their quality healthcare, well-maintained roads and modern conveniences. The low cost of living is also one of the advantages of retirees here in Vietnam. Whether you prefer to live on a budget or luxuriously, you'll get a good conversion rate out of your dollar. No wonder, people from all around the world have Vietnam on their bucket list, while travellers from nearby countries keep on coming back for short getaways.

Why Retire in Vietnam:

- ★ You can get a good stretch out of your dollar
- ★ Cities are progressive and developed
- ★ The locals are welcoming and friendly
- ★ Healthy food options are widely available

Culture

It is good to keep in mind that Vietnamese culture stems from the teachings of Confucius. This is apparent in family structure, worship and education. Children are expected to take care of their parents when they are old, and every family aims for their children to excel in school.

The Vietnamese are free to choose any religion. Most of them choose to be either Buddhist, Christian or atheist. There is also the concept of "face" that reflects a person's dignity, integrity and prestige. The locals also see themselves as part of a larger group. The concept of collectivism includes family, community and country. Thus, you may find them using the words "I" and "Me" less.

There are a total of 54 ethnic groups throughout the country, each with its own cultural identity. Just keep in mind that if you decide to move out of the tourist places where a great percentage of locals speak English, be prepared to learn the local language. Aside from meeting the locals, there are also growing expat communities throughout Vietnam.

Living in Vietnam also requires you to know the basic etiquette in dealing with them. For example, if you are invited to a home, you should never rest your chopsticks point-down in a bowl; also, the oldest person at the table must sit and initiate the meal first.

Climate

The climate varies from the north, central, and south. From November to March, Northern Vietnam experiences the northeast monsoon, and then a warm, wet season from April to October.

Travel further down to Central Vietnam and you'll find coastlines shielded by the Truong Son mountain range. It receives a considerable amount of rain from the Western Pacific. The UNESCO town of Hoi An often floods in October or November. The months of May to August are when tourists flock to the beach for the sun.

Meanwhile, Southern Vietnam experiences hot, humid weather with plenty of rain during the monsoon from April to September. Otherwise, November to April is dry and hot.

Cost of Living

The cost of living always depends on the lifestyle you opt for. Plenty of expatriates enjoy a good life without having to spend a fortune. It is also a food lover's paradise because one can simply enjoy a huge range of local restaurants at a low cost. Transportation wise, there are different, cost-effective options to choose from such as taxis and motorcycle rides, in case you don't prefer to drive because of the chaotic roads.

A couple can live comfortably with AUD 1,960 a month. Here are some expenses for reference:

Expenses	Prices
Local beer	AUD 0.68
Local wine	AUD 15
Local meal	AUD 2.70
Tourist meal	AUD 20.25
Monthly groceries	AUD 270

Housing

A one-bedroom apartment in Nha Trang costs AUD 532 per month, while a house would range

from AUD 651 per month. This price usually includes the cost of water, Wi-Fi and gas.

Buying a house will cost you at least AUD 270,270, so compared to the cost of rent, it does not really make fiscal sense to make a purchase. There are also retirement villages in Vietnam, such as the Tuyet Thai Center.

Healthcare in Vietnam

You can expect high-quality healthcare at a low cost in the big cities such as Hanoi and Ho Chi Minh. We recommend going to public hospitals because they are better equipped and the staff speaks in English or French. Consultation in private hospitals starts at AUD 40.50, or purchase health insurance at AUD 81 a month.

The healthcare system is not developed on the par of Western standards. If you have serious illnesses or injury, you may consider going to Thailand or Singapore instead.

How to Retire in Vietnam (Retirement Visa)*

The bad news is Vietnam does not offer a retirement visa for foreigners. Fortunately, this can be solved:

1. Take the tourist visa that allows you to stay in the country for three months at a time, and then do a visa run to nearby countries (Thailand, Laos, Cambodia, Philippines), or exit so you can get a visa extension.

2. If you don't prefer to exit every three months, you can have an agency manage the visa extension for you.

3. Try a visa by investment, where you can get a temporary residence card. This will require an investment of USD 130,000–4,300,000. This will get you a visa not exceeding twelve months, so if you are not intending to start a business, going through all this trouble may not be worth it for you.

Most foreigners living in Vietnam take the first option because it is the cheapest and the paperwork is comparatively non-existent. There are border-run serviced trips for as low as AUD 47.

* USD has been retained as default currency for all immigration investment figures. Currency exchange rate USD1 = AUD1.36.

Work

You can look for jobs while on a tourist visa. Once you find a job, you can get a work permit with the sponsorship of an employer. There are limited jobs that can be offered to foreigners here, unless you can speak the local language. You may consider teaching English or take volunteering opportunities. It is possible for foreigners to start a business in Vietnam as long as you supply all the business requirements.

Tax

Becoming a resident in Vietnam means you will be subject to 5% taxes on any income whether you earn it in Vietnam or not. Inheritance or gifts get taxed at 10%. Non-residents don't get taxed unless they earn it inside the country at a rate of 20%.

Food

Food in Vietnam is a fusion of French flavours with that of neighbouring countries Thailand, Cambodia and China. Each of Vietnam's dishes encompasses a distinctive flavour that reflects its influences. Traditional cooking features fresh ingredients and minimal use of dairy products and oil.

Common ingredients are usually herbs, vegetables, shrimp paste, fish sauce and rice. You will often find lemongrass, ginger, mint, coriander, basil leaves and lime. The lack of sugar in these meals guarantees a healthy meal. They are sold at reasonable prices too – for instance, healthy traditional street food costs AUD 1.35 per meal. Here are some of Vietnam's signature dishes and drinks:

- **Banh mi** is a sandwich that consists of an air baguette, sour pickled daikon, carrot, cilantro, chillies and cucumber, with your choice of meat.

- **Pho** (pronounced "fuh") is a Vietnamese soup filled with banh pho noodles and thinly sliced beef, served with bean sprouts and fresh herbs on the side.

- **Spring rolls** are made with rice vermicelli, raw vegetables and lean protein. This is a very healthy meal you can enjoy with peanut dipping or fish sauce.

- **Cha ca** is such an obsession amongst the Hanoians that you can find a street dedicated to these fried morsels of fish, seasoned with garlic, turmeric, ginger and dill.

- **Banh xeo** refers to a crispy crepe filled with pork, shrimp and bean sprouts. These ingredients are cut into thin slices, rolled into rice paper and dunked in a special sauce.

- **Cao lau** is a pork noodle dish from Hoi An. It features a thicker noodle, pork and wonton crackers. Although its influences came from China, its broth and herbs are obviously very Vietnamese.

- **Banh goi** is deep-fried Vietnamese samosa. It has a crispy exterior filled with minced pork, vermicelli noodles and mushrooms.

- **Bun cha** is the prime choice when it comes to lunchtime in the capital. It consists of small patties of seasoned pork, charred and crispy and served with a large bowl of heavy broth.

- **Vietnamese pizza** is not your typical pizza. It is made of rice paper, grilled in charcoal topped with pork, shrimp, egg and sauce.

- **Vietnamese coffee** has a thick and lingering distinctive taste, served with sweetened condensed milk. It is traditionally brewed in individual portions with the use of a phin filter or a small cup, a filter chamber and a lid. Because coffee is a huge part of Vietnam's daily life, you can find cafes everywhere.

If you are craving different cuisines, you won't have any trouble finding international restaurants in the big cities of Hanoi, Da Nang and Ho Chi Minh.

Recommended Cities in Vietnam

Hanoi

Welcome to the unique capital city of Hanoi, founded a thousand years ago! It has been a melting pot of culture from the Chinese and French – an eclectic mix of East and West. In the heart of it all is the serenity of Hoan Kiem Lake, surrounded by walkable parks and a maze that is the Old Quarter.

Retiring here can fill your days with pleasant surprises every day. It offers convenience with grocery stores, restaurants and coffee shops at almost every corner. Locals are used to tourists so it will not be difficult to find someone who can speak English. Another advantage is its close proximity to the country's most visited sites and best international hospitals too. Most retired foreigners in Vietnam choose to live alone and spend more time with the locals. You will find them in the Old Quarter, the French Quarter, and Ba Dinh District.

Essentials in Hanoi:

- **Healthcare:** Here is a list of hospitals you can choose from in Hanoi:
    - Hanoi French Hospital
    - Vinmec International General Hospital
    - Japanese International Eye Hospital
    - Thu Cuc International General Hospital
    - Hanoi Medical University Hospital
- **Accessibility:** There are direct flights from Noi Bai International Airport to all the major cities in the world, including Sydney, Moscow and Hong Kong. The airport also connects to local destinations across the country in no time.

Things You Can Do in Hanoi

Hanoi is a city where you will never run out of things to do. From cooking classes, reiki classes to rock climbing, the list goes on and on. Just because you are retiring does not mean you should skip these attractions. Your advantage is that you never have to rush and you can visit them more than once:

- Vietnamese Women's Museum
- Ho Chi Minh Mausoleum
- Ho Chi Minh Museum
- The Presidential palace Area
- One-Pillar Pagoda
- Fine Arts Museum
- Army Museum
- Air Force Museum
- National Museum of Vietnamese History
- Museum of the Vietnamese Revolution
- Museum of Ethnology
- Hanoi Museum
- Temple of Literature
- Ngoc Son temple

- ★ Bach Ma Temple
- ★ Hani Temple
- ★ Hoan Kiem Lake
- ★ Ho Tay West Lake
- ★ Lenin Statue & Park
- ★ Ly Thai To Statue and Park
- ★ Hoa Lo Prison
- ★ Huu Tiep Lake
- ★ Downed Aircraft Memorial
- ★ Army Museum

Da Nang

This coastal city is one of the most liveable places in the country. Anything you can ask for is here, from the growing skyline, parks, promenades, beaches and three UNESCO sites around it. It has around a million people who call it home, and yet Da Nang offers a small-town feel. It has some of the hustle and bustle of a city while being laidback like in the countryside.

Foreigners who chose to retire here enjoy the luxury at an affordable price tag. Living close to the beach is manageable with a budget of AUD 1,351 a month.

Essentials in Da Nang

- ★ **Healthcare:** Da Nang is catching up with Hanoi and Ho Chi Minh because of the excellent reputation of its hospitals. Living in Da Nang can be hassle-free with the following hospitals:
    - ★ Hoan My Da Nang Hospital
    - ★ Family Medical Practice Da Nang
    - ★ Cancel Hospital (Da Nang Oncology Hospital)
    - ★ Hoi An Medical Service
    - ★ VinMec Hospital

- ★ **Accessibility:** Although Da Nang is the smallest of Vietnam's international airports, there are frequent flights to and from Hanoi and Ho Chi Minh. This airport can also connect you to major cities in China, Siem Reap, Singapore and Taipei.

Things You Can Do in Da Nang

If you love to play golf, then consider Da Nang your paradise. Aside from resort-hopping, going to a spa or exploring the UNESCO sites of Hoi An, My Son and Hue, here are the Da Nang's other top attractions:

- ★ Cham Museum
- ★ Marble Mountains
- ★ Ba Na Hill Station
- ★ Cham Island
- ★ Linh Ung Buddhist Temple
- ★ Bach Ma National Park
  Dragon Bridge
- ★ Son Tra Peninsula

Keep in mind that the dialect spoken in Da Nang is different from Hanoi and Ho Chi Minh. You can learn the language for as low as AUD 6.75 per hour.

Ho Chi Minh

From dawn to the wee hours of the morning, there is always something interesting about Ho Chi Minh. It is Vietnam's version of a city that never sleeps. Everyone is in a hurry to work, to eat or to shop. Walking around the city, you'll find skyscrapers next to French colonial villas, art galleries, temples and markets.

Imagine 9 million people, each with their own motorbikes – indeed! Don't worry because

Vietnam also has an operational public bus system if you think driving motorbikes in its chaotic streets is not for you. If you want to get away from the traffic, there are also beautiful parks in which to take shelter.

There is always something new happening in the city. With a thriving art and music scene, you'll find something that will suit your style whether it be rock music, jazz or opera. If you are into history and culture, museums never come short.

Essentials in Ho Chi Minh

- **Healthcare:** This city offers the best healthcare in Vietnam, with two internationally accredited general hospitals. Most of the procedures are at 10% of what you would pay in the USA or Australia. For example, an appointment with a specialist will cost you about AUD 48.

  You will also find the most advanced dental care here, rivalling Bangkok and Singapore. In the future, there might be a chance that it can compete in the growing medical tourism industry in Asia. Here are the top hospitals in Ho Chi Minh:
    - Franco-Vietnamese Hospital (FV Hospital)
    - Vinmec International Hospital
- **Accessibility:** Traveling from Ho Chi Minh is convenient – thanks to Tan Son Nhat International airport which connects to major overseas destinations, including Sydney!

Things to do in Ho Chi Minh

The lifestyle in Ho Chi Minh is a seamless blend of French, American and Vietnamese influences, producing a unique culture of its own. You can experience all these within a day as you walk the streets of the city.

Commonly known as Saigon, the city offers plenty of things to see and do. You may fill your days exploring either a museum or a gallery, followed by a walk in the market and ending in a nice café. Here's a list of what you shouldn't miss in this city:

- Reunification Palace
- War Remnants Museum
- City Hall
- People's Committee Hall
- Museum of Vietnamese History
- Ho Chi Minh Museum
- Central Mosque
- Notre Dame Cathedral
- Thien Hau pagoda
- Quan Am Pagoda
- Phung Son Tu Pagoda
- Saigon Opera House
- The Bitexco Financial Tower
- Saigon Skydeck
- Cu Chi Tunnels
- Mekong Delta
- Ben Thanh Market

Vũng Tàu

Travel southeast of Vietnam, and you will find the gem that is Vũng Tàu, which lies on a peninsula separated from the mainland by the Co May river. With only 527,000 locals living here, you may find a growing population of Americans and Australians. Some expats put up small restaurants and bars.

What makes Vũng Tàu attractive for retirees is its easy access from Ho Chi Minh City (only a two-hour drive or a 90-minute hydrofoil boat ride). It is also one of the sunniest places in the country, but the temperature does not get too humid or hot. You will find plenty of seafood restaurants that cost only AUD 13.50 for two.

Vũng Tàu may not be a large city, but it features some rocky hills and headlands on both ends of the city center. The expatriates who live here navigate the island by walking or taking a bike. Otherwise, taxis are also available and would cost AUD 4 a ride.

Essentials in Vũng Tàu

- **Healthcare:** There are limited but adequate choices of hospitals in the town. Dental clinics are not a problem – they can be clean and efficient. However, for any serious concern, it might be better to drive two hours to Ho Chi Minh and get the necessary healthcare you need there.
    - Raffles Medical
    - Le Loi General Hospital
- **Accessibility:** Residents who live in Vũng Tàu would travel to Ho Chi Minh to fly out of the country or visit a place locally.

Things to do in Vũng Tàu

The lifestyle in Vũng Tàu includes lots of sunny days, fresh seafood and organised activities from soccer games, golfing networks to charitable events. Being on the front beach by the west side of the peninsula, you can find a calm harbor with a nice park, sculpture garden and promenade, perfect for a stroll.

Unlike other cities in Vietnam, there are lesser monuments and sites to see in Vũng Tàu. Residents are more drawn to going to the beach or walking in a nice park or hiking the little mountain. Still, if you are looking for something to see, check out the following:

- Vũng Tàu Lighthouse
- Thang Tam Temple
- Martyr's Memorial
- Small Mount Top pagoda
- Niết Bàn Tịnh Xá Pagoda
- Thích Ca Phật Đài Pagoda
- Villa Blanche

Nha Trang

If you are looking for a true beach haven for snorkelling or sunbathing, you are in the right place. For almost a hundred years, Nha Trang has been a famous resort town for local and international travellers, for its coastal area offering dramatic bay views and golden-sand beaches, as well as luxurious resorts. It is known as a popular stop between Hanoi and Ho Chi Minh with an expat population of around 4,000. Some of them own small businesses, while others spend their time diving, snorkeling, sunbathing or socializing.

Foreigners get by with small motorbikes, bikes, walking or, sometimes, by taxi. Just avoid the tourists on the weekends and holidays, but otherwise the streets can be manageable. Because Nha Trang is a popular tourist destination, you can find a variety of markets, restaurants, bars and activities to choose from.

Essentials in Nha Trang

- **Healthcare:** Adequate healthcare is available in Nha Trang and can cover most medical conditions. Several dental clinics with English-speaking staff are also available. Expatriates living here for a long time recommended the following hospitals:
    - Vinmec International Hospital
    - Tam Tri Hospital
- **Accessibility:** The Cam Ranh International Airport can take you to either Hanoi or Ho Chi Minh to connect to long-haul destinations. There are also weekly flights to some nearby overseas destinations such as Hong Kong.

Things to do in Nha Trang

Because Nha Trang has established itself as a tourist destination, you will never run out of things to do here. The city also features a great choice of traditional markets that includes large supermarkets and malls and movie theatres. The beach alone can offer hundreds of things to do, from surfing to sailing, but there are things beyond the beach Nha Trang can offer too:

- National Oceanographic Museum
- Alexandre Yersin Museum
- Long Son Pagoda
- Po Nagar Cham Towers
- Fishing villages
- Bao Dai Villa
- Vinpearl la
- Chong rock
- Nha Trang Cathedral
- Thanh Dien Khanh Fortress
- Monkey Island
- Yang Bay Waterfalls
- Ban Ho Waterfalls
- Fairy Spring Waterfalls
- Thap Ba Hot Springs and Mud Baths

Is Vietnam LGBT-friendly?

Vietnam is a hassle-free destination for lesbian, gay, bisexual and transgender (LGBT) travellers. The country has improved with its acceptance and legislation, and the ban on same-sex marriages was lifted. Same-sex relationships are legal. You will also find queer bars and clubs in the big cities. Hurrah! Ho Chi Minh is one of the best places for the active LGBT community.

Keep in mind, however, that the country remains socially conservative. While the Vietnamese are friendly and hospitable, public displays of affection of any kind may draw some disapproving glares.

Senior Discounts

There is not much information about senior discounts in Vietnam. Maybe because the country has a young population, with the median age at 30.5 years old in 2015. Nevertheless, with a very low cost of living, you may not need it.

Living in Vietnam: What to Watch Out For

With common sense, Vietnam is a safe place to travel and retire to. However, there are only a few things to complain about:

- ★ **There are safety risks with getting around the busy cities mainly because of motorbikes.**
  Imagine 58 million people ride motorbikes in Vietnam. That's a lot! Chaos reigns and crossing the streets can be traumatic. If you are planning to learn how to ride motorbikes, don't do it in Vietnam. Everyone rides motorbikes here because they are cheap (a used one can cost AUD 405).

- ★ **Smog in the big cities**
  Because of millions of motorbikes roaming in Vietnam, there is no wonder why air pollution is a big challenge for Vietnam. There are also industrial emissions and coal combustion to blame. According to WHO's guidelines, the air quality in the country is considered moderately unsafe. If you have a health problem, particularly respiratory illnesses, you may have to rethink living in its bustling cities.

- ★ **Language barrier is a concern**
  If you can't speak or understand basic Vietnamese, it can be difficult to fully integrate into a new environment. Since Vietnamese is a tonal language, you have to pay attention to how a word is pronounced and it takes a lot of practice. You may want to allocate the time to study the language and learn a few words to survive in dealing with the locals.

- ★ **Mosquito-related disease is an issue.**
  Watch out for mosquito-borne diseases that tend to be prevalent during the rainy season. This includes malaria and dengue fever. Take precautions and make sure that your vaccinations are up to date.

Summary

Vietnam offers the best value for money in Southeast Asia. It only proves that you can enjoy a good life even for less!

Healthcare: ★★★
Culture: ★★★★★
Cost of Living: ★★★★★
Housing: ★★★★
Accessibility: ★★★★
Safety: ★★★

TOTAL STARS: 24 ★

CENTRAL AND SOUTH AMERICA

Houses and yachts at a sea coast in Belize City

Reasons to Retire in Belize

The last on our Central American list is the tropical paradise in the Caribbean: Belize. To its north is Mexico and to the south is Guatemala. Belize—which also emerged from the Mayan civilization and was subsequently conquered by Spain and Britain—has developed a diverse society that you will find apparent in their culture and languages.

Although the national language is Belizean Creole, English remains the official language – making it convenient to relocate, adjust, and live here.

You can also still practice your Spanish here as you enjoy the September celebrations, while dancing along to punta music or as you explore its barrier reefs. The latter is perfect for divers and snorkelers, and pretty much anyone who loves the ocean. The Belize Barrier Reef is a 300-kilometer-long reef that is a continuation of what you will find from Cancun, Mexico, and which extends all the way down to Honduras—making it the second-largest coral reef system in the world.

In addition to its coast, Belize also features a rich variety of wildlife. Due to the low human population, there is sufficient habitat for over 5,000 species of flora and fauna. The government also makes sure that its treasured nature continues to be protected and preserved.

The weather is perfect, too. Because of its location, any period of rainfall during the rainy season from June to November usually only lasts for a couple of days.

The country is also a safe haven for foreign retirees to live in. There are virtually no crowds because it is still a hidden gem as a retirement destination. One of the common reasons to retire overseas is to have a different ambiance and to explore another culture. Sometimes, being away from it all—yes, that includes the people you're used to seeing in your own country—is the best treat.

Another good reason is Belize's retiree program. While other countries would require you to be 65 years old and above, Belize only requires you to be at least 45 years old to enjoy the QRP program.

Why Retire in Belize:

★ It is easy to fit in this Central American country where most speak English.
★ You are surrounded by amazing beaches and exotic rainforests.
★ The tropical climate is just perfect!
★ It is a safe country to live in.
★ Belize offers the best retiree program.

Culture

Do you know that Belize was previously called British Honduras in 1862? Belize was the last continental possession of the United Kingdom in the Americas. With so many cultures blending together, the country is a good definition of a melting pot.

This has lent itself to the people having an open-minded attitude towards interracial marriages. Thus, when you come to live here, you will see a mix of Creoles, East Indians, Chinese, Garifuna, Maya, European Mennonites, and Mestizo. All these influences blend harmoniously. The Creoles, who were descendants of African enslaved peoples during the colonial period, make up 2/5 of the population.

Belize is an English-speaking country, which also means that the major businesses, as well as the government, conduct transactions in English. This is because their roots are more British than Spanish. Yes, you can survive with just being equipped with English in this country. Plus, the Belizeans are welcoming, too.

Religion-wise, the majority are Roman Catholic. What you need to keep in mind, however, is that they are still quite conservative. It may be better, if you are a woman, to wear a dress, except if you need to go to work; try not to be revealing.

Otherwise, the country has a laid back attitude, so if you want to be accepted in the community, you also must be relaxed and patient. People rarely tip here, but try not to haggle as that is uncommon in Belize and can be considered as rude.

In the countryside, classes and castes still exist, especially in the ethnic groups. Those who belong in the highest level tend to have lighter skin such as the Creoles and mestizos, while the lower levels are those who have darker skins. Gender roles also still exist in the country, with women participating less in its politics and economics.

Climate

This small country in Central America enjoys a tropical climate, with the hot and rainy seasons

lasting from June to October, and the cooler season from November to February. The driest period covers the months of February to April, as the heat gradually increases.

Even if it does rain in Belize, it is mainly in the form of downpours or thunderstorms in the late afternoon, which means even in this period, the sun still shines. Meanwhile, the temperature is at an average of 25 degrees Celsius all year round. Hurricanes are more frequent in September and October, so when you plan to live here, we recommend finding a property with stable hardware that can protect you from the weather.

Expenses	Prices
Housing rent (one-bedroom in Cayo)	AUD 811
High-speed internet	AUD 176
Electricity and water	AUD 119
Phone with basic data plan	AUD 20
Loaf of white bread	AUD 2.50
A dozen eggs	AUD 2.70
Local beer	AUD 3.26
Taxi per kilometer	AUD 4.75

Cost of Living

Because of its size and housing limitations, Belize is not the cheapest country to live in, in Central America. The good news is, this country is not overly materialistic and you can save a lot of your money here. There are smaller shops covering only necessary items, so you don't get tempted to spend. Transportation-wise, you can ride a bike for transportation, as having a car is not necessary.

When it comes to food, all you need to do is avoid the imported American food and stick with the local produce. You can buy directly from farmers and fishermen that cut the middlemen's cost. A good budget is AUD 2,028 per month to cover your rent and necessities. Again, it will depend on where you live and your lifestyle of choice. Here's a quick look at the common expenses in Belize:

Housing

Foreigners are allowed to buy land in the country—even a beachfront property. The least expensive areas for foreigners living in Belize are Cayo, Corozal, and Punta Gorda. It is possible to buy a lot and build your house for under AUD 135,190. If you have a bigger budget, you may consider Ambergris Caye, where you can allocate AUD 270,380 for a resort-style living, complete with a pool and a sea view.

Renting depends on your budget. A one-bedroom apartment is priced at AUD 811, while a three-bedroom apartment can cost AUD 1757.

As for nursing homes, there are only a handful available. It is not yet common to have a daycare facility here for the elderly. Instead, it will be better to rent a housekeeper if you ever require any assistance.

Healthcare in Belize

Although the country has tried to improve in recent years, Belize still does not have a well-developed medical care system. With its low population, the government can't allocate enough budget to build better healthcare facilities and equipment.

It is worth mentioning, however, that there are doctors in the country who are passionate and dedicated to their patients, so that you can feel enough medical attention is being given to you. The minor ailments and most emergencies are treated by Red Cross or by physicians at public clinics, which are available throughout the country.

Alternatively, there is excellent healthcare in its neighboring countries, so some foreigners and residents would choose to fly to get medical treatment. This means that you need to have international health insurance before moving to Belize. Private hospitals also exist in Belize City to provide comprehensive care, so be prepared to travel to the capital for better healthcare if not abroad.

If you are foreseeing that this will be a problem for you given your health condition, you may need to rethink moving to Belize altogether. You should know yourself, your lifestyle, and your health and don't risk moving to a city by yourself.

How to Retire in Belize (Retirement Visa)*

There are two visa options to retire in Belize. There is an option to become a permanent resident or to apply for the Qualified Retirement Persons (QRP) program.

The first option will require you to live in the country for at least fifty consecutive weeks in a year as you use a visitor's visa or a tourist card, which you need to renew every month until you get your permanent residency application approved. Normally, Belize will permit you to stay for thirty days. This option allows you to work in the country even without a working permit, plus you can travel in and out of the country. Once you get the approval, you may try to apply for citizenship after five years.

Any individual over the age of 45 can apply for the QRP option, which can also benefit your spouse and children. As long as you spend one month in a year in Belize, and hold a proof of deposit amounting to USD 24,000 a year in a local bank account, you can maintain your QRP status. The proof of money can be through retirement savings, pension, or social security-related funds. However, keep in mind that this option will not permit you to work in Belize.

* USD has been retained as default currency for all tax and immigration investment figures in this article. Currency exchange rate USD1 = AUD1.36.

Work

It is possible to work and set up a business in Belize with a permanent resident status. If you don't belong in this category, you need to apply for a working visa or approach the Belize Trade and Investment Development Service to help you establish a business. With its small population, you will find that the majority of businesses here are small businesses. There are also plenty of expatriates who are making a living by setting up their businesses here.

Tax**

Belize is said to be a tax haven for privacy and profits. Tax havens are used by many individuals and international companies to reduce their tax

liabilities, and the country has legislation, such as the International Business Companies Act and the Offshore Banking Act, that has put Belize at the forefront of having shell companies.

Secondly, to attract foreigners into the country, Belize adopted a "qualified permanent residence law" that lets retirees enjoy a tax-free lifestyle. That means pension income is exempt from taxes. Meanwhile, income tax is subject to 25% rate, with the exception of the first USD 14,500

** USD has been retained as default currency for all tax and immigration investment figures in this article. Currency exchange rate USD1 = AUD1.36.

Food

Belize's cuisine is a combination of all the nationalities and their influences in the country, resulting in a sumptuous medley of Caribbean classics, seafood, fresh fruit, and other treats. The Mestizo with its Spanish, Mexican and Mayan influences, dominates the local cuisine. A typical breakfast consists of bread or tortillas, eaten alongside various cheeses and eggs. Later midday meals range from lighter food such as fried meat pies, escabeche, stew chicken, while dinner features rice with beans, meat, and salad.

Chinese food, descended from 480 Chinese immigrants in 1865, has adapted to the Belizean setting. It has maintained its richness with fresh ingredients, such as Chinese pumpkin, cabbage, and bitter melon. Noodles are still much consumed along with potatoes and beans. Then there's the Garifuna with hudut and darasa, while the Maya who have always been hunters and progressive farmers brought in a variety of fruits, vegetables, and spices. And of course, the East Indians with their turmeric-based curry and dhal roti.

Now, imagine stirring all these influences in one giant pan, and you'll definitely have a unique culinary journey as you spend your retirement days here in Belize. Some people who visit the country find it difficult to distinguish the Belizean cuisine, but perhaps they only need to stay longer to truly understand the country's palette. Here is a list of food you should not miss in Belize:

- ★ **Chimole**, also called the black dinner, is a chunky stew that combines Mexican and Mayan cultures. It is made with chicken and local spices such as achiote.

- ★ **Sere** is a popular cuisine among the Garinagu. This is a type of fish soup that consists of fried fish, plantains, and coconut milk.

- ★ **Salbutes** is a local's favorite snack that consists of corn tortillas topped with meat, cabbage, avocado, and hot sauce.

- ★ **Rice and beans** is a classic staple in Belize, and is sometimes called the national dish of the country. Although it has a lot of variation from light and bright to peppery and fiery, it is always served with a type of meat and salad.

- ★ **Tamales** is a traditional Maya and Mestizo food. The Belizean version is cooked chicken or meat wrapped in plantain leaves, instead of the commonly used corn husks in Mexico.

- ★ **Panades**, or **Belizean Empanadas** is another classic snack filled with smoked fish, cheese, and curtido. It is then covered in flour and fried until it's crispy.

- ★ **Boil Up** is a Belizean version of hot pot. One only needs to bring all the ingredients (eggs, fish, pigtail, yams, cassava, sweet potatoes, plantain) together and boil them up. This feast you can make at home will surely bring the family together.

* **Pibil** refers to marinated meat wrapped in banana leaf before it is smoldered in a pit lined with stones. This results in meat falling apart easily releasing a rich flavor.

* **Cow's Foot Soup** may not sound appetizing to many, but it is one of the signature dishes in the country. The meal which includes a cow's foot or a pig's tail is actually tasty as long as it is served with carrots, potatoes, pepper, cilantro, okra, and onions.

There is a wide range of food choices in Belize, whether you prefer cheap eats, mid-range or fine dining, or whether you want European or Chinese, Belize has it. However, choices are still quite limited outside the city.

Recommended Cities in Belize

Placencia

Placencia has become one of the desirable locations in Belize, after Ambergris Caye. With its location at the top of a peninsula, off the coast of the mainland, many people refer to it as the "caye you can drive to." Placencia offers the same vibe and activities but at a more relaxed pace.

Its central and southern coasts are breathtaking even if there are tons of new resorts sprouting here and there. There are also condominiums and restaurants around. It may sound that there have been plenty of infrastructures built over the years, it is good to know that the residents are keen to conserve its authenticity and natural beauty. With only less than 5,000 in population, the Placencia Peninsula offers both relaxation and adventure in its beach paradise.

Its topography and convenience of being located on the main island attract foreigners to live and retire here. Placencia also has a small-town vibe, so wandering around the main road would give you a feeling of being in an authentic Central American Village.

As for the cost of living, Placencia is a little cheaper than Ambergris Caye, although still a little expensive compared to the rest of the country. Here, you can rent a property for only AUD 676 a month. Purchasing a property here would cost a little over a hundred thousand dollars.

Essentials in Placencia:

* **Healthcare:** Placencia has a better choice of hospitals and clinics compared to Ambergris Caye. Here are some of them:
  * Placencia Medical Services
  * Placencia Health Center
  * Southern Belize Medical Clinic
  * Independence Poly Clinic
  * Punta Gorda Hospital

- **Accessibility:** Placencia is three hours drive away from Belize City. The most economical and popular option to reach Placencia is by taking a shuttle at a reasonable cost. Alternatively, you can also take a flight on a seat Cessna plane with only about 9 – 13 seats.

Things You Can Do in Placencia

Luckily, there is a good number of activities and establishments here. One can't get lost as you walk around the loop of the village. You may stop by the local woodworking and witness them working, then a local café for an aromatic coffee. If you prefer, you can even stop at a gelato place before proceeding to the farmer's market stands.

Nearby Placencia is the Maya King Waterfalls so you may consider renting a car. You may also go for a hike at Bocawina, plus a stop at the Los Reef. In this tiny village of Placencia, you also have a choice to go on a food tour or simply enjoy the beach. Here are places you can visit:

- Monkey River
- Jaguar Preserve
- Silk Caye
- Actun Tunichil Muknal
- Mojo Caye
- Ranguana Caye
- King Lewey's Caye

Ambergris Caye

Ambergris Caye (pronounced as key), is one of the most famous tourist destinations in the country. It is also home to most of the expatriates in Belize, that they refer to it as Isla Bonita after a Madonna song about the island. What draws people to this area are its natural beauty and the activities it offers. Aside from its turquoise ambiance, the lively Caribbean island is also home to plenty of nightlife options and social activities.

In recent years, because of the increase in tourism, proper infrastructure and amenities were built on this island. It also boasts festivals and live music sessions. Nowadays, it is hard to imagine how it was a humble fishing village a long time ago.

The cost of living here is higher compared to other areas in the country because everything needs to be transported. The traffic on the island also tends to be hectic especially in the tourist high season. Otherwise, it is comfortable to walk around the vibrant town of San Pedro with its paved streets and fishing village charm. The mode of transportation on this island is a golf cart, whether it is from home to shops, cafes, and restaurants.

Essentials in Ambergris Caye:

- **Healthcare:** Aside from a Polyclinic, there are no hospitals on the island. Doctors who are on call for 24 hours are available. These doctors spend as much time as needed during an appointment with a patient, which would only cost you AUD 41. These doctors are trained in a specialty and have received their training in countries like the USA, Cuba, and the UK.

- **Accessibility:** The island of Ambergris Caye can be accessed via domestic flights operated by Tropic Air and Maya Island Air. The hourly flights take only 20 minutes from the capital. A water taxi is also another option but takes 90 minutes.

Things You Can Do in Ambergris Caye

Its location, with the Caribbean to its east and San Pedro Lagoon on the opposite side, gives the island its charm unique on its own. Aside from the sea activities you can enjoy, you can also find festivals, live music, nightlife, and restaurants.

Aside from being a party town, Ambergris Caye is also home to several health clubs, yoga studios, and other healthy activities. If you ever get bored, there are always art galleries and coffee shops where you can pass time. There are also churches and volunteer opportunities. Here are the top places to visit on the island:

- ★ Hol Chan Marine Reserve
- ★ Shark Ray Alley
- ★ Secret Beach
- ★ Belizean Arts
- ★ Mexico Rocks
- ★ The Gallery of San Pedro
- ★ Bacalar Chico National Park and Marine Reserve
- ★ Ambergris Museum
- ★ Marco Gonzalez Maya Site
- ★ Belizean Melody Art Gallery

Cayo District

If you want to escape the beach life, you only have to travel two hours away from the capital and you will find a quiet and more affordable alternative to living in Belize. The Cayo District is located in the jungle-covered Maya mountains with three rivers. The river of Mopan and Macal come together in the town just outside of the Bullet Tree Falls.

Cayo District has it all, from reefs, rivers, and ruins. The region is dotted with Mayan ruins and herbal medicine trails in its rich rainforest.

A quarter of the country's population (90,000 people) live in this peaceful city. There is also a good size of expatriates here who learned how to be self-sufficient in this part of the world.

One advantage of living in Cayo is the cost of living. It is possible to purchase a riverfront lot for less than AUD 47,317. Renting an apartment is also cheaper with a two-bedroom apartment only costing about AUD 676 a month. Food is also even more affordable here compared to the beach towns because most of the produce comes from here. The ground is fertile so you may also consider planting your own food.

Essentials in Cayo District:

- **Healthcare:** The healthcare system is adequate in Cayo, with American-trained doctors. Plus, there are two major hospitals in the region:
    - San Ignacio Hospital
    - Belmopan Hospital Cayo
- **Accessibility:** The Cayo District is only a couple of hours away from Belize City, and it is most reasonable to simply drive there.

Things You Can Do in Cayo District

The weather in Cayo is more bearable given its location. It has an average temperature of 21 - 26 degrees Celsius that you may not require air conditioning when you go to sleep. It also gives the perfect opportunity to pleasantly explore the surroundings. You may fill your retirement days with a food trip at the Saturday market, visiting one of the ruins, going for cave tubing, or a chill time in Chaa Creek Resort. Another option is exploring the caves such as Actun Tunichil Muknal and Barton Creek Cave. Here are other things you can see in Cayo District's vast rolling hills and rainforest:

- Cahal Pech
- Green Iguana Conservation Project
- Xunantunich
- Blue Hole National Park
- San Ignacio Market
- Actun Tunichil Muknal
- Belize Botanic Garden
- St. Herman's Cave
- The Maya Ruins of Caracol
- 1,000-foot falls
- Crystal Cave

Is Belize LGBT-friendly?

Belize is still adjusting to the LGBT community. It was only in 2016 when same-sex sexual activity was decriminalized and it was only a few years ago when the first Pride week was held. Since then, anti-discrimination laws in employment, hate speeches, etc. were passed.

The country has become a famous destination for the LGBT community. It is a safe destination, however, living here may be a different story. An LGBT couple may not have smooth sailing living here.

Senior Discounts

The senior citizens in Belize enjoy discounts from medical services, taxes, and transportation, to name a few. With these reasonable deals, it is still uncommon to offer senior discounts that you actually have to ask for it yourself. Make sure to bring your ID that shows your date of birth to enjoy these benefits.

Living in Belize: What to Watch Out For

The white sand and the Caribbean waters easily draw foreigners to leave behind the life they are used to and move to Belize. However, before deciding whether it is a good place for retirement, you have to understand what Belize can and can't offer.

- ★ **It is not as developed compared to its neighbors, Mexico and Costa Rica.**
  Infrastructure, services, and amenities are limited in Belize. Here, you enjoy life's simplicities—you get back to the basics of appreciating and conserving what it has to offer. If that's the lifestyle you are after, then Belize is for you; otherwise, you may find it boring in the long run.

- ★ **The party culture is too much!**
  You will never run out of parties and festivals to attend. And when Belizeans party, the music is so loud and it lasts until morning. Partying has always been a part of their culture—even the churches love their amplifiers.

- ★ **The country's healthcare system is not fully developed yet.**
  If you have serious health issues, then Belize with its limited healthcare resources may not be the best country for you. For serious illnesses, you may have to fly to Mexico or the US to make sure you get the necessary healthcare you need.

Summary

As a young and developing nation, Belize has a long way to go to catch up to its neighboring countries. Give it another decade or two, and hopefully, its healthcare system can improve. Other than that, Belize enters the 'not bad' category, as its culture and safety remain top-notch.

Healthcare: ★★
Culture: ★★★★
Cost of Living: ★★★
Housing: ★★★★
Accessibility: ★★★★
Safety: ★★★★★

TOTAL STARS: 22 ★

A typical colourful Colombian streetscape

Retire in Colombia

Reasons to Retire in Colombia

Touching both the Caribbean Sea and the Pacific Ocean, and with a good percentage of the Amazon rainforest and three ranges of the Andes mountain, Colombia makes for one of the most picturesque places to spend your retirement days. It is home to 50 million people; neighboring countries Panama and Ecuador are among its competitors.

Do you prefer to stay in a warm, tropical, ocean-side community or cities with spring-like temperatures? How about in the cooler mountain areas? Colombia has it all, being the second-most biodiverse country in the world, so you can choose whichever will suit you.

What makes it perfect for retirement is its affordable healthcare system. 20 out of 49 Latin American hospitals are situated in the country so you will be assured access to the best healthcare for you. If you are from the USA, accessibility will not be an issue either. It is located in the northernmost tip of South America and a three-hour flight will bring you to Florida.

Living in Colombia will also give you the best value for your money, guaranteeing a better quality of life compared to what you'll have at home. A three-bedroom apartment costs AUD 121671 just a little outside of Medellin. Plus, fresh produce is also available—fruits, vegetables, beef, and fish are all inexpensive and of abundance.

Contrary to the misconceptions, because of Pablo Escobar's fame around the world, Colombia is no longer a dangerous country filled with drugs. Rather, it is a country with warm and welcoming people that has the fourth-largest economy on the continent. It has transformed into a thriving country that attracts travelers and retirees. There is no doubt that the country has become a rising star in the tourism sector and yet it is still often overlooked.

Why Retire in Colombia:

- ★ It offers great diversity where you can experience everything.
- ★ The weather is perfect.
- ★ An abundance of produce.
- ★ Low cost of living.

Culture

There is no better way to learn and understand the culture but by immersing yourself in it. Interestingly, Colombian culture contains a lot of contradictions.

Let us first introduce you to Colombian pride—there is a lot of national love of positivity, from the people to its country. The intense patriotism towards the country makes Colombians avoid chatting about anything negative, especially when it pertains to their society and politics, with foreigners. Thus, if you want to make friends, you might want to avoid the above topics. Instead, start with what they're proud of—from Colombian food, weather, or tourist attractions. Colombians are also fond of sporting events and beauty pageants.

Colombia retains its traditional culture despite the increase of modernity in the country. Colombians still prioritize family ties and traditional household roles, with family as the main building block of the society. There are constant interactions with relatives and endless family gatherings. Young people stay close to home and live with their parents until they get married.

A big percentage of the population are Catholics and this influence goes all the way to their language. For example, "si dios quiere" which means "God willing" or "dios te bendiga" as "God bless you."

However, this does not mean that their behavior is always beyond reproach. Like many countries around the world, infidelity still happens, while some adapt to the narco-culture. Because of its long history with the mafia and drug trafficking, the locals accept crime as part of everyday life.

Spanish is the official language as imposed in the colonial period. English is still spoken in the major cities such as Cartagena and the Caribbean islands of San Andres and Providencia, but if you prefer to live outside these cities, it is best to study Spanish to take part in everyday conversations.

Climate

Because of Colombia's geographical location near the equator, the country experiences tropical and isothermal climate with variations within its natural regions. Its climate is influenced by its tropical rainforests, deserts, mountains, savannas, and steppes. Sometimes, it gets altered by the seasons. From March to June is spring time, June to August is the hot summer, while autumn occurs from September to December, then winter from December to March.

For Spring-like temperatures, Bogota, the largest city and the capital, is the best place to be with its location in the Eastern Andes region. Throughout the year, the temperature hovers around 18 – 20 degrees Celsius. If you prefer somewhere warmer, then proceed to Cartagena, with temperatures rarely dropping below 30 degrees during the day.

Cost of Living

One of the best benefits Colombia has to offer is the low cost of living with first-world amenities. Your cost of living will still depend on several factors such as the city and neighborhood of your choice. Medellin and the capital Bogota have the most expensive areas. You can find apartments for rent from AUD 676 – AUD 1,690 for starters.

Keep in mind that the country uses the estrato system to check the cost of utilities. The system would assign an estrato number to the neighborhoods that is based on the income of the residents. Lower estrato neighborhoods pay lower compared to the higher estrato neighborhoods. If you want big monthly savings on utilities, you may consider mid- to low-level estrato. Estrato 3 is comfortable enough for most foreigners living in Colombia. Living with AUD 1,352 a month is sufficient for most retirees in Colombia. Here's a quick look on the below sample list of expenses:

Expenses	Prices
Housing rent (one-bedroom in city centre)	AUD 541
High-speed internet	AUD 20
Electricity and water	AUD 47
Phone with basic data plan	AUD 20
Loaf of white bread	AUD 1.10
A dozen eggs	AUD 2.25
Local beer	AUD 1.15
Taxi per kilometer	AUD 1.85

Housing

Home and apartment prices in Medellin and Bogota can definitely compete with the home prices in the United States. For example, a three-bedroom high-rise apartment can cost AUD 1,690 per month. There are other cheaper and smaller options too if you decide to live in these cities so keep looking. If you have a lower budget, you can find a three-bedroom apartment in Barranquilla and Santa Marta at AUD 608 per month. These two cities are two important locations for retirement-age real estate investment.

Purchasing a two-story home in the capital will cost a million, but in cities like Manizales or Pereira, it will only cost you AUD 337,975. An apartment is even less expensive. The view will also influence the price, for example, oceanfront or ocean view properties are more expensive than those miles away from the water.

Upscale assisted living is available in Medellin. One good option is Habitat Adulto Mayor, a large and upscale area for retirees, boasting an open and bright set-up and supportive social setting. At AUD 2,163 a month, it offers residential services that include six balanced meals a day and 24-hour nursing.

Healthcare in Colombia

Colombia ranks 22nd out of 191 countries in the World Health Organization's list of countries with the best healthcare systems. After all, the country has 40% of the top Latin American hospitals in the continent. Four of these hospitals are Joint Commission International-accredited with the gold standard. These hospitals are located in Bogota, Medellin, and Bucaramanga.

Excellent hospitals are spread throughout the country, offering essential services from general check-ups, joint replacements, and organ transplants to ICU to cancer treatments. To enjoy the public healthcare plan, also called EPS or Entidades Promotoras de Salud, you must have a resident Cedula or an identity card. It will cost retirees 12% of their pension income.

To get a Cedula, you must first obtain a visa. Once it is stamped in your passport, you can then apply for the Cedula and apply for EPS insurance. Meanwhile, if you want to choose your own specialist, then you better pay for a private policy. Having a private policy will still require you to get an EPS. This will give you direct access to specialists, private hospital room stays, and other coverages that are not covered by EPS. Anyway, even if you decide to not get any of the above insurance, the cost of the consultation will remain reasonable. For instance, a check-up with a specialist will cost you around AUD 68.

How to Retire in Colombia (Retirement Visa)*

The country has a straightforward retirement visa procedure. Colombia offers retirement visas for foreigners who are receiving a retirement income and want to retire in Colombia. The M-11 retirement visa is valid for one to three years, depending on your health insurance, and costs USD 282. The M-11 retirement visa will lose its validity if you leave the country for a period of over six months.

The requirements to get the M-11 visa includes an income that exceeds three times the minimum wage in Colombia. The minimum wage is USD 25, thus, you need to have three times that amount to be granted a retirement visa. You are also required to show an international health insurance certificate that has at least USD 70,000 in coverage.

If you want to live in Colombia permanently, you need to take a citizenship test related to Colombian history, geography, and the constitution. You will also need a basic Spanish oral test. If you are not yet ready to take the above examination, you can keep on extending your M-11 visa in the meantime.

Work*

You are not allowed to work under the M-11 retirement visa. If you want to work, then you have to get a work visa. An investment visa for business is possible and will require at least USD 25,428 in investment.

* **USD has been retained as default currency for all tax and immigration investment figures in this article. Currency exchange rate USD1 = AUD1.36.**

Tax**

Since you are not permitted to work in the country, you are not going to be taxed for your income. If you are somehow earning in the country, it can be a little complicated to understand the tax system, but it is essential to avoid any future penalties. Firstly, you have to determine if your situation can be classified as fiscal residency which is only confirmed when:

- ★ You spend more than 183 days in Colombia
- ★ More than 50% of your income comes from any kind of economic activity in Colombia
- ★ More than 50% of your equity is managed in Colombia
- ★ More than 50% of your assets are within the country

If you answer yes in any of these categories, you need to declare taxes in the country. Here's a sample table of how tax is progressively charged in Colombia:

Income	Tax Rate
USD 0 – USD 1,090	0
USD 1,090 – USD 1,700	(Taxable income or taxable occasional gain translated into TVU less TVU 1,090) x 19%
USD 1,700 – USD 4,100	(Taxable income or taxable occasional gain translated into TVU less TVU 1,700) x 28% + TVU 116
USD 4,100 – USD 8,670	(Taxable income or taxable occasional gain translated into TVU less TVU 4,100) x 33% + TVU 788
USD 8,670 – USD 18,970	(Taxable income translated into TVU less TVU 8,670) x 35% + TVU 2,296
USD 18,970 – USD 31,000	(Taxable income translated into TVU less TVU 18,970) x 37% + TVU 5,901
USD 31,000+	(Taxable income translated into TVU less TVU 31,000) x 39% + TVU 10,352

** USD has been retained as default currency for all tax and immigration investment figures in this article. Currency exchange rate USD1 = AUD1.36.

Food

Though the country's cuisine does not normally top the list of renowned cuisine internationally, if you look closely then you will find a jam-packed variety built on the foundation of its influences—from indigenous food to the European palate. There are also slight Arab and African influences in some regions.

The most common ingredients in Colombia's cuisine are rice, maize, potato, cassava, legumes, and meats. It also features a variety of tropical fruits like papaya, guava, araza, and passionfruit.

Its six regions have their own culinary tradition. In the city of Medellin, it is typical to find beans, chorizo, and chicharron. In Cali, you will find sancocho de gallina, a soup of chicken and plantain. On the Caribbean coast, there are more spicy dishes that include fish and lobsters. Travel into the Amazonas and you will taste the influences of Brazil and Peru. Living in Colombia, you have to experience eating at piqueteaderos, rustic eateries that serve specialties in platters to share. Here is a list of food you can't escape from:

★ **Arepa** is probably the most Colombian cuisine ever. It is a circular bread made from cornmeal pan-fried or grilled with toppings ranging from butter and cheese to meat and vegetables.

★ **Bandeja Paisa** is the country's national dish, which comes from the Antioquia region. This is a plate filled with steak, ground beef, chicharrones, beans, rice, egg, avocado, arepa, and plantains—an amazing combination!

★ **Sancocho** refers to a hearty stew you will find in other South American countries too. But the one in Colombia includes a lot of ingredients, oftentimes a few different kinds of meat, plantains, potatoes, and yucca. It is usually served with white rice and avocado.

- **Empanadas** are the default street food found on every street corner. The Colombian version is filled with chorizo, beef, chicken, cheese, and spinach.

- **Buñuelos** is another popular street food that you'll often find in the holiday months of November and December. These are fried dough balls that will come out as sweet and savory. The Colombian Buñuelos is fairly plain and topped with sugar.

- **Mondongo Soup** is a very filling soup made from the stomach lining of a pig or a cow. Often served as an appetizer, the Colombian version is made with tons of peas, carrots, onion, and cilantro.

- **Lechona** is also common in Colombia like in any other South American country. This is pig roasted for twelve hours, stuffed with rice, onions, peas, and spices.

- **Ajiaco** is another hearty stew filled with chicken, three types of potatoes, corn, avocado, and sour cream. The interesting part is it also includes guasca, an herb considered to be a weed in the US.

- **Cazuela de Marisco**s is a thick soup filled with lobster, shrimp, white fish, and vegetables. It also has creamy coconut milk for broth.

It will take time to get used to South American dishes and, once in a while, you will crave international food. Don't worry because you can find a variety of restaurants especially in the major cities to satisfy your cravings.

Recommended Cities in Colombia

Medellin

Surrounded by the Andes Mountains in the middle of the country is the city of Medellin, the second-largest city of Colombia. It is also known as the City of Flowers and has attracted a lot of retirees in recent years. If you want to live an active lifestyle in a city with spring-like weather, Medellin should be your top choice! Every Sunday, the city transforms the large sections of the major roads into pedestrian walkways. Thus, you'll find plenty of families, joggers, and cyclists enjoying the outdoors.

The city has a lot of green spaces with flowers always in bloom, brooks, and a huge variety of birds. It feels more intimate than the big metropolis it really is.

Two decades ago, it had a reputation as one of the most dangerous cities in the world, but it currently has a new story to tell. It has been undergoing a transformation and has gained for itself recognition as the City of Innovation.

Foreign retirees can be found throughout the city but most of the expatriates are living in Laureles, which is a flat neighborhood that makes walking around effortless.

Essentials in Medellin:

- **Healthcare:** High-quality and affordable healthcare—what else can you ask for? The city has eight hospitals that are ranked among the top 43 in the Joint Commission International accreditation. Here are the best hospitals in the city:
  - Hospital Pablo Tobon Uribe
  - Hospital Universitario de San Vicente Fundación
  - Clinica las Americas
  - Hospital General de Medellín
  - Clinica Universitaria Bolivariana
  - Clinica Medellin
  - Clinica El Rosario
  - Clinica Cardio Vid

- **Accessibility:** The Jose Maria Cordova International Airport is one of the biggest airports in the country, serving several destinations with the route to Miami as the busiest. It connects the city to Mexico City, Madrid, Santiago, Lima, and other parts of the country. It is also the hub of the low-cost airline Viva Colombia.

Things You Can Do in Medellin

Medellin offers all transport conveniences, starting from the metro system to over thirty universities, art galleries, history museums, theaters, sports complexes, and restaurants. You may spend your time at the Metropolitan Theater, which offers a varied program of classical music, or wander around the Museo de Antioquia that features a large collection of paintings and sculptures. If you love festivals, Medellin offers a unique line-up throughout the year, from Colombiamoda or fashion week and the flower festival to Christmas. Retiring here means there will never be a dull moment with the following things you can see:

- 3 Cruces
- Museo del Castillo
- Señor Botero
- Museo Moderno del Arte
- Museo Casa de la Memoria
- Parque Explora
- Jardin Botanico
- La Peña
- Rio Claro
- Guatape and El Peñol
- Santa Fe de Antioquia
- Horizontes
- Jerico
- Jardin
- Paramo de Belmiro
- Cerro Tusa

Cartagena

With a million in population, Cartagena is the fifth-largest city in Colombia. It has a strategic location along the Caribbean coast, making it a major seaport for commercial and cruise ships. It sees more than 3,000 ships and a hundred thousand tourists every year.

It is also a UNESCO World Heritage Site, having retained its original colonial architecture after gaining independence from Spain in November 1811. Walking around, you'll find cobbled-stoned streets, amazing churches, museums, and a variety of restaurants in colonial-style buildings. The center is also surrounded by the historic city wall where many residents would stroll feeling the warmth of the ocean breeze.

Many choose to retire in this city because of the variety of its recreational activities from boating, swimming to playing golf.

There is no shortage of happenings in Cartagena. There is the International Music Festival every January, the Film Festival in March and the Jazz Festival in December. There are also plenty of museums and art galleries throughout the city. The common neighborhoods to live in for expatriates are Bocagrande with its high-rise apartments or Manga which is a more laidback residential neighborhood.

Essentials in Cartagena:

- ★ **Healthcare:** Like the other parts of the country, Cartagena enjoys the benefits of Colombia's top-notch healthcare system. Here are the hospitals that made it in our list:
    - ★ Hospital Naval de Cartagen
    - ★ Medihelp Clinic Services
    - ★ Hospital Universitario de Cartagena
    - ★ Nuevo Hospital De Bocagrande

- ★ **Accessibility:** Named after the former Colombian president who wrote the National Anthem of Colombia, the Rafael Nuñez International Airport, located fifteen minutes outside the city, offers direct flights to Miami, New York, and Fort Lauderdale.

Things You Can Do in Cartagena

The city of Cartagena is known for its colorful walled city. Living here will give you the opportunity to see it from a different angle, and not least because it's a cruise hub. You get to explore the city with its warm, tropical climate as you immerse in the vibrant city and enjoy the white-sand beaches. A usual retirement day can also include island hopping, dancing all night in the salsa clubs or simply taking a mud bath. Here are other things to explore as you call this your new home:

- ★ Castillo de San Felipe de Barajas
- ★ Rosario Islands
- ★ Palace of the Inquisition Cartagena Historical Museum
- ★ Las Bovedas
- ★ Cathedral de Santa Catalina de Alejandria
- ★ Plaza de Santo Domingo
- ★ Santuario de San Pedro Claver
- ★ Clock Tower Monument
- ★ Museo del Oro Zenu
- ★ Convent of Santa Cruz de la Popa
- ★ Plaza of Customs
- ★ Ciudad Amurallada
- ★ Walled City
- ★ Plaza de Los Coches
- ★ La India Catalina
- ★ Bahia de Cartagena de Indias
- ★ Plaza de Bolivar
- ★ Las Botas Viejas
- ★ Museo Naval del Caribe

Santa Marta

Santa Marta is another city in Colombia meant for the sun and sea worshippers. It is smaller in size and in population compared to Cartagena but it does not mean it offers less. It has been a sought-after destination not only for tourists but also for retirees. This city of half a million population can offer you an active and healthy lifestyle as you enjoy its cultural offerings. For instance, the city's flat streets make it a great

haven for cyclists. The warm and tropical climate makes it perfect to enjoy the beach where you can also scuba dive for hours to explore the amazing array of coral reefs and sunken wrecks. To top it all, you can eat a sumptuous seafood meal with fresh seafood caught right off the beaches.

Santa Marta offers all the conveniences from banks, pharmacies, and malls to affordable restaurants. Retiring here will include spending time in one of its eco-parks, or strolling along its tree-lined neighborhood towards the beach. The cost of living is also reasonable, with savings from accommodation if you choose to live a block or two away from the beach.

Essentials in Santa Marta:

- **Healthcare:** There are both public and private hospitals in Santa Marta. Here are the top-rated hospitals in the city:
    - Instituto del Corazón de Santa Marta
    - Hospital Universitario Fernando Troconis
    - Clinical Caribbean Sea
    - Uromed, Centros Medicos Santa Marta
- **Accessibility:** The Simon Bolivar International Airport is only half an hour away from the city center. Although it does not offer any direct flights to the US, it can connect you to the main hub cities such as Bogota and Medellin.

Things You Can Do in Santa Marta

Santa Marta is the country's premier beach destination, and it offers many fun things to keep your retirement days busy. You can trek to sites of lesser-known ruins and explore marine life. Do you know that this is also the home to South America's only Island Global Yachting? You may choose to have your own boat or rent one for a day. The marina itself is one of its greatest attractions. The life here is casual and laid back. Even in the wet season from May to November, you'll have plenty of things to do, and one of them can be studying the Spanish language.

- Tayrona National Natural Park
- Lost City
- Taganga
- Playa Blanca
- Museo del Oro Tairona
- Quinta de San Pedro Alejandrino
- El Rodadero
- Minca
- Santa Marta Market
- Simon Bolivar Metropolitan Park
- Rodadero Sea Aquarium
- Parque del Agua
- Pico Cristobal Colon
- Parque San Miguel

Is Colombia LGBT-friendly?

Fortunately, the country embraces diversity. Same-sex marriage and adoption for same-sex couples are allowed. There are anti-discrimination laws that protect the community. Trans people are allowed to change their gender in their identity documents.

Colombia is at the forefront of the LGBT movement among the Latin American countries. Television programs continue to feature LGBT characters and members of the LGBT community are government officials too. Claudia Lopez, for instance, is the first woman and lesbian mayor in the country elected in Bogota.

Senior Discounts

The country passed a law in 2007 that ensures protection and discounts to all of its senior citizens who are 62 years old and above. If you are a foreigner with a legal residency in the country, you can enjoy discounts on public buses in all the cities, as well as preferential seating.

Government offices and utility companies also provide senior priority. Seniors can also benefit from discounts offered by any tourism organization. That means 50% for all state monuments and attractions. You can also get free entrance to museums and other cultural centers. If you want to take classes, a 50% discount is offered too!

Living in Colombia: What to Watch Out For

Colombia is not all paradise, like all countries in the world. It is still important to understand the negative things that come with it too before finally deciding to live and retire in the country. What to watch out for before migrating to Colombia? Read on!

- ★ **Corruption is common.**
  Want to get things done fast and efficient in Colombia? You will have to bribe, otherwise you have to rely on your local lawyers to do the job for you. Many transactions are done under the table so adjust your mentality and adapt accordingly.

- ★ **Beware of dangerous areas.**
  There are parts of the country where you should not go because they are still ravaged by war between the government and the guerillas. This includes Arauca, Cauca, Choco, Nariño, and Norte de Santander.

- ★ **You need to brush up on some Spanish.**
  Living in the country requires you to speak Spanish. Unfortunately, most locals don't speak English so if you want to live an independent life, you have to learn how to speak the language, or it will be difficult to get by. Before moving to Colombia, you might want to get a student visa that will allow you to stay in the country while practicing the language.

Summary

Colombia is an undiscovered gem for retirees from the ease of retirement visa application, top-notch healthcare, accessibility, and the cost of living. To top it all, the quality of life is getting better in the country—if only we look beyond its past.

Healthcare: ★ ★ ★ ★ ★
Culture: ★ ★ ★ ★ ★
Cost of Living: ★ ★ ★ ★
Housing: ★ ★ ★ ★
Accessibility: ★ ★ ★ ★
Safety: ★ ★ ★

TOTAL STARS: 25 ★

Tamarindo Beach, Guanacaste

Reasons to Retire in Costa Rica

There are hundreds of reasons why Costa Rica remains as one of the best retirement destinations in the world, from the ease of residency to affordable healthcare, not to mention its natural beauty. The country has stayed true to its motto of Pura Vida, which translates to "pure life" or "life is good." It is also a greeting in Costa Rica. If someone asks you how you're doing, all you need to say is, "Pura vida."

This country of 5 million is tucked between Nicaragua and Panama, with the Pacific Ocean to its west and the Caribbean to its east. It is probably the country that's got it all – from a year-round tropical climate, hillside villages, contemporary cities, rainforests, beaches – you name it! You can enjoy its natural beauty and fill your days with bird watching, gardening, hiking – and you can do it with the locals or with a thriving expat community that continues to grow every year.

Costa Rica is also known to offer one of the highest standards of living in Central America. It has theaters, museums, and amazing restaurants, plus the essentials, of course: from exceptional healthcare, stable internet to reliable electricity. It even has clean water you can drink directly from the tap. Compared to its neighboring countries, you can enjoy a good quality of life in Costa Rica at a lower cost. Taxes are also low so you can save more money and spend on what's important for you instead. Costa Rica's accessibility to North America is also commendable with regular direct non-stop flights to the United States and Canada.

Why Retire in Costa Rica:

★ Known for its natural beauty, Costa Rica features volcanoes, beaches, and rainforests.
★ It has a thriving community of expatriates.
★ There is political stability.

Culture

The country has a lot of strong traditions – things you must be aware of before you decide to move and retire here. Like many countries in Central and South America, there is a strong influence from the Catholic Church here. 70% of its population are identified as Catholic so you may expect religious events during Easter and Christmas. The Holy Week is when the whole country shuts down, with locals often taking their family vacations. Same thing goes during the Christmas holidays.

If there's one unshakable tradition Costa Ricans have, it is being deep-rooted in Ticos or the Costa Rican natives. You'll find this in their friendly and welcoming attitude towards foreigners, that you get to be treated as a family member right away as they invite you to their gatherings and celebrations. The Ticos always act with exceptional humility so try not to be arrogant when you are around them. Their tranquil nature also comes naturally that there is rarely violence and hostility.

Everyone in Costa Rica treasures their democracy, and they value their personal liberty so much. This has manifested in daily living in different ways. For example, keep in mind that being on time is considered strange. Except for a doctor's appointment or the movies, the Tico hour always applies. People are always late so extend your patience as much as you can.

Costa Ricans also love to dance, and you will find all sorts of clubs in the major and rural cities. They are in love with their theaters so don't be surprised to find them dotted around across the country.

Should you learn to speak Spanish while living in Costa Rica? It is not necessary to learn and speak Spanish in Costa Rica. Many locals speak English so the chance of you surviving with just English is high, however, if you want to fit in the neighborhood, you may want to brush up with some basic Spanish.

Climate

With the country lying down on the Caribbean Plate, just a little north of the equator, Costa Rica enjoys a tropical and subtropical climate as well as two primary seasons. From the winter in December to summer in April is when the dry season lasts, while from May to November is when the wet season happens. The latter period is when conditions are humid and overcast.

The temperature varies with a range between 17 – 27 degrees Celsius. It is by the month of January when the lowest temperature is recorded, while April is the hottest. Microclimates also exist based on altitude, local geography, rainfall, and topography. The annual rainfall reaches 1,981 mm and September to October are the wettest months.

Cost of Living

There are plenty of inexpensive things you can enjoy in Costa Rica. Luxuries are also available and if you have any extra budget for that, it can add up to your monthly expenses. A comfortable budget is AUD 2,028 or even less monthly, which allows for bus rides and occasional taxis, and even trips to the farmers' market and few restaurant meals. A 3-course menu in a moderately-priced sit-down restaurant costs AUD 20 – 27 per person. A trip to the farmers' market will cost you about AUD 27 – 54 which can fill a week's worth of meals from fruits, vegetables, meats, and fish. Here's a sample list of expenses for your references:

Expenses	Prices
Housing rent (One-bedroom in city centre, Arenal)	AUD 439
High-speed internet	AUD 77
Electricity and water	AUD 93
Phone with basic data plan	AUD 20
Loaf of white bread	AUD 3.65
A dozen eggs	AUD 4.40
Local beer	AUD 3.75
Taxi per kilometer	AUD 1.45

Housing

Renting a well-furnished apartment in the urban areas costs around AUD 406 – AUD 811. This may include a laundry, and a heater in the shower. If you are looking at a lavish three-bedroom house in the Central Valley with Jacuzzi, you may expect to pay AUD 2,028 a month.

Buying a house is permitted for foreigners, whether they are residents or non-residents. A two-bedroom house in Arenal can cost you AUD 168988+, while a one-bedroom apartment in San Jose is more expensive at AUD 216,304.. Just continue looking and you'll be able to find good deals.

There are long-term care facilities and nursing homes available in the country too, that provide activities, meals, laundry, and healthcare. Some cater to expatriates with English-speaking staff, costing AUD 1,351.90 – AUD 6,760 a month.

Healthcare in Costa Rica

Do you know that on its northern Pacific coast, where the Nicoya Peninsula region is, residents live longer than average? In fact, the World Health Organization has always placed Costa Rica at the top when it comes to long life expectancy – and that says a lot about the health of the people living here. Perhaps one of the reasons is their relaxed way of living combined with healthy and fresh food.

Expatriates can access two healthcare systems in Costa Rica. First is the government-run universal system called Caja Costarricense de Seguro Social, which is also known as Caja. They offer more than enough advancements at a low cost compared to their North American and European counterparts. If you are under the residency programs such as Pensionado, Rentista, or Inversionista, then you can join this program by paying a small monthly fee based on your income. Usually, it is between 7% - 11% of your earnings.

The second option is private healthcare which is of a higher quality and also affordable. You can pay cash out of your pocket or use your health insurance. The doctors also speak in English, especially those who are in private healthcare. We recommend using both systems just to make sure they will be fully covered.

How to Retire in Costa Rica (Retirement Visa)*

There are a few options to become a resident in Costa Rica. The good news is, after three years as a temporary resident in any of the below categories, you can then apply for permanent resident status.

The Pensionado Program requires proof that you earn at least USD 1,000 a month from

Social Security, pension, or any other kind of retirement plan. This will not allow you to work as an employee in the country but owning a company and receiving dividends is okay. This permit is valid for two years and can only be renewed if you still meet the requirements. You must also prove that the income has been received in the country and you have lived in the country for at least four months per year.

The Rentista Program is suitable for people without a fixed retirement income. This will provide proof of USD 2,5000 monthly income for at least a couple of years. Alternatively, you must deposit an amount of USD 60,000 in a local bank approved by immigration authorities.

Inversionista Program is for those who can invest at least USD 200,000 in the country. However, keep in mind that this only applies to the investors and not their families.

* USD has been retained as default currency for all immigration investment figures in this article. Currency exchange rate USD1 = AUD1.36.

Work

As stated above, you are not permitted to work under the Pensionado and Rentista Program. Owning a business is possible but you cannot run it yourself. You may only receive dividends, otherwise you must apply for a work or a proper business permit.

Tax**

Both residents and non-residents are subject to tax on income they earn within Costa Rica. If you are earning income from foreign sources, don't worry because you will not be subjected to taxes in the country. That means your pension is safe and will not be subjected to tax. If you have permanent work in the country, then expect to pay a progressive tax between 0% - 25%. Here's a quick guide:

Income	Tax Rate
Below CRC 619,000	0%
CRC 619,001 – CRC 929,000	10%
CRC 929,001+	15%

** CRC has been retained as default currency for all tax figures in this article. Currency exchange rate CRC1 = AUD0.0022.

Food

Costa Rica has a fairly mild cuisine – no wonder it is often underappreciated. Here, you'll find plenty of fruits and vegetables, as well as rice and black beans because they are a staple in almost all traditional cuisines. Pork and beef are often found in their dishes, while fish and chicken are usually more accessible on the Caribbean coast. Other basic elements include plantain and potatoes.

Their cuisine is an amazing mix of cultures with influences coming from Spain, Guinea, Ghana, and later on, Jamaica. There are also influences from the indigenous descendants of Mayas in the north and Chibchas in the south. The United States has also left a mark.

Living in Costa Rica, you will surely encounter Salsa Lizano, which was created in 1920. It is the most common condiment in the country boasting the elements of Tico cooking. You may recognize it with its tangy flavor and its ingredients such as onion, carrot, cauliflower, cucumber, pepper, mustard, and turmeric. It is often compared to Worcestershire sauce.

Here are the dishes you will get the chance to know:

- **Gallo Pinto** is claimed by both Costa Rica and Nicaragua. It is a variation of rice and beans seasoned with cilantro, onions, and bell peppers. The name itself translates to "spotted rooster" which means spots of beans standing out against the white rice. It is often served with fried egg in the morning, or with meat or fish for lunch and dinner time.

- **Chifrijo** or fried pork with red beans is present in nearly every canteen. From the name itself, it consists of two signature ingredients: the fried pork or the chicharron and beans. It is perfectly paired with rice, salad, or nachos.

- **Rondon** is your typical seafood and coconut stew. You may use any kind of fish and vegetables and throw them into a pot of coconut milk and herbs.

- **Casado**, which literally means "married man," is a usual lunch meal. It is basically a mix of vegetables and protein served with rice, beans, and coleslaw.

- **Olla de carne** is beef and vegetable stew. It is a weekend meal in Costa Rican homes, and is usually served in family gatherings. It is simmered for at least four hours, sometimes longer, with lots of vegetables from potatoes, carrots to plantains.

- **Picadillos** is a mix of chopped vegetables sauteed with onion, stock, and other seasonings. It is a side dish served with rice and meat.

- **Chorreadas** are savory and sweet pancakes made from corn. This is a typical breakfast, drizzled with honey or syrup.

- **Ceviche** is a common cuisine in many Latin American countries but what sets it apart in Costa Rica is that the seafood must be marinated in lime juice for at least an hour which results in less raw-tasting fish.

- **Tamales** is a dish of seasoned meat wrapped in banana leaves and usually prepared during Christmas. It is one of the most time-honored traditions in the country.

- **Peach Palm Soup** or sopa de pejibaye is a starchy, orange palm fruit. It is usually boiled for at least an hour, before peeling. Then it can be pureed into a soup along with meat stock, cream, and herbs.

- **Sweetened Squash Paste** or miel de chiverre is a typical pan-Latin sweet. It is similar to a flan, but chunkier because it is made from chiverre or the fig leaf gourd.

In the urban areas such as San Jose and other beach destinations frequented by tourists, there are other varieties of cuisine available such as Peruvian, Japanese, Chinese, and Italian.

Recommended Cities in Costa Rica

The Central Valley

Encompassing the capital city of San Jose, San Ramon to Cartago, this 90-mile area where 70% of the country's population choose to live, is an elevated plateau ranging from 900 – 1,524 meters above sea level. This makes for perfect weather, which is one of the main attractions of living in this area. And because the temperature is so pleasant, many of the homes don't come with air conditioning or heating.

Living in San Jose means you can access plenty of museums, art galleries, entertainment and shopping. Some of the popular suburb areas are Sana Fe and Escazu where one can escape the hustle of the city and enjoy the spectacular mountain view.

San Jose is also the focal point of educational, political, and economic activity. It has been the capital since 1820, thus, you will find planned neighborhoods or barrios exhibiting different architectural styles, built slowly over the centuries.

You may also consider smaller towns such as Grecia, Cartago, Atenas or San Ramon with its own charm, personality, and a tight expat community. Here, you can find coffee plantations and sugar canes – it is an escape from the beach too.

The main international airport is also in Central Valley, which makes it the perfect base if you prefer to travel and explore other countries.

Essentials in The Central Valley:

- ★ **Healthcare:** There are two hospitals in San Jose with JCI accreditation, which means they meet a set of quality standards required to improve patient care. Along with the first two that are JCI accredited, there are also other hospitals you may consider:
    - ★ Hospital Clínica Bíblica
    - ★ Hospital Clínica La Católica
    - ★ Hospital San Juan de Dios
    - ★ Hospital CIMA
    - ★ Hospital Calderón Guardia
- ★ **Accessibility:** The Juan Santamaria International Airport is the primary airport in Costa Rica. Named after the national hero, it connects the country to many different cities in North, Central, and South America.

Things You Can Do in The Central Valley

Focusing on San Jose, retiring here guarantees a vibrant lifestyle and one that you will never get tired of. You can spend your months and years here, and there will still be plenty to discover. It has an amazing transportation system – the rail and the bus.

It has an impressive pedestrian mall, one-of-a-kind barrios, and quaint neighborhoods – that even if there is a big city atmosphere, it is still

possible to lead a stress-free life. San Jose boasts a wide variety of markets from the Central Market to the weekly farmers' market. Living in San Jose gives you the opportunity to explore extraordinary treasures that tourists tend to miss. Here are some of those:

- Municipal Rose Garden
- Rosicrucian Egyptian Museum
- Santana Row
- Winchester Mystery House
- Cathedral Basilica of St. Joseph
- SAP Center
- Los Gatos Creek
- Sikh Gurdwara
- San Jose Center for the Performing Arts
- Willow Glen
- Alum Rock Park
- San Pedro Square Market
- Avaya Stadium
- San Jose Museum of Art

Arenal

Located in the northwestern part of the country, Lake Arenal is the country's largest freshwater lake nestled between Alajuela and Guanacaste. There is no large-scale development so it is a total escape from the city, where you can relax in one of the small towns. The most popular is Nuevo Arenal that offers rural country living and yet it has all the modern conveniences from restaurants, shopping centers, pharmacies, banks, and many more.

La Fortuna is another town at the far side and closer to the volcano, with an airport and even a multitude of different restaurants. It is a tourist destination with sufficient facilities making it the perfect sanctuary for expatriates too.

Arenal has a Spring-like climate which makes it pleasant to explore the outdoors. It does rain heavily sometimes, but it's what nourishes the lush environment. Plus, you can enjoy the beautiful landscape with the serenity of the pristine lake.

If you are looking for bargain real estate, then Arsenal may be the perfect fit for you. Lots of homes in this area maximize an outdoor lifestyle so you will find large covered patios, with windows facing the lake. The cost of living is also cheaper here compared to the Central Valley.

Essentials in Arenal:

- **Healthcare:** The standard of healthcare offered in Arenal area remains, and here is a list of hospitals that you may consider shall the situation call:
    - Clinica Medicenter Fortuna
    - Centro Medico Sanar La Fortuna
    - Clinical Internacional la Fortuna

- **Accessibility:** La Fortuna in Arenal is only three hours drive from San Jose. It also features its own airport, La Fortuna Airport that has regular quick flights to San Jose.

Things You Can Do in Arenal

Located three hours' drive from the capital, La Fortuna, one of the places to be in Arenal, makes a perfect getaway for city-dwellers. Living here will provide you more chances of living in peace and complete serenity. Say goodbye to heavy traffic and crowds and say hello to the small-village atmosphere.

One of the side benefits of volcanic activity is that countless thermal hot springs abound in the area. Here, you can enjoy dipping into the hot springs while enjoying the view of the Arenal Volcano. It is believed to have medicinal properties that can alleviate arthritis and heart conditions.

Aside from the natural scenery and possible health benefits, there are plenty of adventures waiting for you in Arenal. Here are some that are not to be missed:

- ★ La Fortuna Waterfall
- ★ Arenal Hanging Bridges
- ★ Ecotermales Fortuna
- ★ Baldi Hot Springs
- ★ Proyecto Asis
- ★ Arenal Volcano
- ★ Lake Arenal
- ★ Venado Caves
- ★ Cerro Chato
- ★ Rio Chollin
- ★ Paradise Hot Springs
- ★ Arenal Oasis Wildlife Refuge
- ★ Natura Eco Park

Central Pacific

Stretching from Puntarenas to Manuel Antonio, the Central Pacific Coast is one of the most popular places for expatriates and retirees. There has been large upscale development in recent years in this area. It is also strategically located an hour away from San Jose. One can also find two big marinas here: Herradura at Los Sueños and another in Quepos. This means a variety of great sportfishing is available.

The weather in the Central Coast is more tropical, although not dry as there is a bit more rain in this part of the country, but again, it only makes the region greener and lusher. There are also good surfing spots and one of them is Playa Hermosa, which organizes many international surfing competitions.

If you prefer living in the Vegas of Costa Rica by the beach, just head over to Jaco where you will find casinos and all kinds of shopping and nightlife. Lying between several mountains, and flanked by the beaches of Herradura Bay and Playa Hermosa, this town of over 10,000 people boasts an exciting vibe like no other. But if you are fond of a nice and quieter retirement place, then it should be Esterillos Este with affordable housing too!

Check out Manuel Antonio, which is one of the most visited national parks accessible from here. There are gorgeous beaches with lovely housing options along the coast.

Essentials in Central Pacific:

- ★ **Healthcare:** There is an adequate number of hospitals along the coast, but with its proximity to San Jose, the hospitals in the city are more preferred. The most popular is Hospital CIMA which is a part of a group of international hospitals based in the USA. Here are other hospitals you may consider in the area:
  - ★ Hospital Clínica Bíblica
  - ★ Hospital de Ciudad Neily
  - ★ Golfito Hospital Manuel Mora Valverde
  - ★ Hospital Monseñor Victor Manuel Sanabria Martinez

- ★ **Accessibility:** The Chacarita Airport offers 30-minute flights to San Jose. However, the 1.5-hour drive into the international airport is also a good alternative to access the rest of the world.

Things You Can Do in Central Pacific

Living in the Central Pacific towns means an abundance of excellent restaurants, as these are often visited by both local and international tourists. There are also countless hotels and recreational activities that retiring here will give you enough things to do, beyond swimming by the beach and sunbathing.

The Central Pacific remains the top choice for retirement destination because it is only here where tropical forests meet the Pacific Ocean, which also means spectacular sunsets! Baby Boomers and Gen Xers who are landing in the bustling beach towns can access the following places too:

- ★ Ballena Marine National Park
- ★ Chirripo National park
- ★ Dominical Beaches
- ★ Carara National Park
- ★ Mount Chirripo
- ★ Manuel Antonio National Park
- ★ Nauyaca Waterfalls
- ★ San Mateo City
- ★ Jaco
- ★ Tarcoles Beach
- ★ Punta Leona Beaches
- ★ Herradura Beach
- ★ Hermosa Beach
- ★ Palma Beach
- ★ Bejuco Beach
- ★ Quepos City
- ★ Palo Seco Beach
- ★ Savegre River
- ★ Naranjo River
- ★ Baru Beach
- ★ Matapalo Beach

Is Costa Rica LGBT-friendly?

There are areas in the country that have been vacation destinations for LGBT individuals for over two decades. These are Quepos and Parque Nacional Manuel Antonio – it makes living here convenient and comfortable for LGBT couples. LGBT rights have evolved in the past decades in Costa Rica, with sexual relations legal since 1971.

Same-sex marriages have been allowed since 2020, and discrimination on the basis of sexual orientation is prohibited. Keep in mind also that although homosexuality is legal in Costa Rica, it is best not to display public affections to avoid unwanted attention.

Senior Discounts

Senior citizens are well-respected and valued in Costa Rica. That's why they have an amazing senior citizen discount program. If you are 65 years old and older and a legal resident of the country, you may apply for a Ciudadano de Oro ID card with quite a few benefits. It is run by Caja or the Department of Social Security with the following benefits:

- ★ Free bus rides
- ★ Commercial discounts in shoe stores, pharmacies, optical stores, hotels, appliance stores, etc.

This discount varies between 2% - 20% so make sure to bring your card anywhere you go to enjoy these benefits.

Living in Costa Rica: What to Watch Out For

There are always two sides to the coin. Despite the things that make Costa Rica a paradise, there are also little consequences that come with it.

★ **You can't escape the untamed natural surroundings.**
Because Costa Rica's wildlife is so rich, this means you can spot anything from monkeys to toucans in your garden. There are also chances of finding bats and other critters in your toilet too. They are unavoidable unless you live in a high-rise building with closed windows.

★ **When it rains, it pours.**
Because of so much rain the country experiences, power and water outages are common. It is best to select a city with all the amenities. It will be better if you experience living there yourself for a few weeks before deciding if the place can adapt in a good way.

★ **It is getting saturated with North Americans.**
There is an advantage to this, of course. It means social gatherings, gardening clubs, gringo poker night, etc. We're guessing that this kind of lifestyle is what you probably want to escape from. If you can tolerate it, then it's all right, otherwise, choose a less-developed spot with fewer expatriates.

Summary

Costa Rica has been among the best choices for retirement for decades now. Whichever area you choose in the country, you will find thriving expat communities making it easier to fit in and adjust to your new home.

Healthcare: ★ ★ ★ ★
Culture: ★ ★ ★ ★
Cost of Living: ★ ★ ★ ★
Housing: ★ ★ ★ ★
Accessibility: ★ ★ ★ ★
Safety: ★ ★ ★ ★

TOTAL STARS: 24 ★

Quito, Ecuador

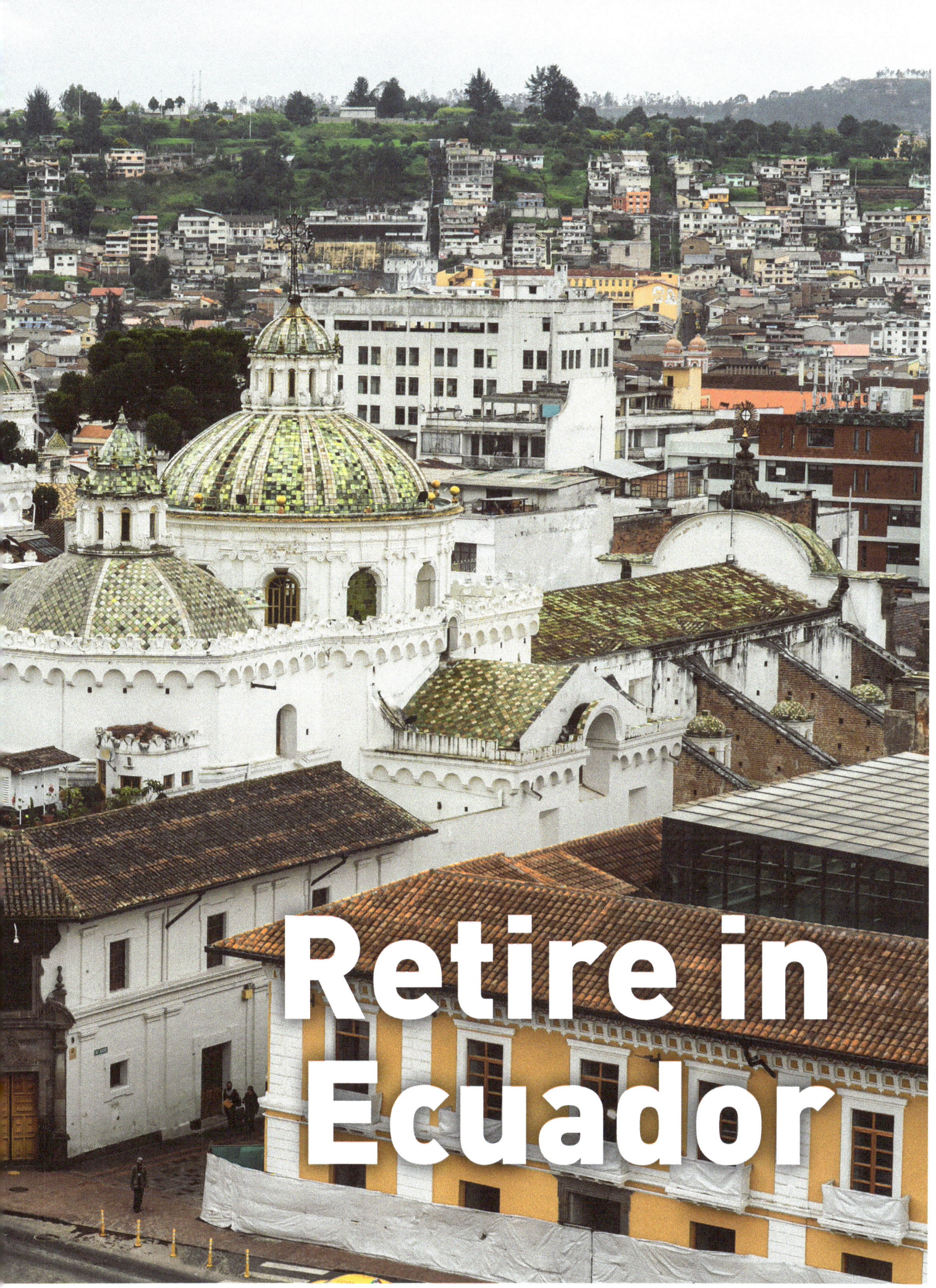

Reasons to Retire in Ecuador

In Ecuador – known as the land of eternal spring given the surrounding mountains – you will not feel too hot nor too cold, as the weather is comfortable all year round. There is plenty of fresh produce available in the country so that every meal can feel like a feast. You can enjoy fresh fruits and vegetables throughout the year.

Ecuadorians are also warm and welcoming. You will find a lot of support when you decide to move and retire here. Compared to its neighboring countries, Ecuador is a safe country to retire in, given that it has the lowest homicide rates in the world. As long as you carry your common sense with you, you'll be okay.

Ecuador's geography also offers plenty of fun activities during your retirement. If you are into adventure, you can choose to trek the rainforest or walk along the rim of the volcano. With 1,400 miles of coastline, you can do lots of water activities, from snorkeling and diving to surfing, or you can charter a boat on the weekend for some whale-watching.

If you are looking to retire with little money saved, then living in Ecuador may be one of the best options for you. With less than AUD 2,307.87 a month, you can live a comfortable lifestyle here. Most expatriates who live in Ecuador choose to have both a main home in the city, as well as a country home or a beach property. This way, they can have the best of both worlds. Also, expect to pay minimal healthcare fees that are still cheaper compared to the rest of the world.

Why Retire in Ecuador:

★ Spring-like temperature all year round.
★ Cheap cost of living.
★ There is an abundance of fresh fruit and vegetables with lots of exotic things to explore and try.

Culture

In Ecuador's population of 11 million, about 65% is mixed European and Indian blood, also known as mestizo, 25% is Amerindian, while the remaining portion is a Black minority.

The Catholic religion has a strong influence on Ecuadorians' personal and social behavior. The church is also wrapped up with government processes. With 50% of its population practicing Catholics, living here may require your understanding of the religion as you attend the festivals celebrated throughout the year.

Another thing to take note of is the machismo in the country. Traditional gender roles remain in Ecuador, which means the man is the breadwinner, while the wife takes care of the home.

As you retire in Ecuador, keep in mind that there is a low proficiency of English in the country so you better equip yourself with some Spanish. Quichua is the official language, but it is only spoken by the Indian population. If you decide to live in the city, English will be okay to get by as it is common among professionals. However, not learning the language may not get you into the locals' inner circle. If you want to make more friends, then Spanish is the way to go.

While people are warm and polite, some can be tactile and stand too close to you when they speak. Ecuadorians also tend to communicate indirectly. They prefer not to confront anyone and even if they want to say no, they will still go out of their way. Still, be careful with whatever you say. Blunt communication is viewed as extremely rude. If they flatter you, you may expect that they want something from you.

One of the best things about Ecuadorians is they are very optimistic people. They tend to see the glass half full in all kinds of situations.

Climate

With Ecuador's geographic location directly on the equator, the country enjoys twelve hours of daylight all year round. However, it will depend on wherever you decide to locate in the country that will dictate the climate you will experience. There are four geographical areas in Ecuador: Sierra or the mountains, the La Costa or the Pacific coastal plains, the Oriente or the eastern rainforests, and the Galapagos Islands.

The capital Quito is situated in the Central Valley at 2,900 meters above sea level, thus the Spring-like weather makes it comfortable to walk around the city with just a shirt and shorts. Other cities such as Cuenca, Loja, and Cotacachi have similar climates to Quito.

If you prefer to have a warmer climate, then better head to the coast – to the West of the Andes, which has a tropical climate. July to November experience the dry season, while the rest of the year is the wet season. Still, the coasts remain drier than the areas at the foothills of the Andes.

For warmer weather, then head towards the Amazon basin, with towns such as Tena and Puyo where you can live in a rainforest environment of lush jungles and tropical birds.

Cost of Living

This will depend on your needs and wants but, typically, a couple can afford a comfortable lifestyle in Ecuador for AUD 2,172.11 a month. It can even be lower if you decide to live in a more remote area.

Rent-wise in an upscale two-bedroom apartment will cost you AUD 815 a month. If you prefer to live frugally, it can even go down to AUD 543. Utilities can be as little as AUD 27 – 41 a month

covering electricity and gas. It is not necessary to own cars because some towns are walkable. If you want to indulge in food then expect to allocate AUD 679 from your budget. Pampering oneself does not cost much in Ecuador. A haircut costs AUD 27 while a massage runs from AUD 20.

Here is a quick summary of what necessities will cost you while living in Ecuador:

Expenses	Prices
Housing rent (One-bedroom in an average area)	AUD 541
High-speed internet	AUD 54
Electricity and water	AUD 54
Phone with basic data plan	AUD 20
Loaf of white bread	AUD 2.15
A dozen eggs	AUD 2.35
Local beer	AUD 1.90
Taxi per kilometer	AUD 2.03

Housing

Fortunately, there are no restrictions on foreign investment in Ecuador. You can purchase a property as long as it is within 50 km of the border or the coastline. Ecuador can be a real estate bargain, but we still recommend you take precautions when buying a property here as there are scams in the industry. Most of the properties for sale are not listed because it is highly localized in the country. It will be best to consult a real estate agent for assistance if you are keen. A nice 100 sqm apartment in Quito can costs about AUD 155,468.50, while a 3-story home of 285 sqm can cost AUD 344734.50.

Renting an apartment can start from AUD 540.75. With such cheap rent, you may want to wait before buying your home in Ecuador. Keep in mind that apartments often have an alicuota or a condo fee, which costs around AUD 54.

There are retirement communities where expats thrive in Ecuador. Cuenca is the most popular place with over 5,000 expatriates living here. With the affordability Ecuador offers, it may be better to live in your own home or apartment in the country and hire a maid for assistance.

Healthcare in Ecuador

One of the reasons why Ecuador is one of the top retirement countries is its healthcare system. Healthcare cost is the lowest compared to the USA, China, Malaysia, and Panama. For instance, surgeries cost 25% of what you would have paid in the US. The same thing goes with dental care and regular check-ups.

Ecuador is still a developing country but it does not mean you can't find first-rate medical care here, especially in the major cities. A lot of doctors are educated overseas and yet they don't expect to be paid much. A general practitioner will cost you around AUD 34, while a specialist will charge from AUD 41.

Ecuador recently passed a bill where people 65 years old and above are required to get health insurance. The cost of health insurance remains a bargain, where you can expect to pay at least AUD 95 per year.

Alternatively, you can also choose to buy in the social security healthcare option. You only have to pay 17.6% of your income, which covers in-hospital care, extended care, home care, outpatient care, prescription drugs, eye care, and dental care.

How to Retire in Ecuador (Retirement Visa)*

Ecuador offers a straightforward procedure to become a resident of the country. You have three options: first is staying on a tourist entry, which allows you to stay for ninety days; the 12-IX visa, which is referred to as the tourist, commercial, or sports visa, can allow you to stay in the country for up to 180 days in one year.

Another choice of visa is the temporary visa that is valid for two years. Remember that it can be renewed at one time only, so during this period, you can try to get a permanent visa that does not have an expiration date. Also, keep in mind that temporary visa holders may go out of the country no more than three months every year.

The main choice for foreigners who want to retire here is the 60-III: Pensioner, where you only need to show proof of permanent income from sources outside of Ecuador amounting to USD 800 per month. If you have any dependents with you, then that's an additional USD 100 per month. If you have a pension, social security, or any fixed-income annuity, you can apply for the 60-III: Pensioner. The main benefits are you no longer have to pay taxes on foreign homes and you can import your household goods duty-free six months after obtaining residency.

* USD has been retained as default currency for all tax and immigration investment figures in this article. Currency exchange rate USD1 = AUD1.36.

Work

If you intend to work in Ecuador, you must apply for a working permit and you can still bring along your family with you. The other type of visa is an investor visa if you intend to start a business or invest in an existing business here.

Tax**

Your tax liability as a foreign resident of Ecuador is still low unless you are running a business here. You will only be taxed in any income earned from Ecuador, not from the income you earn from other countries. Income tax is charged in progressive rates from 5% - 35%. Here's a guide for your reference:

Income	Tax Rate
0 – USD 11,315	0%
USD 11,315 – USD 14,416	5%
USD 14,416.01 – USD 18,018	10%
USD 18,018.01 – USD 21,639	12%
USD 21,639.01 – USD 43,268	15%
USD 43,268.01 – USD 64,887	20%
USD 64,887.01 – USD 86,516	25%
USD 86,516.01 – USD 115.338	30%
USD 115,338.01 onwards	35%

** USD has been retained as default currency for all tax and immigration investment figures in this article. Currency exchange rate USD1 = AUD1.36.

Food

There is an abundance of native ingredients in Ecuador from its Pacific shore, Amazon rainforest, flatlands, and high-altitude valley. In the coastal region, beef, chicken, and seafood are popular, while rice and pasta are common in the mountainous region, served with pork, chicken, beef, and cuy (guinea pig). A typical meal follows a 3-course meal of soup, rice or pasta with protein, and dessert.

Other usual staples include potatoes, fish, yuca, rice, beans, and plantains. Ecuadorians also use a lot of aji or spicy chile pepper hot sauce. With the cuisine's diversity and flavor, Ecuador's food is one reason to stay. Here are some of the cuisines you can try while spending your retirement days here in Ecuador:

- ★ **Locro de papa** is the Ecuadorian version of potato stew. It contains cheese and rinds, served with toasted corn and avocado.

- ★ **Cuy Asado** or roasted guinea pig is something that worries a lot of people coming into the country and trying this cute animal for the first time. Eating cuy asado is like eating KFC, although it is not a very meaty animal that you have to eat it with your hands. This is often served with rice and potatoes.

- ★ **Llapingachos**, or fried potato pancakes, are made with boiled potatoes and cheese, bathed in peanut sauce, chorizo, fried egg, vegetables, and avocado.

- ★ **Currasco ecuatoriano** or Ecuadorian grilled meat is a delicious dish of beef served with white rice, French fries, egg, and avocado.

- ★ **Ceviche de camaron** is one of the most traditional dishes in South America, and shrimp ceviche is the best quality in Ecuador. Some prepare ceviche with beans, mushrooms, and palm hearts. This is perfectly paired with a nice local beer.

- ★ **Bolones de verde**, or stuffed green plantain dumplings, is a delicious meal filled with cheese and/or deep-fried pork. It is often paired with scrambled eggs and a cup of coffee.

- ★ **Encebollado,** also known as chuchaqui, helps to alleviate hangovers. It is a fish-based broth, and contains yuca, pepper, tomato, and onion.

- ★ **Encocado de pescado** is a traditional dish on the Ecuadorian coast, made of coconut and fish. It is served with white rice, patacones or a flattened slice of fried green plantain or maduro frito.

There are plenty of international restaurants in Ecuador, even fast-food chains such as McDonalds or KFC. If you are craving for Asian or Western meals, there are a lot of options in the main cities.

Recommended Cities in Ecuador

Cuenca

As the largest city in Ecuador, Cuenca has turned into an economic center of the southern sierra. It is known for its colorful festivals, amazing cuisine, and glorious scenery. It is also a UNESCO World Heritage Trust site. The name of the city itself means "basin" in Spanish, which aptly describes its geographical features. Cuenca sits on a plateau with four rivers running in and around it. At 2,500 meters, it gets Spring-like temperature, with rainfall averaging at three inches per month.

The city has been growing since 2000 and now has over half a million in population. New Town is developed, featuring suburbs and modern mid-rise condominiums. There are several malls, hospitals, markets, and cinemas.

Cuenca is also a mecca for artists, with artisans producing fine leather goods, musical instruments, jewelry, and ceramics. There is a growing expatriate community here – some of them running their businesses, from restaurants to massage services.

Essentials in Cuenca:

- **Healthcare:** Excellent healthcare is offered in Cuenca with top-notch hospitals and bilingual doctors. Here are some of the hospitals we recommend in Cuenca:
    - Mount Sinai Hospital
    - Hospital Universitario del Rio
    - Hospital Vicente Corral Moscosco
    - Clinica Humanitaria
    - Hospital San Martin de Porres

- **Accessibility:** Mariscal Lamar International Airport, a high elevation airport that serves the Azuay Province. Avianca and LATAM Ecuador connect the province to Quito.

Things You Can Do in Cuenca

You will never run out of interesting and fun things to do in Cuenca. It has history, culture, and many adventurous activities. If you are looking for a culture-rich life combined with a modern feel, Cuenca is a great place and it is attracting more and more expats every year.

For the adventurous retirees, there are plenty of opportunities to hike, trout fish, and bike. Exploring the city at a relaxed pace is also an option. Walk along in its lovely cobblestone streets and discover something new in every turn such as the following:

- Cathedral de la Inmaculada
- Tomebamba Riverfront
- Homero Ortega Museum
- Museo Sombrero De Paja Toquilla
- Mirador de Turi
- Pumapungo Archaeological Park
- Amaru Biopark
- Flower Market

- Plaza de San Francisco
- Mercado de Artesanias Rotary
- Parque Calderon
- Cajas National Park
- Garden of Azuay
- Chordeleg Museum
- Artisan Towns
- Ingapirca

Quito

The capital is a 14,000-acre world-class metropolis and is often called the most beautiful city on the continent. It is situated in the palm of a valley between Andean peaks, filled with parks and plazas. You will find a maze of forested paths and on a clear summer day, you can see the snow-topped Antisana, Cotopaxi, and Cayambe volcanoes.

If you are an urban-lover, and being at the center of action, then a retirement in Quito is recommended. It is filled with the best restaurants and malls where you can find anything you'll need. With its 2.6 million population, it is the second-largest city after Guayaquil. Embassies are all located here and healthcare with the most modern and attentive medical care is available.

The city continues to put great effort into expanding and improving its park system. A good example is Parque Carolina, a celebrated park in the financial district. With its 160 acres, you'll find walking and jogging trails, sporting areas, as well as a Vivarium.

Essentials in Quito

- **Healthcare:** The capital of Ecuador offers first-rate healthcare with the best hospitals and medical clinics in the country. Here are our recommended hospitals:
  - Hospital Baca Ortiz
  - Hospital Especializo San Juan de Dios
  - Clinica la Merced
  - Dr. Orlando Suarez CMI Traumatologia
  - Centro de Referencias Medicas Club de Leones Quito Luz de America
- **Accessibility:** Mariscal Sucre International Airport is the busiest airport in the country. It connects the airport to South American countries, Panama, USA, Madrid, and Amsterdam.

Things You Can Do in Quito

Quito has a great diversity of modern things and preserved history and culture. Retirement days here can be filled with so many things to see and do throughout the town. There are dozens of museums that can take you back to the past. Or there are also huge shopping malls and artisan markets for shopping. The entertainment never runs short, with symphonies, ballets, and art exhibitions. Here are other points of interest in Quito:

- Basilica Towers
- Equator Line
- Quito Central Park
- Plaza Foch
- La Ronda
- El Panecillo
- Ciudad Mitad del Mundo
- La Campaña
- The Crystal Palace

- ★ La Forest Street
- ★ Plaza Grande
- ★ Basilica del Voto Nacional
- ★ Casa del Alabado Museo
- ★ Chapel of Man
- ★ Convent and Monastery San Francisco

Loja

This is a modern city with all the amenities you need, but with added cultural richness – making it one of the most ideal places to live in Ecuador. Imagine: a dramatic countryside, with green mountain peaks and rivers! It is located in the southern part of Ecuador, bordering Peru. There is a good number of town squares where you can walk around and socialize. There are also nice cafes to relax in. It is also the safest place to live in the country, where residents can walk the streets in the evening without fear.

The temperature during the day is 22 degrees Celsius and 8 degrees in the evening. So, you don't need the air conditioning, but at least prepare your winter clothes.

The locals are friendly and welcoming, and polite and courteous, too. You can find indigenous presence but not as omnipresent as in Quito. If you enjoy music, then you'd be happy to hear that it is a big part of the culture of the city, that it boasts two orchestras and a music conservatory.

The cost of living is also very affordable in Loja, that AUD 1,352 would be sufficient for a couple.

Essentials in Loja:

- ★ **Healthcare:** The city has dental and medical schools which run clinics. It also has a number of hospitals, from a large public hospital to modern private hospitals linked to the universities. The standard is high for what you pay. Here is a list of hospitals we recommend in Loja:
    - ★ Isidro Ayora Hospital
    - ★ Hospital Clinica MEDILAB
    - ★ Centro Quirurigico Ambilatorio
    - ★ San Jose Hospital
    - ★ Clinica de Especialidades Médicas Mogrovejo
    - ★ Hospital UTPL

- ★ **Accessibility:** Ciudad de Catamayo Airport is an airport serving the Loja province. It connects the region to Quito with about fifteen flights a week.

Things You Can Do in Loja

Being one of the oldest cities in Ecuador, Loja now is home to three major universities and many museums. It has a population of quarter a million and yet it keeps a small-town atmosphere and a sense of community. In the downtown area, you will find the main cathedral of Virgin de Cisne. There are also squares like San Francisco and Santo Domingo with tree-lined walkways along the rivers. There are several parks to explore too.

- ★ City Gate
- ★ Rio Malacatos
- ★ Plaza Parque Central
- ★ The Loja Cathedral
- ★ Botanical Garden
- ★ Calle Lourdes
- ★ Santuario de Nuestra Señora de El Cisne
- ★ Vilcabamba
- ★ Cascada de Los Incas
- ★ Podocarpus National Park
- ★ Museo de la Música

Vilcabamba

In the southern part of Ecuador, Vilcabamba is tucked away. Also known as the Sacred Valley of the country and with only 4,000 inhabitants, it offers a mellow lifestyle and a small village atmosphere. It is also clean and friendly and with a growing number of expatriates.

If you are the type who appreciates nature and the outdoors, and wants to have a back-to-basics lifestyle, away from the hustle and bustle of the city, then living in Vilcabamba is perfect for you. If you want the freshest air and maybe try your hand at farming, then this is also the place it be. Vilcabamba is often called the healthiest place in the world to live.

Boredom will not be a problem because you will find nice shops in the square. People are also ready to socialize around here. You will meet all kinds of people, especially those well-traveled and free thinkers, thus conversations will be more diverse and interesting. Modern conveniences have reached the area so high-speed internet and cable TV are available. The cost of living is low, and you can still get a two-bedroom house at AUD 148,709. If you have a garden where you can plant your vegetables, you may not need to go to the market again.

Essentials in Vilcabamba:

- ★ **Healthcare:** There are several hospitals and clinics in the valley of Vilcabamba. From the feedback we gathered, the care was personal and very professional, plus inexpensive too. Here are some of the hospitals and clinics in the area:
    - ★ Hospital Vilcabamba
    - ★ Subcentro de Salud Yangana
    - ★ Health subcentre Daniel Alvarez
    - ★ Hospital Basico "Jose Miguel Rosillo"
- ★ **Accessibility:** Getting to Vilcabamba can be a little difficult. The nearest airport is from Loja, which is a four-hour drive to Vilcabamba with winding mountain roads.

Things You Can Do in Vilcabamba

The village is also called the playground of the Incas. The town itself is easily walkable and is set around a beautiful church. Excellent restaurants are also available with international cuisines. Since people are very social here, you will never run out of things to see and do. There is live music, dancing, sports like tennis, and a diner-theater. You can hike, bike, and ride horseback across its beautiful valley. Here are other things you cannot miss while living in Vilcabamba:

- ★ Sendero Cerro Mandango
- ★ Cascada El Pato
- ★ Garden of Paradise
- ★ Parque de Vilcabamba
- ★ Rumi Wilco Nature Reserve
- ★ Cascada El Palto
- ★ Mirador Mandango
- ★ Parque Nacional Podocarpus

Is Ecuador LGBT-friendly?

With the majority of the population identifies as Catholic, homosexuality is usually frowned upon in Ecuador. Even tourists who visit the country must exercise caution and must exercise discretion upon revealing their orientation.

In 2008, the government recognized same-sex unions, but it is still unusual to meet someone who is openly homosexual in the country. Cities like Guayaquil and Quito are more liberated so if you are members of the LGBT community and decide to retire in Ecuador, then you may consider these two cities.

Ecuador has more LGBT rights' protection, but it will not make you immune from the old-fashioned machismo. The good news is since 2009, same-sex marriage is permitted in Ecuador so that means the country is still progressing towards their view with people from the LGBT.

Senior Discounts

If you are 65 years and above and a citizen of Ecuador, you can enjoy the following benefits:

★ Access to discounted price health care.
★ 50% discount on both public and private transportation.
★ Discount on cinemas and sporting events.
★ Special tax.

Living in Ecuador: What to Watch Out For

No place is paradise. Like anywhere else in the world, there are some things you have to factor in before deciding that Ecuador is for you. Here are some things to watch out for:

★ **Unannounced electricity black-out**
If you are working online, you will need a backup power source. Unfortunately, Ecuador experiences unannounced black-outs. Not just the electricity, but also standard utilities such as internet, telephone service, and water.

★ **Rain is common**
Spring in Ecuador comes with rain showers. That's what keeps the jungles lush and green. It can rain for days and weeks. Thus, living here means you have to learn how to embrace the rain that comes with the pleasant weather.

★ **Litter is a big problem**
Aside from the many street cats and dogs wherever you go, you will find plenty of trash in rural areas. There is litter on the side of the road, like discarded plastic. The country is trying to improve its laws with plastic, but Ecuador still has a long way to go. You may not encounter this problem in bigger cities like Quito where there are assigned sweepers.

★ **Theft and Pickpocketing**
Although Ecuador has the lowest homicide rates in the world, petty crimes such as pickpocketing are common in the country. Just be wary of your belongings whenever you go into public transport or crowded places.

Summary

Ecuador is a paradise. It hits five stars in almost all of our criteria, from nature, culture, healthcare, cost of living, it is hard to say no to it. If only housing and safety are not issues to deal with, it'll get to the top of our retirement destinations.

Healthcare: ★★★★★
Culture: ★★★★★
Cost of Living: ★★★★★
Housing: ★★★★
Accessibility: ★★★★
Safety: ★★★

TOTAL STARS: 27 ★

Plaza de la liberacion, Guadalajara, Mexico

Reasons to Retire in Mexico

The common stereotype for Mexico, especially if you have not been to the country, is that crime is prevalent. Surprisingly, however, it has the same crime rate as in the US and if you look beyond that (though we're not telling you to close your eyes altogether), Mexico is one of the best destinations to retire. For years, millions of foreign retirees have called it their home. Its accessibility to the US is one of the advantages, where you can easily drive or fly in a few hours.

With the low cost of living the country offers, most people would choose to earn dollars and spend in peso. You will find yourself paying only 50% of the price you'll pay in the US. Mexico also has exceptional healthcare that is also not as expensive.

And because of its huge size, it has varied geography – whether you prefer a retirement lifestyle by the city, by the sea, by the mountains, or in its UNESCO towns, you will find something that will suit your taste. If you prefer to be warm, then live by the coasts bathed by the Gulf of Mexico or by the Caribbean Sea. If you prefer to live somewhere cooler, then we recommend Mexico City, sitting at 2,200 meters, which experiences cooler temperatures since it is surrounded by the snow-capped mountains especially in the winter months.

You can also find amazing activities on its coasts. Mexico is the home of some of the world's best beaches, where you can swim, snorkel, boat, fish, and dive. If you are a fan of water-filled caves, also known as cenotes, just head to the Yucatan Peninsula.

It is also a country rich in history, so you can easily fill up your time visiting its UNESCO sites. Or why not experience the country's culture and its friendly people with their relaxed lifestyle?

Why Retire in Mexico:

- ★ Huge country to explore, with a variety of things to do.
- ★ The cost for almost everything is lower in Mexico.
- ★ Mexico offers excellent and affordable healthcare.

Culture

With 127 million people and counting, Mexico is known to be the 12th most populous country in the world. It has several ethnic groups, with the majority of the population Amerindian Spanish, while the rest are Amerindian or white. Most of the locals speak Spanish, while a small percentage speak other indigenous languages. Because the country is also a popular tourist destination, English is widely spoken. You will survive just speaking English in Cancun, Playa del Carmen, Tulum, Cozumel, Acapulco, Puerto Vallarta, Sayulita, Cabo San Lucas, Mexico's coastal areas, and Mexico City.

Elsewhere, you'll find that English is used less and less, so a few basic Spanish words will be of great help. Also, keep in mind that bank clerks don't speak much English so you may need assistance: find someone who can go with you or find someone from the bank who can speak.

Mexicans, like most of the Spanish colonial countries, are Catholic, so their culture revolves around the religion's values. Family is the most valuable element in the country's culture, thus the family units with traditional gender roles. The elderly and the parents are treated with respect. Retiring in Mexico will give you a chance to attend huge events such as the quinceañera, the celebration of a young lady's fifteenth birthday, where there will be plenty of people, food, and dancing.

Mexican families are always so close that they consider it their duty to help relatives in finding a job or making big purchases. Machismo is still very much practiced in the country, with Mexican males believing that nothing should tarnish their image as a man. People are often late and if you get invited to a party, arriving thirty minutes late will not hurt.

Climate

Mexico enjoys two seasons: the dry season during November to May and the rainy season during June to October. Temperatures range between 10 to 32 degrees Celsius. Still, the climate varies, with the northern part experiencing lower temperatures and lesser precipitation during the winter months, while the south's temperature is fairly consistent all year round.

Mexico also lies within the hurricane belt, making the coastal region susceptible to storms during the rainy season. Hurricanes on the Pacific coast are usually less violent, but watch out for the ones that hit the eastern coastline. Several hurricanes, bringing high winds and heavy rain and causing great damage, strike the Gulf of Mexico and the Caribbean in a year. Therefore, in choosing an area to retire to in Mexico, it is essential to learn which areas are safer from this kind of calamity.

Cost of Living

A comfortable amount to retire in Mexico for a couple is AUD 2,578 a month, covering a two-bedroom house, a maid service, groceries, utilities, entertainment, and healthcare. If you can live away from the tourist cities, you may expect to lower your expenses even more. Some even reported spending only AUD 814 per month (e.g., living in Oaxaca without a helper).

It is also good to keep in mind that not everything is priced in pesos. Some merchants will price their products in dollars too. A meal in an inexpensive restaurant will cost about AUD 6.80, while a mid-range restaurant serving a three-course meal will be at AUD 34 per person. Here is a quick guide on how much you will spend on your monthly necessities in Mexico:

Expenses	Prices
Housing rent (One-bedroom in city centre)	AUD 882
High-speed internet	AUD 30
Electricity and water	AUD 75
Phone with basic data plan	AUD 20
Loaf of white bread	AUD 2.15
A dozen eggs	AUD 1.85
Local beer	AUD 2.40
Taxi per kilometer	AUD 2.20

Housing

Location-wise, there is a lot to consider while looking for a place to stay in Mexico. Should you live near the beach or in its colonial cities? Should you go for short-term rentals or purchase your own property? Some of the most common places to live for expatriates in Mexico are Puerto Vallarta, which is known as a haven by the sea, the colonial town of San Miguel de Allende, and Lake Chapala, which has one of the largest expat communities.

You have to be more cautious in purchasing a house in Mexico because sometimes, there are scams with property owners deciding to claim back the home. House prices in Mexico City start at around AUD 135,722.

Renting a house or an apartment comes in either short-term, six-month, or long-term contracts. A large furnished apartment in Mexico City costs AUD 1,262, while a small apartment costs AUD 597. If you go further to Cancun, then rent will be 35% cheaper.

Upon retiring in Mexico, you may also choose to live in a community living area, co-housing with other seniors, or with assisted living if you have a higher level of need. The latter is still a new concept in Mexico because the locals tend to take care of their parents when they are old. These living facilities are not regulated by the government, and the price is about the same price as what you pay in the US, which is about AUD 2,714 per month.

Healthcare in Mexico

Plenty of doctors and dentists in the country received their training in the US, especially those from Mexico City and Guadalajara, so you will not have any issues communicating with them. First-rate hospitals can be found in every medium to large city in the country, and we can't reiterate enough that it is incredibly affordable.

The healthcare system of Mexico is made up of two primary paths. The first is the IMSS system, which is a part of the social security process and is mainly for employees in the country. If you are holding a temporary or a permanent resident status then you can apply for this program as well, but having pre-existing conditions may prohibit you from joining. If you get in, then you need to pay AUD 54 a month.

The second option is Seguro Popular, which is better suited to people who have pre-existing conditions. It has its own clinics and participating hospitals with annual fees between AUD 0 – AUD 679 annually. The amount will depend on your income.

Or you can pay out of your pocket. The general doctor visit costs AUD 16 – 20, while a specialist check-up will cost AUD 54 – 68. Dental check-up ranges from AUD 34 – 68.

How to Retire in Mexico (Retirement Visa)*

Most nationalities are permitted to stay in Mexico for six months. For those who want to stay longer, getting a temporary or a permanent visa is the next step. Most documents are in Spanish so you may require some assistance along the way, but it is a rather straightforward process. As long as you provide the requirements, then you are eligible to stay in Mexico and retire here.

The temporary resident visa lasts up to four years, and you need to show proof of income at USD 1,400 per month. Or if you have a bank statement for the last twelve months with an average balance of USD 23,500 , that may do, too. If you intend to stay longer than four years, then you must apply for a permanent resident visa.

If you've been living in Mexico for four years, you can easily change that visa into one of permanent status. You only have to show your investment statements with a balance of USD 93,000 or a monthly net income of USD 2,300 in the last six months.

* USD has been retained as default currency for all immigration investment figures in this article. Currency exchange rate USD1 = AUD1.36.

Work

Foreign nationals who have a temporary resident visa can live, study, and work in the country. The same thing goes if you have a permanent visa. You can also open an account and start a business in the country.

Tax**

Your tax will depend on the amount you earn in Mexico, whether you earn it from working, running a business, or renting out a property you own. Your interest-bearing bank account will also incur taxes in the country. Mexican tax varies, is progressive, and will depend on the amount of your earnings and deductions. Every sale transaction incurs a 16% Value-added tax.

Income	Tax Rate
MXN 0.01 – 7,735	1.92%
MXN 7,735.01 – 65,651.07	6.40%
MXN 65,651.08 – 115,375.90	10.88%
MXN 115,375.91 – 134,119.41	16%
MXN 134,119.42 – 160,577.65	17.92%
MXN 160,577.66 – 323,862	21.36%
MXN 323,862.01 – 510,451	23.52%
MXN 510,451.01 – 974,535.03	30%
MXN 974,535.04 – 1,299,380.04	32%
MXN 1,299,380.05 – 3,898,140.12	34%
MXN 3,898,140.13 and above	35%

** MXN has been retained as default currency for all tax figures in this article. Currency exchange rate MXN 1 = AUD 0.068.

Food

The roots of Mexican cuisine lie in the roots of Mesoamerican cuisine, with ingredients and methods coming all the way from agricultural communities, like the Maya. The staples include corn, beans, chia, avocados, squash, amaranth, sweet potato, vanilla, cacao, tomatoes, and chili pepper. After the Spanish colonization, a number of other foods were introduced, from meat, dairy products, rice, olive oil, and sugar to other fruits and vegetables. One can also find Asian and African influences in Mexican cuisine.

Throughout the country, corn remains the most commonly consumed, and you'll find it in dishes such as menudo, pozole and tortillas. Mexican food is also known for being spicy. They've been using chilies for thousands of years so the locals are used to the flavors. Here is a list of food you should not miss in the country:

* **Chilaquiles** came from a Nahuatl word *chilaquilitl,* is a traditional breakfast featuring lightly fried corn tortillas topped with salsa. It is often served with fried eggs and chicken.

* **Pozole** is a pre-Hispanic soup that is now cooked with either chicken, pork, or vegetarian substitutes, with many herbs and spices, stewed for a long time – sometimes overnight. Once ready, lettuce, radish, lime, onion, and chili are put on top.

* **Tacos al pastor** is another traditional dish that goes back to the 1920s during the arrival of immigrants from Lebanon and Syria. It is made of thin strips of pork, placed on a tortilla sprinkled with onions, coriander, and pineapple.

* **Tostadas** literally means toasted. Tortillas are fried until crunchy and golden, then topped with a pile of garnishes such as cheese, meat, seafood, and ceviche.

* **Chiles en nogada** is probably the most patriotic dish in the world. It features the three colors of the Mexican flag – the sauce is white, picadillo represents the green, and pomegranate seeds are for the red.

* **Enchiladas** came from the Valley of Mexico. It refers to a small fish wrapped with tortillas and filled with goodness such as meat, cheese, beans, and vegetables.

* **Mole** refers to a rich sauce popular in Mexican cooking. It contains about twenty or even more ingredients that require a great amount of stirring.

* **Guacamole** is made from mashed-up avocados, tomatoes, onion, lemon juice, and chili peppers. It is often served with tortilla chips.

* **Tamales** is another traditional dish and was first developed for the tribes who needed healthy food before going into battle. It is corn dough filled with corn husks, fruit and vegetables filling, chilies and mole, then steamed.

International restaurants never come short in Mexico. You can find anything from Asian, American, African to European cuisine, making it the perfect country to retire to. You don't have to travel out of the country to satisfy your cravings.

Recommended Cities in Mexico

Merida

Merida is one of the Spanish-colonial cities in Mexico, a sprawling metropolitan with universities, museums, and major corporations. Just half an hour drive from the Yucatan Gulf Coast, it is also one of the safest cities in the country.

With about a million in population, Merida offers a small city feel especially upon walking its tree-lined streets. The expat community here is also smaller, but it also guarantees an authentic local ambiance to it. Merida is also the home to the Yucatan Symphony Orchestra. Music lovers can easily find traditional performances combined with jazz and opera in one of Merida's six theatres.

The sun shines all year round, and once summer comes, it will even be warmer. This historic center is filled with hundred-year-old homes, churches, and other buildings. Charming plazas and squares are also part of its colonial charm.

Cost of living-wise, Merida offers a better stretch of your dollar compared to other cities in Mexico. For instance, a three-bedroom in the downtown area starts at AUD 814. Fresh fruits and vegetables are available and are cheaper than what you would pay in the capital. Other necessities such as a haircut would only cost you AUD 4.

Is Merida a safe city? Absolutely. There is a great deal of police presence making one comfortable to walk even at night. The people are also so friendly that strangers greeting you with a smile is very common.

Essentials in Merida:

- ★ **Healthcare:** There are a number of fine hospitals and clinics in Merida. Whether you need a minor issue or a major procedure, Merida offers more than adequate healthcare. Here are the most recommended hospitals:
    - ★ Clinica Merida
    - ★ Star medica
    - ★ Centro Médico de las Américas
    - ★ Centro de Especialidades Médicas
    - ★ Centro Medico Pensiones

- ★ **Accessibility:** with Merida situated on the northern coast of the Yucatan Peninsula, the Merida International Airport helps connect the city to central America, South America, the Caribbean, USA, and Canada.

Things You Can Do in Merida

Because Merida is not a touristy town, you may want to fill your time practicing your Spanish as you choose the city to be your retirement haven. Don't worry because you can still find English books in places like the Merida English Library – the usual hub for expatriates who want to socialize. This is where meetings and functions are often held.

Keep in mind also that the Spanish spoken in this city is different from the rest of the peninsula. Yucatan Spanish has a heavy Maya influence making it more challenging to study the language – at least it will keep you stimulated as you blend and explore the city.

- ★ Dzibilchaltun
- ★ Catedral de Merida
- ★ Paseo de Montejo
- ★ Plaza Grande
- ★ Casa de Montejo
- ★ Mayan World Museum of Merida
- ★ G. Canton Palace
- ★ Museo Fernando Garcia
- ★ Parque Zoológico del Centenario
- ★ Palacio de la Música
- ★ Museo de Arte Popular de Yucatán
- ★ Nahualli house artists
- ★ Museo De Arte Sacro

San Miguel de Allende

A charming town four hours drive from Mexico City, you can find the UNESCO town of San Miguel de Allende. If you don't intend to sunbathe by the beaches, this town will entertain you with a temperate climate, a welcoming active expat community, low cost of living, and rich arts and tradition. What else can you ask for?

San Miguel de Allende offers a beautiful setting for retirees. If you are the type who loves wandering around colonial architecture along narrow cobblestone streets, then this one's for you. You will find baroque churches and grand homes, with gorgeous, wooden doors. Walk further and you'll find plazas and parks with trees and benches.

It is cheap to live in a colonial home, which starts at AUD 679, that may look historic outside, but with a renovated inside with updated plumbing, electricity, and Wi-Fi. There is plenty of fresh produce in the local market at a cheap price. And because the air is fresh and clean, it is not necessary to turn the air conditioning on, thus keeping your electric bills low.

What makes it most interesting for foreign retirees is the thriving art scene. San Miguel de Allende has been a favorite destination for lovers of arts and music. Artists and musicians from all over the world come to visit the city to appreciate all that it has to offer.

Essentials in San Miguel de Allende:

- ★ **Healthcare:** It may sound unusual for its size, but San Miguel de Allende has three private hospitals. There are also over 20 medical specialties and pharmacies, which is sufficient enough for the city's size. Here are our recommended hospitals:
    - ★ Hospital Joya
    - ★ Unimed
    - ★ MAC
    - ★ General Hospital Dr. Felipe G. Gobarganes
    - ★ Centro de Especialidades Médicas de Allende
- ★ **Accessibility:** San Miguel de Allende is well-connected with an hour-drive from two airports: Queretaro Intercontinental Airport and Leon-Bajio International Airport or a three-hour drive from Mexico City Airport.

Things You Can Do in San Miguel de Allende

Walking along this famous town, you will find countless galleries showcasing both folkloric and contemporary art. There are also book clubs, live music performances, and theaters - there is something new happening every week. It is also home to great restaurants, both local and international. All these help in leading an interesting lifestyle in this UNESCO town. Here are other amazing things to do in San Miguel de Allende shall you choose to retire here:

- Mercados
- Craft Market
- Viñedo Dos Búhos
- Fabrica La Aurora
- La Gruta Hot Springs
- La Parroquia Church
- Charco el Ingenio
- Canada de la Virgen
- El Jardin
- Chapel of Jimmy Ray Gallery
- Santuario de Atotonilco
- Mask Museum
- Parque Benito Juárez

Puerto Vallarta

In the foothills of the Sierra Madre Mountains, condominium buildings sit along the shoreline by the Pacific Ocean. It became well known in the 1960s when it appeared in a film titled *Night of the Iguana*. Since then, it has become a big attraction to both travelers and retirees.

There is always something new going on, with lots of entertainment and dining options. Shops, bakeries, restaurants, and historical buildings also fill the narrow streets of Zona Romantica, or the Old Town. Meanwhile, modern and huge shopping malls are found on the outskirts of the town.

One of the advantages of living here, aside from enjoying the beach, is the warm and humid temperature, especially in summertime. The cost of living is also reasonable, even if it is a tourist spot. For example, a one-bedroom apartment that is walking distance from the beach starts at AUD 814. If you prefer something bigger, then allocate at least AUD 1,222 per month for rent.

The community of expatriates living here is also very active; activities such as get-togethers, beach days, and brunches are organized. There are also volunteering activities and fundraisers.

Essentials in Puerto Vallarta:

- **Healthcare:** Puerto Vallarta is also a convenient place for retirees because of its top-notch medical care. Similar to other cities in Mexico, excellent healthcare is available in Puerto Vallarta where doctor visits only cost about AUD 54. Here is a list of our recommended hospitals in the city:
    - CMQ Hospital
    - Hospiten Puerto Vallarta
    - Regional Hospital Puerto Vallarta
    - Hospital Joya

- **Accessibility:** The Licenciado Gustavo Diaz Ordaz International Airport serves the region of Puerto Vallarta. It is mainly a tourist airport connecting the city to Mexico City and to international cities in the USA, Canada, and Panama.

Things You Can Do in Puerto Vallarta

The usual day of a retiree in Puerto Vallarta includes enjoying a meal on Los Muertos beach with amazing eateries on the sand, listening to live music from jazz to acoustic music, and going to the beach to lounge around, or to swim. The beach, after all, is the hub of activity even in the winter months. It is also a bird haven, with snowbirds flocking here from January to April. Here are things that can fill your time in Puerto Vallarta:

- ★ Los Arcos
- ★ Zona Romantica
- ★ Playa de los Muertos
- ★ Bucerias
- ★ Yelapa
- ★ Vallarta Botanical Gardens
- ★ Playa Palmares
- ★ Playa las Gemelas
- ★ Playa Las animas
- ★ Isla Rio Cuale
- ★ Malecon
- ★ Mirador Cerro de la Cruz
- ★ San Sebastián del Oeste

Is Mexico LGBT-friendly?

Mexico allows same-sex marriage. In fact, it decriminalized homosexuality in 1871. Even if the country is strongly Catholic, members of the LGBT community are still faith-driven. As long as one does not display same-sex affection such as handholding in public or kissing, it won't invite any potential backlash – a similar reaction from what you can get in a small, conservative town anywhere in the world.

There are also areas popular with the community, and annual parades such as Mexico City Pride scheduled every June. Puerto Vallarta is the country's gay capital with plenty of hotels and venues marketed towards the community. There are also gay bars scattered in Cancun, Acapulco, and Playa del Carmen.

Senior Discounts

A foreign retiree who is sixty years and above is eligible to apply for an INAPAM discount card. This is a card issued to enjoy discounts for a wide range of goods and services. This covers food, medicine, transportation, utility bills, and leisure activities. Discount varies between 10 – 15%.

Living in Mexico: What to Watch Out For

Is living in Mexico the best thing for you? Before deciding to spend your retirement days here, it is best to get yourself acquainted with the following:

- ★ **Storm in Mexico's Coast**
  Living on Mexico's coasts, you can easily find yourself in the path of a damaging storm or even a hurricane. The worst part is that the government would only give at least a week's notice that you won't have much time to prepare. If you choose to live by the coast, make sure that the accommodation you are choosing can stand hurricanes.

- ★ **Common Crime in Mexico**
  Theft and assault are the common crimes in Mexico, and the urban areas usually get a higher crime rate. There are hot spots to be avoided, but secure communities also exist. The places mentioned above are some of the safest places to stay in Mexico – still, carry your common sense with you wherever you go and you'll be fine.

- ★ **Too Many Speed Bumps on the Roads**
  Driving the local roads can be a struggle especially with a great number of large speed bumps that can sometimes damage tires. Sometimes, a two-way street becomes a one-way street with unmarked intersections so watch out whenever you're driving, especially in the evening.

Summary

As long as one knows, understands, and embraces the ins and outs of Mexico, it can be a dream paradise for retirees. Having a temporary visa does not stop you from working and studying at the same time, plus you can enjoy its many treasures from nature, activities, food, and people. Here's our overall rating for the country!

Healthcare: ★★★★★
Culture: ★★★★★
Cost of Living: ★★★★
Housing: ★★★★
Accessibility: ★★★★★
Safety: ★★★

TOTAL STARS: 27 ★

Rosemary Beach, Panama City

Reasons to Retire in Panama

Panama is probably the best retirement destination you can consider, especially if you are a fan of sunshine, tropical beaches, and warm people. Given its stable economy and government, there are also modern amenities that will make for convenient living. It is also much more developed compared to other countries in Central America, with towering skyscrapers greeting you by Panama Bay. And if you look closer, you'll see that this modernity and polish is not just on the surface.

The country has built a good reputation as a world-class destination. It boasts accessibility to life's essentials—such as low cost of healthcare, transportation, insurance, and entertainment—that you will be able to include life's little luxuries in your budget. Imagine an Uber fare or a haircut at AUD 6.70, or a bottle of wine for AUD 11?

In the previous years, there has been constant economic growth. Nearly everywhere, you will find high-speed internet, stable electricity, and clean water from the tap. Its government may not be perfect, but it has done great improvements for the country.

You will find that life is quite active, with plenty of expat-organized activities across the country that feature live music and outdoor adventures. Retiring here in Panama will never be boring with the growing community and what it has to offer. Depending on your preference, you can either live in an apartment by the ocean or a Swiss-style chalet by the mountain. You can choose from among Panama's diverse regions, from cities, mountains, and beaches—and the price is not bad either. Panama offers quality housing at an affordable price.

Healthcare is the most pleasant advantage you'll get out of Panama. It has more than adequate modern and affordable healthcare facilities. There are also smaller clinics that can offer all kinds of check-ups, from dental to eye exams.

Why Retire in Panama:

★ There is a good level of political and economic stability.
★ It offers enough value and variety.
★ Infrastructures are well-maintained.
★ There is an adequate supply of amenities like potable drinking water, reliable power supply, and improved healthcare centers.

Culture

The population of Panama is so diverse that you can find people from China, Africa, India, the Middle East, Europe, and North America, in addition to the indigenous groups. There has been a constant number of immigrants over the last 500 years because of the country's role as a commercial transit point. The population is 70% mestizo or mixed Amerindian and Caucasian and 10% Amerindian, while the rest are either of African or European ancestry.

The country's most powerful people are those from elite families with lighter skin and Spanish ancestry, also called as rabiblancos or white tails. The poorest in the country are those from indigenous groups or of African descent. Unfortunately, the discrimination against people of African descent people still continues to today. Bloodlines are also considered, where prominent families tend to marry other prominent families. For those unlucky, your family name might hinder your success.

Panamanians love everything about their country, from its climate, culture, and tradition. The dominant culture retains its Spanish origins, with family as the most important unit and the machismo concept still existing. The Catholic religion is the most prevalent in the population.

Panama is a very laid back country and people are treated with respect. They are warm and always greet each other with a handshake. Moving here means you have to put extra attention to your personal appearance and hygiene because the locals always try to maintain a neat appearance in public. If you are addressing someone directly, keep in mind that titles are important. Don't forget to add Don for men and Doña for women, which are equivalent to Sir, Mister, or Mrs.

Although the official language is Spanish, there are areas with a high concentration of expats that it is possible to get by just speaking in English. However, we recommend being equipped with a little Spanish to communicate with the locals too.

Climate

With Panama's proximity to the equator, lying between 7 and 10 degrees north of it, its daily temperatures are fairly consistent throughout the year. The sun rises at 6 am and sets at 6 pm. In the lowlands, the temperature ranges around 32 degrees Celsius in the daytime and 21 degrees Celsius at night. Meanwhile, in the highlands, be prepared for the 10 – 20 degrees Celsius range.

The country has a rainy season that lasts from mid-April to mid-December and in this period, rain usually comes in the afternoon or early evening. The rain is at its heaviest towards the end of the season, which is from October to December, with the Caribbean side wetter than the Pacific side. The dry season is from mid-December through mid-April, which is the perfect time to enjoy the outdoors, especially the beaches.

Cost of Living

Fortunately, despite all the conveniences the country offers, the cost of living in Panama is low. Although the rent in Panama City is at least AUD 1,086, if you decide to live beyond the capital, you'll get plenty of savings by paying AUD 407 for rent. Utilities are also cheap, with water bills under AUD 27 a month. With these expenses, if you are wise and savvy, you can live comfortably for only AUD 1,357 a month.

Imported food can be expensive, but if you visit the local market with its native fruits like mango, papaya, and pineapple, you will find them amazingly cheap. Check out Panama's Super 99 supermarket chain with reasonable prices for canned goods. Here is a sample budget for essential expenses of living in Panama:

Expenses	Prices
Housing rent (One-bedroom in city centre, Boquete)	AUD 747
High-speed internet	AUD 49
Electricity and water	AUD 153
Phone with basic data plan	AUD 20
Loaf of white bread	AUD 2.60
A dozen eggs	AUD 2.70
Local beer	AUD 1.70
Taxi per kilometer	AUD 4

Housing

Foreigners are permitted to own properties in Panama. What attracts a lot of foreigners to buying properties here is the price. You can expect to pay less than one-third or one-half of what you would pay in North America. In Panama City, you can get a two-bedroom apartment for AUD 183,225. A house may be double the price.

It is a safe and easy procedure, with laws protecting foreign investors. The government takes 2% tax for the transfer of a property title plus other legal fees.

Renting prices in Panama will depend on the location. In the capital itself, you can get a two-bedroom apartment at AUD 1,154, but in areas like Pedasi, you can get the same size for half the price.

There are also assisted retirement centers in the country, such as Residencial Casa Blanca, that offer meals, laundry, organized activities, and nursing assistance. Or you can simply hire a nurse which is AUD 1,629 – AUD 2,714 monthly.

Healthcare in Panama

There is no shortage of clinics and hospitals in the country – they are strategically located in major and minor hubs. The next hospital is always half an hour away since the country is so small. Many doctors in Panama are trained in the US and can speak English so there will be no trouble communicating. Their methodologies are also on the same level as what you will find in the United States or in Europe. Its major private facilities are affiliated with excellent hospitals from the US.

Panama is famous in Latin America for having excellent clinics and hospitals. For instance, in the cosmopolitan area of Panama City, there are four major private hospitals, and one of them is known for being the most technologically advanced – Hospital Punta Pacifica, which has US affiliations. Foreign retirees and expatriates also reported that they received better care compared to what they'd get in their countries. There are plenty of pharmacies, with the popular El Rey chain offering 23-hour services in most supermarkets.

Affordable private health insurance is also available for foreigners living in Panama. We recommend purchasing even if hospital fees are cheap. This is because the basic salary in the country is still low.

How to Retire in Panama (Retirement Visa)*

There are three visa options available in Panama:

1. **Friendly Nations Visa**
   Officially named the Permanent Residence for Nationals of Specific Countries, it is available for professionals and entrepreneurs from forty-seven countries that maintain professional, economic, and investment relationships with Panama. That includes the USA and Canada. All you need to do is open a local bank account with a minimum balance of USD 5,000, plus any of the following: open a business, find employment, or purchase real estate with a minimum investment of USD 10,000.

2. **Professional Residence Permit**
   This is ideal for those who want to work in the country as long as they don't take professions meant for the locals such as medical, accounting, real estate, and law. An applicant must have a university education and must apply twice two years apart. Upon applying the latter application, you must show that you have been employed in Panama for the last nine months and have been paying local social security.

3. **Pensionado Visa**
   As long as you can prove that you will have a lifetime pension of at least USD 1,000 a month, you can apply for a permanent pensionado permit. The best thing about this visa is you can keep your status even if the rules change later on.

* USD has been retained as default currency for all tax and immigration investment figures in this article. Currency exchange rate USD1 = AUD1.36.

Work

You are permitted to work in Panama with the Friendly Nations Visa and Professional Residence Permit, as long as you don't take any professions meant for Panamanians. You may also start a business in the country.

Tax**

You are only subject to pay income tax if you are working in Panama, but if your money comes from a foreign country, you don't have to report or pay taxes in the country. In case you decide to work or start a business in Panama, you are liable to the following progressive tax rate:

Income	Tax Rate
USD 0 – USD 11,000	0%
USD 11,001 – USD 50,000	15%
USD 50,001+	15% on the first USD 50,000 and 25% on the remainder

** USD has been retained as default currency for all tax and immigration investment figures in this article. Currency exchange rate USD1 = AUD1.36.

There are also other taxes to think about such as property tax, transfer tax, and capital gains. For sales tax, there are 7% additional charges on most goods and services, though essentials like food and medicine are exempted.

Food

Retiring in a country means you need to embrace its cuisine too. Panama's cuisine is a mix of African, Spanish, and Native American dishes, ingredients, and techniques. This means there is a variety of fruits, vegetables, and herbs too. It is similar to Latin American dishes with common ingredients such as yuca, wheat flour, rice, maize, and plantains.

There is plenty of fresh seafood too especially in areas along the Caribbean coast, along with the usual meat of chicken, pork, and beef. Sometimes, it's hot and spicy, but most of the time you can expect a hearty meal.

If there's one thing you should never miss, it will be the country's national dish called sancocho which is a chicken and vegetable stew. At Christmas time, the traditional dish that will be on every home's table will include chicken tamales, arroz con pollo, turkey, and relleno. You can also find bowls of fruits and fruitcakes and who would forget Ron Ponche or the eggnog? Here is a list of the most incredible food you must try:

- ★ **Arroz Con Pollo** is a simple recipe of chicken and rice – that's all! There are several versions of this dish and it is common to use annatto or onoto to color the dish too. Sometimes, commercial soups for flavoring or natural seasonings and vegetables are added.

- ★ **Sancocho** is a staple food, also made of chicken and vegetables boiled in a wholesome broth. It is very popular despite its simplicity because of its unique flavor. Sancocho is usually served with a great portion of sweet plantains and white rice and most restaurants in the city put their own little twist.

- **Ceviche** is fish cooked with onion, pepper, lime juice, and cilantro for the whole day. This method ensures that the seafood will absorb all the zest from the ingredients. It is served with fried plantains, soda crackers, or a bottle of cold beer!

- **Guacho de Mariscos** is a little hard to find nowadays. It is a dish combining pork tails, beans, rice, and yuca. Sometimes, in some restaurants, it is served with seafood.

- **Chorizo Tableño** will never disappoint. Originating from the province of Los Santos, each bite of this smoked pork sausage is a journey in the uniqueness of the Panamanian flavor. Go for the traditional recipe!

- **Carimañolas** is a common breakfast staple. It is a crunchy yuca roll, filled with ground beef and deeply fried.

- **Panama Fresh Fish** is served either baked, fried, or grilled. The freshness and abundance in Panama will keep you asking for more! Make sure to try the Caribbean king crab, octopus, lobster, and corvina. On the Caribbean coast, it is often mixed with coconut milk from its West Indian influence.

- **Hojaldra** is a popular fried food in the country. This is delicious fried bread that you can eat on its own or pair with cheese or cinnamon sugar.

- **Papas** is Panama's version of fries. The term comes from Spain meaning potatoes and it is served in a variety of ways.

- **Tortillas de Maiz** which you'll find in Panama are thicker and deep-fried cornmeal cakes, compared to what you can find in Mexico and Guatemala. It goes nicely with eggs and roasted meat.

Panama offers a wide range of dining options from humble roadside grills to world-class restaurants, however, there will be fewer options outside the tourist attractions. International cuisines are available too just in case you crave something different.

Recommended Cities in Panama

Bocas del Toro

Consisting of six islands by the western coast, Bocas del Toro is one of the popular sites in Panama. The tropical rains keep this region lush and green throughout the year. Its residents and tourists can't get enough of its turquoise blue water, so taking day trips to its surrounding islands is one of the common things to do.

It is also a vibrant town known for its parties and lively social life. If you prefer an active lifestyle, Bocas del Toro is for you – take note, its transportation system is mainly by bikes or skateboards. Expatriates who choose this area as their home are more inclined to volunteer opportunities, diving, Spanish lessons, fitness classes, or attend music venues. They are more adventurous. Most of the foreigners who live

here lead a bohemian-type lifestyle. You can enjoy the beach and if you are fortunate, you can spot some dolphins.

With accommodating people and a low cost of living, Bocas del Toro has attracted more and more retirees. If shopping is your thing, you will have several places to go, from markets to delis, but you will not find any shopping malls. Floating restaurants are common to go to at any time of the day, from breakfast to dinner. You are guaranteed an amazing view!

Essentials in Bocas del Toro:

- **Healthcare:** There are hospitals in both the islands and the mainland offering quality healthcare to its residents. Here are our recommended hospitals:
    - Isla Colón Regional Hospital
    - Hospital Guillermo Sanchez Borbon
    - Clinica La Mar
    - Hospital Point
    - Hospital de Almirante
    - Hospital Raul Davila Mena

- **Accessibility:** There are a few ways to reach Bocas del Toro. It can be accessed by air with a 45-minute flight from Panama City or a 10-hour journey by road. The best option is by flight that runs daily.

Things You Can Do in Bocas del Toro

There is always something new to see on the islands, and interesting people to meet. The scenery never gets old too, especially for those who prefer island living. From white sand beaches to green rainforests, Bocas del Toro is just beautiful anywhere you look. And you don't even have to be a diver to appreciate its beauty.

The same thing goes with Bocas Town, which makes an excellent base. You may kayak on Saigon Bay, take on a culinary adventure – particularly with its chocolate production, or simply savor the beach and relax. Here are things you can see and visit as you spend your retirement days here:

- Starfish Beach
- Isla Zapatillas
- Plastic Bottle Village
- Boca del Drago
- Parque Nacional Marino Isla Bastimentos
- Dolphin Bay Preserve
- Red Frog Beach
- Smithsonian Tropical Research Institute
- Random Art
- Polo Beach
- Isla Bastimentos
- Isla Pajaros

Pedasi

Another paradise for ocean lovers is located on the south-eastern tip of Azuero Peninsula by the Pacific coast called Pedasi. It is a small town of 4,000 residents that was a fishing village once upon a time, until Panama's first woman president Mireya Moscoso Rodriguez de Arias helped build better roads, lighting, and internet. There has been an increase in developments in recent years, with more housing and hotels in the region. The main source of income of the locals here is fishing; it is considered the tuna coast of Panama.

Pedasi has a central road, a town center, and a residential area. Here, you have a choice of living in luxury homes on the water at AUD 1,086 a month. Meanwhile purchasing an inland home is also affordable under AUD 271,444. Condominium properties are available too.

Pedasi is known for its annual carnivals and beach activities that range from sport fishing, diving, and surfing. If you like to explore the country's national parks and reserves, you may consider basing yourself here. It is also a clean neighborhood, which features a hospital, library, small airport, and a few restaurants and supermarkets. Retiring in Pedasi means you can get to experience the driest part of Panama with only 39 inches of precipitation annually.

Essentials in Pedasi:

- **Healthcare:** Hospitals in Pedasi are just about 30 minutes away from each other. There are several choices in Pedasi and here are our top ones:
    - Minsa Capsi de Pedasí
    - Hospital De Tonosi
    - Joaquin Pablo Franco Sayas Hospital
    - Centro de Salud San Jose
- **Accessibility:** Panama City is about five hours away by car and 45 minutes by flight which is served by the Tocumen International Airport.

Things You Can Do in Pedasi

Expatriates who live here choose to enjoy the beach in the morning as the sun rises. There are plenty of activities to enjoy, from scuba diving and snorkeling to windsurfing. If you are fond of whales, be sure to be on the lookout from May to November.

There are eleven different, clean, and accessible beaches with sand varying from deep bronze to sparkling black. Other things to do aside from exploring its beaches is horseback riding in the rolling hills or bike riding on its country roads and rolling hills. Or why not go to the town square where you can find markets, concerts, and art shows? Living in this charming town will give you plenty of opportunities to visit the following places:

- ★ Playa Venao Beach
- ★ Playa Arenal
- ★ Playa Los Destiladeros
- ★ Playa Toro
- ★ Artemania
- ★ Alaya Panama
- ★ Isla Iguana

Panama City

If you prefer to live in a bustling city and if you have extra budget, then Panama City is your best bet. The city of Panama is on the coast so you may expect breezy and warm weather. The expatriates who live here love it because of its convenience and the availability of shops, theaters, and a variety of restaurants. We recommend exploring areas like El Cangrejo, which features vibrant nightlife, laid-back pubs, and casinos.

The capital is also a growing city, with over four million in population. Its downtown is the core filled with high-rise buildings. A two-bedroom apartment costs under AUD 1,357 a month, with the best infrastructure in the region with drinkable tap water and reliable electricity supply.

There is also a good mix of hospitals and clinics. This includes the affiliated hospital of Johns Hopkins. Although its land area makes traffic a challenge, the metro has made transportation better since it opened. The top neighborhoods are El Cangrejo, which is the most central area that you won't need a car; Casco Antiguo, which is the capital's historic district; and Santa Maria, which features a self-contained and green neighborhood. The latter is walkable with lots of parks and plazas. The cost of living may be the most expensive here, but compared to capital cities around the world, Panama City offers the most value for money.

Essentials in Panama City:

- **Healthcare:** Panama City has superb healthcare facilities, attracting patients from nearby countries from dental work to joint replacement surgeries. Here are our top picks in the city:
    - Punta Pacifica
    - Hospital Nacional
    - Clinical Hospital San Fernando
    - Centro Medico Paitilla
- **Accessibility:** The Tocumen International Airport is the international airport of the capital city. It serves most South American countries, Miami, Toronto, Paris and Madrid, via Copa Airlines, Avianca and American Airlines.

Things You Can Do in Panama City

Experience the perfect mix of the old and the new with Central America's first-world capital. A retirement day can consist of eating in a gourmet restaurant while attending a jazz festival. There is a rich cultural tapestry, which is the result of its history – you can experience it in the colonial buildings of Casco Viejo and the many festivals in the city, not to mention its thriving art scene. If ever you are looking for an escape from the city, the best options are just an hour's drive away, whether it is the beach town of Coronado or the lush mountain scenery of Cerro Azul.

- Panama Canal
- Casco Viejo
- Miraflores Visitor Center
- Amador Causeway
- Monkey Island
- Avenida Balboa
- Biomuseo
- Albrook Mall
- Metropolitan National Park
- Gatun Lake
- Multiplaza Pacific
- Soberania National Park
- Panama La Vieja
- Bridge of the Americas
- Panama Viejo
- Iglesia del Carmen
- Bahai Temple
- Iglesia de la Merced

Is Panama LGBT-friendly?

The country is more tolerant and accepting, compared to its neighboring Latin American countries. Same-sex activity has been legal in the country since 2008, with 18 as the age of consent. However, the LGBT community may still face legal challenges not experienced by non-LGBT residents. Currently, there is no recognition of same-sex couples in Panama because of the pressure from the Catholic

Church. This was reconfirmed in 2014 when the Code of Private International Law, which prohibits same-sex marriage in the country, was approved. Unfortunately, Panama does not recognize same-sex marriages performed in other countries.

Senior Discounts

Panama has designed an appealing program called pensionados for local and foreign retirees in the country. The benefits include the following:

- 50% off entertainment anywhere in the country (movies, theaters, concerts, sporting events)
- 30% off bus, boat, and train fares
- 25% off airline tickets
- 25% off monthly energy bills
- 30% to 50% off hotel stays
- 15% off hospital bills

Aside from the above, you can also benefit from the one-time exemption of duties when you import household goods up to AUD 13,572. There will also be tax exemptions every couple of years when you import or purchase a car.

Living in Panama: What to Watch Out For

Sometimes, the positive can turn into negative, especially if you are not prepared. Even if Panama seems to have it all, you still need to adjust your mentality before moving all the way down here. Here are the things to expect:

- **The locals will always tell you what you want to hear.**
  Need opinions and advice? Better not ask a local because they may give you an answer that is not necessarily the correct one. Even if they don't know the correct answer, they will still give you a piece of advice. This is their way of being polite so be careful with what you're told.

- **Nothing moves fast.**
  The whole country embraces the mañana effect which is, "when they say they'll do it tomorrow, it means not today." The inefficiency can be frustrating especially if you are not used to a slower lifestyle. Before moving here, you have to adjust your expectations because not everything will be done at your pace. Not to mention the bureaucratic problems that add up.

- **Panamanians' parties are a norm.**
  Their motto has always been "work to live and not otherwise." Even if you choose to live away from a party area, there is a tendency that your neighbor will start the party at night to last until the early hours of the morning. "If you can't beat them, join them" seems to be the best solution to this.

Summary

It's hard to beat Panama in every factor of consideration in choosing a place to retire – it ticks everything in flying colors. This puts Panama on top of our list!

Healthcare: ★ ★ ★ ★ ★
Culture: ★ ★ ★ ★ ★
Cost of Living: ★ ★ ★ ★ ★
Housing: ★ ★ ★ ★ ★
Accessibility: ★ ★ ★ ★
Safety: ★ ★ ★ ★

TOTAL STARS: 27 ★

Historic Center, Lima Peru

Reasons to Retire in Peru

For decades now, more and more people have been discovering Peru's charm. Some of them have traveled to Peru countless times, while others choose to stay. It has become one of the best destinations in South America for the variety it offers — from colonial towns, modern cities, beaches, and fields. The whole country is twice the size of Texas so whatever living lifestyle you prefer, you will surely find something that will suit your taste.

Aside from the 54 UNESCO sites that can be found here, there's also the spectacular Andes Mountains that split the country with the Amazon on one side and the desert on the other. The Amazon rainforest covers two-thirds of the country, and the highest sand dune in the world can also be found here near the Nazca Lines. To the coast, you can experience all kinds of activities. If you prefer to explore the world's deepest canyon, Peru's also got it.

Another reason to live in Peru is its low cost of living. It offers a good quality of life for less, even in the capital itself. There are houses and apartments that cost only AUD 339 a month. Private healthcare is also inexpensive. And, of course, the variety of food. Its influences are from all over the world, served with the freshest ingredients from the mountains, sea, and jungle. Every block in the city has a bakery or a café. You may either choose to eat at a restaurant for AUD 41 or in a local picanteria for AUD 4.

Last but not least is its straightforward visa processing. The Rentista Visa is almost unbeatable. As long as you can prove that you get AUD 1,357 a month, you'll be fine —and three years later, you can apply for a permanent residency and you can call Peru your home.

Why Retire in Peru:

★ With 54 UNESCO sites and counting, there is plenty to explore especially for history buffs.
★ The cost of living is low.
★ There is a variety of landscapes to explore.
★ The culinary scene is superb!

Culture

The culture of Peru enjoys a beautiful combination of Hispanic and native traditions. The two main native cultures with their own native languages are Quechua and Aymara. Their attitude is strongly influenced by their religion, given that 80% of the population is Catholic.

Peruvian families, like those in countries in Central and South America, are close-knit. Machismo is a concept widely accepted, although more women now are working outside the home. The elderly are well-respected in the country, and there are separate queues in banks and supermarkets. When using public transportation, you may expect that younger people will always offer their seats to you.

If there's one thing to know, it's that Peruvians don't like it when they lose face. They also don't like making others feel uncomfortable so they avoid confrontation, and as much as possible, they maintain their composure at all times. You will also notice how Peruvians care about what they wear. They tend to dress a bit more formally, so seeing people in their Sunday best is normal.

Like any other South American country influenced by Spain, it is normal to arrive late for a party or dinner. Half an hour late is actually normal, but keep an ear when they say "hora inglesa" which means they want you there on time. When you get invited to a home, it is nice to bring a small gift like flowers or a bottle of wine.

Knowing how to speak Spanish makes a big difference to your quality of life. Do you need to learn Spanish upon retiring in Peru? It may not be necessary, but we strongly recommend that you do so. English is not widely spoken, so if you can communicate with the locals by speaking Spanish, then better. It will not limit your social experiences and understanding of the culture.

Climate

Peru enjoys four seasons with it located in the southern hemisphere. Summer lasts from December to March, autumn is from March to June, while winter lasts until September. Spring, meanwhile, is from September to December.

The climate of Peru is also influenced by the presence of the Cordillera of the communal Andes, which explains the variety of temperatures across the country. For example, by the Coast, warm temperate climate can be experienced, but with high humidity acquainted with thick mist by winter. By summer there is little mist with the temperature reaching 30 degrees Celsius. The Highlands only experiences two seasons, summer and winter, while the jungle or the Amazon area is only defined by the rainy and dry season.

Cost of Living

The country is one of the least expensive countries to live in on the continent. Living in the capital Lima is more expensive compared to the rural areas, especially in real estate, whether you plan to purchase or to rent. Food is affordable and cheaper, with modern supermarkets filled with local and international items. Dining at an upscale restaurant with a three-course meal would only cost AUD 41 or even less. A local picanteria will provide decent food for less than AUD 4.

It is not necessary to own a car because of the extensive transportation system that is also priced reasonably. A couple can live comfortably in Lima for AUD 2,715, but it can be cheaper if you explore other cities. Here's a quick look at a possible budget:

Expenses	Prices
Housing rent (one-bedroom in city centre, Trujillo)	AUD 272
High-speed internet	AUD 39
Electricity and water	AUD 100
Phone with basic data plan	AUD 20
Loaf of white bread	AUD 0.88
A dozen eggs	AUD 4.40
Local beer	AUD 2.50
Taxi per kilometer	AUD 1.75

Housing

Both foreign residents and nonresidents can purchase property in Peru. It does not require any government approval unless it is close to Peru's frontiers. Also keep in mind that foreigners are not allowed to own properties near military bases and government installations. Upon purchase, you will incur 3% transfer tax, a notary fee of 0.10%, and a 0.81% registration fee. A three-bedroom apartment in San Isidro, Lima will cost AUD 271,444 or less than AUD 135,722 in the city of Arequipa.

If you don't intend to purchase a property, it is possible to find a two-bedroom apartment to rent for AUD 679 per month in Lima or AUD 271 in the city of Trujillo.

There is a list of retirement and assisted living facilities in the country. One example is Casa de Reposo Unidos in Lima that includes accommodation, activities, and medical care to their tenants.

Healthcare in Peru

The healthcare system of Peru is categorized into two – the public and the private sector. The public hospitals are supported by the Ministry of Health and Social Security, while the latter includes various hospitals and clinics by medical professionals. Unfortunately, the public healthcare system is not properly funded so it does not have sufficient space, especially to treat foreign retirees.

Although anybody can receive care at a public hospital at a low cost, we still recommend purchasing health insurance and consulting a private healthcare provider. This guarantees quality standards especially in the major cities, which is preferred by foreign retirees living in Peru. If you have a serious illness, you may consider flying to another country, so make sure your insurance includes emergency evacuation. Lima has the best hospitals in the country so before retiring here, it is better to locate them just in case. The good news is, large pharmacies are generally well supplied.

How to Retire in Peru (Retirement Visa)*

If you receive USD 1,000 a month in pension, you can acquire the Rentista Visa. This will require an applicant to be in the country at least six months a year. However, it does not permit you to work. After three years, you can then obtain a permanent visa or citizenship if you prefer.

The procedure will take a couple of months, but if you want to save more time, you may consider hiring a lawyer too to avoid the bureaucracy and the long queues. Although the Rentista Visa does not need to be renewed every year, you still need to prove that you are in the country every year.

There are also other options such as the Independent Investor Visa, Student Visa, Religious Visa, and Family Visa.

* USD has been retained as default currency for all tax and immigration investment figures in this article. Currency exchange rate USD1 = AUD1.36.

Work

You are not permitted to work in the country with the Rentista visa, but if you want to, there is an option of setting up a small business for less than AUD 6,786 with an attorney. You may hire yourself and apply for a work visa which will let you legally reside in Peru. Three years later, you can also apply for a permanent resident or citizenship.

Tax**

Since you are not allowed to work in the country with the Rentista Visa, you are not required to pay any income tax. As a holder of a Rentista Visa, you will also benefit from the exemption of tax and duties connected with the import of personal and domestic items, which is usually 12% of the value. Meanwhile, if you decide to work in Peru, you are subject to pay the following tax rate:

Income	Tax Rate
USD 25,000	15%
USD 40,000	16%
USD 80,000	21%
USD 125,000	24%
USD 200,000	26%

VAT at 18% is imposed on transactions such as the sale of movable property, rendering services, sale of property, and the import of goods.

** USD has been retained as default currency for all tax and immigration investment figures in this article. Currency exchange rate USD1 = AUD1.36.

Food

The Peruvian cuisine combines influences from the indigenous population, such as the Inca, and the immigrants that came from overseas. The latter includes Spain, Italy, Germany, Japan, China, and Africa.

The four traditional staples are corn, tubers, legume, and potatoes. Later on, the Spanish brought over rice, wheat, and meat. There are many traditional foods too, such as chili peppers, quinoa, and kiwicha. Peruvians are also used to roots and tubers, which have become popular in recent decades.

The Peruvians had made great progress in their cuisine, with real talent in conserving their traditional culture and adapting to modern styles. Retiring in Peru will give you lots of opportunity to try 7,000 years of history and influences in Peruvian cuisine. It probably has the largest number of dishes in the world. There is so much richness and diversity that it can be on the same level as French, Creole, or Chinese

cuisine. Head over to the 50 Best Restaurants website and you will find a big list of Peruvian restaurants popular in the whole world.

In the capital of Lima, you will find a blend of Peruvian fusion and perhaps the greatest blend was that of Japanese techniques, local ingredients, and flavors. It is easy to find the most innovative dishes anywhere in the big cities. Here are our best choices:

* **Ceviche** is a common cuisine in Central and South American countries. The Peruvians give it a delicate flavor by spicing it with red onions and aji peppers. It is then served with sweet potato or white Andean corn called choclo.

* **Lomo Saltado** is an Asian fusion cuisine with stir-fried beef, tomatoes, onions, and peppers, combined with fried potatoes and soy sauce and served with white rice.

* **Empanadas** are filled with chicken or beef with caramelized onions, olives, and egg. It is then baked, turning out to be flaky, hot, and delicious when fresh from the oven.

* **Cuy** is guinea pig that's either baked or barbecued and one of the staple meats in many households in the Andes.

* **Aji de Gallina** is a rich stew of chicken, aji pepper, and condensed milk, with the addition of white bread producing a thickened version. There is also a vegetarian option which is made of boiled potato with creamy yellow sauce.

* **Papa a la Huancaina** is a dish that uses cheap ingredients such as potatoes, lettuce, and spicy cheese sauce with olives. It is also easy to make and yet it produces complex flavors and textures.

* **Pollo a la Brasa** is another commonly consumed food in Peru, made of marinated chicken that is then roasted. It comes with French fried potatoes, salad, and a variety of creams, from Peruvian mayonnaise to chimichurri.

* **Dulce de Leche**, which is also known as manjar blanco, is often found in birthday cakes, pastries, cookies, and more. It is prepared by boiling milk and sugar that is mixed until it produces a thick and golden caramel sauce.

* **Mazamorra Morada** refers to a popular dessert made from purple corn and fruit, which is thickened into a pudding-like texture. It uses potato flour with cinnamon and cloves and has a beautiful deep morada color which tastes like a blackberry pie filling.

* **Pisco Sour** is a cocktail drink invented by an American bartender named Victor Morris in the 1920s. It is a strong drink of grape distilled brandy not only popular in Peru, but also in Chile.

There is no shortage of restaurants in the big cities that can serve both homey and innovative food. Every day will surely be an adventure that you will never get bored of.

Recommended Cities in Peru

Arequipa

Sitting at an altitude of 2,500 meters, there is no shortage of sunshine in this city with a million in population. Its residents enjoy over 300 days of sunshine a year, with temperatures ranging from 5 – 21 degrees Celsius.

The city was founded in the middle of the 16th century, so you can find an abundance of colonial architecture that combines Spanish and native elements. These buildings were constructed with the use of volcanic rock, thus Arequipa was nicknamed the White City.

The historical city also has a smaller feel, complete with areas to live, work, shop, and play. Narrow streets are filled with churches, plazas, grocery stores, cinemas, and choices of restaurants. It is also a walkable city that most foreigners living here rely on walking.

If you are keen to live in a city rich in culture and history, Arequipa is the place to be. Arequipa is also the home of artisans, where you can purchase woven Alpaca textiles at a cheap price. Fine leather goods and jewelry are also available. It also offers opportunities for nature lovers, with the Salinas y Aguada Blanca National Reserve located a short distance from the city. Fancy going to the beaches? It's only a couple of hours away. Arequipa is also meant for those who seek an active retirement for it is the hub for trekking the nearby canyons and mountains.

Essentials in Arequipa:

★ **Healthcare:** Arequipa is one of the fortunate cities in Peru to have loads of hospitals. Here is a list of private hospitals you may consider in the city:
  - ★ Policlinico Espiritu Santo
  - ★ Policlinico Rodriguez
  - ★ Clinica San Miguel Arequipa
  - ★ Hogar Clinica San Juan de Dios
  - ★ Blue Medical

★ **Accessibility:** The city is served by Rodriguez Ballon International Airport that offers connections to Lima, Cuzco, and Chile. It is one of the main hubs in the south of Peru and serves the increasing tourism industry in the region.

Things You Can Do in Arequipa

There is no reason to get bored in Arequipa. With its affordability, you can try a multitude of cultural activities almost every week. You will find parades and food festivals, plus art exhibits and music events. For a weekend getaway, you may choose to explore the picturesque Colca Valley, along with the ancient Inca ruins, or why not have a go at the hot springs. There are other historical towns scattered in the valley, where you can immerse yourself in how the locals live. You can also go restaurant- or bakery-hopping. After Lima, Arequipa has some of the best restaurants in the country. Here are things that can fill up

your time while enjoying your retirement days in Arequipa:

- ★ Monasterio de Santa Catalina
- ★ Plaza de Armas
- ★ Volcan Misti
- ★ Salinas y Aguada Blanca National Reserve
- ★ Mundo Alpaca
- ★ Museo Santuarios Andinos
- ★ Historic Centre
- ★ Iglesia de la Compania de Jesus
- ★ Yanahuara
- ★ Museo de la Catedral de Arequipa
- ★ Canteras de Sillar
- ★ Mercado Central
- ★ Museo de Arte Virreinal
- ★ La Mansion del Fundador
- ★ Mirador Carmen Alto
- ★ Molino de Sabandia
- ★ Monasterio de la Recoleta

Lima

Travelers often overlook Lima, going straight away to Cusco and Machu Picchu. However, the biggest city in the country is home to world-renowned restaurants, museums, and art galleries. No wonder it's the home of the majority of the expatriates living in Peru. It has a seaside location, which does not only create a dramatic scene but also serves as one of Latin America's largest and major ports.

Try to wander around the tourist districts of Miraflores and Barranco and you'll find the city stretching back into valleys and mountain slopes, offering gorgeous views of the city and the Pacific Ocean.

Lima also has a rich history dating back to the pre-Inca period. A great example is Huaca Pucllana, a pyramid ruin that dates back before the 5th century A.D. The thriving metropolis is made up of thirty districts that feature its own personality. Each district features a special gallery, restaurant or shop.

Lima might be the most expensive city to live in Peru. Still, it's relatively cheap. For instance, one can survive here with AUD 2,715 a month, paying only AUD 678 for rent. Plus, it gives you access to the best private hospitals in the country.

Essentials in Lima:

- ★ **Healthcare:** Lima has 23% of the country's hospitals. Here, you can find the best hospitals in the country so if you are foreseeing any serious medical condition, it is best to base your retirement here. These are the best hospitals in Lima:
    - ★ Javier Prado Hospital
    - ★ National Hospital Arzobispo Loayza Hospital
    - ★ Clinica El Golf
    - ★ Dr Jose Alvarez Blas
- ★ **Accessibility:** The Jorge Chavez International Airport is the country's main international and domestic airport. It connects the country to cities around the world such as Madrid, Toronto, Mexico City, Chile, Bogota, and New York.

Things You Can Do in Lima

Keeping your retirement days busy in Lima is not difficult. With a vibrant theater scene, sprawling art galleries and museums, and easy access to all parts of the country, there is no doubt that you'll find something new to do and explore every day. The big community of foreigners living here frequently organizes activities that you can sign up for as well.

A retirement day can consist of walking throughout Baranco, while enjoying its colorful murals, followed by Malecon which is a scenic cliff-top walkway stretching almost six miles – definitely a good exercise before choosing from the large number of bars and restaurants. If there's one city to get busy with every day, that will be Lima. Here are other places you may include in your daily retirement itinerary:

- ★ Museo Larco
- ★ Circuito Mágico Del Agua
- ★ Barranco
- ★ Huaca Pucllana
- ★ Plaza Mayor
- ★ Miraflores Boardwalk
- ★ Pachacamac
- ★ Museo Convento San Francisco y Catacumbas
- ★ Circuito Mágico del Agua
- ★ Parque Kennedy
- ★ Museo MATE
- ★ Marcahuasi
- ★ Museo de Arte de Lima
- ★ Parque El Olivar
- ★ Casa de Aliaga
- ★ Museo Nacional de Arqueologia
- ★ Costa Verde

Trujillo

The land of eternal spring – that's what they call Trujillo. Located on the coast of the country, just five hours by drive from the capital, Trujillo is one of the most pleasant places to be in the country. It is inexpensive to live here, with apartments as low as AUD 272 a month. Quality healthcare is also available, with private clinics and hospitals with well-equipped facilities.

Although you won't be able to find white sand and warm water in this part of the country, you can still find nice beaches that are perfect for sunbathing and surfing. One option is Las Delicias, only ten minutes south of Trujillo — an upscale beachside area that is clean and quiet.

Trujillo has a thriving art community and the city is filled with cultural events throughout the year. One of the festivals held annually is the National Marinera Festival during the last week of January, drawing participants from all over the country to showcase the marinera dance. The dance involves complex choreography and footwork and is very entertaining to watch. There's also the Spring Festival to watch out for; it is one of the largest in the country, where you'll find Paso horse shows and crowning of the festival queen.

Essentials in Trujillo:

- ★ **Healthcare:** With Trujillo as the third main city in Peru, it features a sufficient number of hospitals that serve the 900,000 people living here. Have a look at our list of recommended private hospitals in Trujillo:
  - ★ Hospital Nacional Daniel A Carrion
  - ★ Clinica Internacional
  - ★ IntegraMedica Clinica
  - ★ Instituto Regional de Enfermedades Neoplásicas
  - ★ Centro Medico Naval Disamar
- ★ **Accessibility:** The Trujillo Airport connects the city to the capital, Lima, Chiclayo, Cajamarcca, Tumbes, and Chagual. There are two airlines that serve the moderately large city: Lan Peru and Avianca.

Things You Can Do in Trujillo

The city is home to several archaeological sites dating back thousands of years. It is also the site of great prehistoric Moche and Chimu cultures and the perfect base for exploring the popular beach town of Huanchaco. Living here will also give you the chance to explore Trujillo's architecture, which is traditionally painted in white. If you want to see Trujillo's centre, the best way is by foot. Make sure to spot the traditional names of its central streets displayed in ornate plaques!

A day in the life of a foreign retiree in this city may consist of walking around in the main plaza, visiting one of the archaeological sites or the museums, followed by a quick surf in Huanchaco before enjoying the traditional Trujillo soup called Shambar. Here are other points of interests in the city:

- ★ Chan Chan
- ★ Complejo Arqueológico El Brujo
- ★ Plaza de Armas de Trujillo
- ★ Catedral de Trujillo
- ★ Museo Huacas de Moche
- ★ Huaca Arco-Iris
- ★ Casa Urquiaga
- ★ Museo del Juguete Antiguo
- ★ Casa de la Emancipación
- ★ Jardín de Los Sentidos
- ★ El Mirador
- ★ Casa Ganoza Chopitea
- ★ Palacio Iturregui

Is Peru LGBT-friendly?

Members of the LGBT community may face challenges while living in Peru. Although it is legal to have same-sex activities, LGBT individuals are not eligible for the same legal protections as heteronormative citizens. It was only in January 2017 that a decree was issued prohibiting all kinds of discrimination and hate crimes on the basis of gender identity and sexual orientation. Although there is a heavy influence from the Roman Catholic Church on the attitude towards the LGBT community, people have become more tolerant in recent years. As of writing, same-sex marriage is not allowed yet in the country.

Senior Discounts

The benefits of senior citizens (65 years old and above) in Peru include getting priority seating on transportation whether by bus or by air, throughout the country, plus discounted fares too. You can also get cheaper tickets to cinemas, museums, and other attractions.

Discounts are not automatically given in Peru so make sure to bring your ID with your birthdate with you wherever you go.

Living in Peru: What to Watch Out For

There are always two sides to the coin. Despite the things that make Peru a paradise, there are some not-so-ideal scenarios that come with it.

★ **Traffic and pollution are terrible in the cities.**
In the capital Lima, the air quality is so bad because of its terrible traffic, that it only comes behind Sao Paulo and Mexico City. If you are suffering from asthma or any other allergies, you better choose other areas of the country to retire to.

★ **All the littering on the streets and the stray dogs.**
Aside from the pollution, people have the attitude of throwing stuff onto the streets, despite the abundance of waste bins in the cities. Stray dogs are also everywhere. It is best to get vaccines against rabies.

★ **Spanish is a must to navigate around the bureaucracy.**
Once you enter the immigration of Peru, you cannot expect any of the officers to speak in English, otherwise, you need to hire an English-speaking Peruvian attorney who can help you with the process. You cannot expect anyone to be in a hurry either so be prepared to bribe.

Summary

Peru is on top of everyone's travel bucket list. And why not? There are more things to experience, see, and do beyond Machu Picchu — which, by the way, is already a wonder of its own. It might still be a developing country, but it promises lots of potential and future growth.

Healthcare: ★★★
Culture: ★★★★
Cost of Living: ★★★★
Housing: ★★★★
Accessibility: ★★★★
Safety: ★★★★

TOTAL STARS: 23 ★

Old San Juan, San Juan Antiguo, San Juan, Puerto Rico

Reasons to Retire in Puerto Rico

For US citizens, the Caribbean Island of Puerto Rico is one of the best destinations to retire in. Since it is a US territory, it comes with many benefits. Let's start with the laidback lifestyle of the tropical island. People are friendly, warm, and relaxed. Puerto Rico is for you if you intend to spend your retirement days sipping piña coladas – the country's famous cocktail composed of rum, coconut cream, and pineapple juice, and which can be perfectly combined with the numerous festivals and parties that Puerto Rico celebrates every month.

Puerto Rico is a beach paradise. Some beaches are not crowded either so you can find a serene time as you enjoy looking at the great landscapes. It is also the best place for water sports enthusiasts. Puerto Rico features a myriad of adventures from snorkeling and diving to flyboarding. Not a beach person? It is also a mecca for adrenaline-filled land attractions.

If you are a history junkie, look no further either. All you have to do is to fly to Ponce, the cultural gem of the south where you will find libraries, galleries, museums, and parks. There are plenty of organized culturally themed events that will fill your months.

There are two official languages in the country, Spanish and English. And since the locals study English in school, you can be understood even in rural areas. You can also use your US dollars here so you don't have to worry about exchange rates. Taxes are low even if it is a commonwealth of the US.

Puerto Rican cuisine is amazing too! It is rich in flavor and has a lot of variety. Plus, Puerto Rican coffee! It may not be as famous as Colombian coffee, but Alto Grande has the highest rank a coffee can achieve and it can be found here!

Why Retire in Puerto Rico:

- ★ Great climate and amazing landscapes.
- ★ It is officially a territory of the USA.
- ★ Attractive tax benefits.

Culture

The country is rich in history and tradition. Because of the interactions between the native Tainio people and the Spanish settlers, the culture is a blend of the two, along with the African culture that was also brought by the Spanish conquistadors. Add the impact of the United States and you'll find a unique mix of people and culture in Puerto Rico.

English may be the official language of the country but only 10% of the population speaks it with native fluency. Spanish remains the dominant language in the country and is always used in daily life. If you want to adjust better as you choose Puerto Rico as the place for your retirement, then we recommend picking up Spanish lessons.

Because Puerto Rico is a melting pot of different cultures from Europe, Africa, and North and South America, the number and variety of festivals, traditions, art, and music will never disappoint. Some interesting traditions are clapping when a plane touches down on the island and the parties on the street during Three Kings' Day. Another tradition not to be missed is drinking the local coquito, which is like eggnog but sweeter and coconut-based.

The country has a long-lasting relationship with art and you'll find evidence of that in their colorful street murals and countless art museums in the country. The music and all the dancing can also be contagious even if you have two left feet, with salsa, trova, and bomba y plena reigning on the dance floors. If there's one thing to pack in retirement in this country, it definitely has to be your dancing shoes. This only proves the vibrant culture Puerto Ricans enjoy.

Climate

Puerto Rico enjoys a tropical marine climate with temperatures ranging from 21 – 26 degrees Celsius. That means a lot of warm, sunny, and humid days. There are no other seasons but summertime. Sometimes, the temperature in the south is a few degrees higher than in the north.

It is also good to keep in mind as you choose Puerto Rico to be your retirement destination, that the country is exposed to the cyclones of the Caribbean. Still, a little less than Jamaica and Cuba. Hurricane Maria, a category 5 major hurricane, made landfall last September 2017 and is regarded as the worst natural disaster in the country.

Some 13 to 16 hurricanes a year occur between August and October so you have to make necessary preparations. Be equipped with a generator and stock up on gas, along with an emergency supplies kit. In the worst-case scenario, be prepared for an evacuation, or find a house that is hurricane-proof. It can be a little pricier, but will definitely protect you from the weather.

Cost of Living

Compared to living in the mainland US, the cost of living in Puerto Rico is a lot lower. For instance, you only have to pay 50% of the amount of rent you will pay in the US. Even the cost of groceries, healthcare, education, and daily expenses are lower in Puerto Rico. Living with AUD 2,700 a month is doable in the country and can provide you with comfortable living.

For an even cheaper way of living, there are smaller cities outside of the capital to choose from, such as Cayey and Dorado, where you can go as low as AUD 1360 a month. Here is a table that shows the basic expenses while living in Puerto Rico:

Expenses	Prices
Housing rent (one-bedroom in city centre)	AUD 855
High-speed internet	AUD 76
Electricity and water	AUD 265
Phone with basic data plan	AUD 21
Loaf of white bread	AUD 3
A dozen eggs	AUD 3.75
Local beer	AUD 2
Taxi per kilometer	AUD 5.50

Housing

Finding the perfect sanctuary is easy in Puerto Rico especially if you prefer to rent a place first. This is recommended if you want to have a better feel of the place before deciding to buy a property. The good news is, the country has well-developed infrastructure. You can rent a fully-furnished one-bedroom apartment for as little as AUD 679 in Ponce. Before signing the contract, you may want to compare it with apartments that include utilities and furnishings.

The housing market in Puerto Rico has been gaining good momentum because of good demand, rising sharply due to new initiatives like tax incentives and other stimulus measures. Foreigners can own a home in Puerto Rico, with the government welcoming investments from overseas buyers. There are no restrictions for foreign retirees in acquiring their own properties in the country. The price of a three-bedroom property is around AUD 312,160 in Palmas Del Mar. Many expatriates prefer to live in gated communities that offer a safe and secured stay.

There are plenty of senior assisted living communities in Puerto Rico such as Hogar Barcelona at Ocean Park, with a starting cost of AUD 2,300 a month. The amount covers full-time non-medical care, daily activities, and assistance with grooming, getting dressed, and eating.

Keep in mind that upon choosing where to live, it is crucial to ask and inspect if the property is susceptible to hurricanes and tropical storms.

Healthcare in Puerto Rico

The healthcare in Puerto Rico is sufficient with standards comparable to the USA. Medical professionals are also knowledgeable and can speak English so you won't have any troubles in case you need a check-up. However, in recent years, there has been a shortage of doctors because they choose to work in the USA for better pay.

There are over 63 hospitals and many more clinics and pharmacies in the country. Outside the major cities, the hospitals can be a bit run down with fewer doctors, equipment, and staff. If you want to get the best healthcare, then it is best to live in San Juan or Ponce.

Public healthcare is managed under a government-run program, providing medical and healthcare services. Even if the quality is good, better manage your expectations regarding the long waiting times even if you set appointments in advance.

Alternatively, opt for a private healthcare provider. It has a higher standard with a shorter waiting time. Of course, we recommend buying insurance – the ones you can get in Puerto Rico tend to cover pre-existing conditions even with small co-payments. Dialing for emergencies?

Don't worry, Puerto Rico has English speakers too. Private companies run ambulances and may require upfront payment – thus again, the importance of health insurance.

How to Retire in Puerto Rico (Retirement Visa)

Puerto Rico has no government body that deals with external affairs since it is under the United States. Any kind of foreign relations, trade, customs administration, and immigration are all subject to US policy. If you are thinking of retiring in Puerto Rico, you have to deal with the US immigration authorities. The same procedure applies as when you apply for a visa to the United States.

It can be difficult to get a residence and work permit unless you have a traditional expat assignment. Retiring here is a different story because unfortunately, Puerto Rico does not offer any retirement visa scheme.

If you are a citizen of the following countries under the Visa Waiver Program that can travel to Puerto Rico without the need for a visa, you might have a better chance. This includes a total of 39 countries: Andorra, Australia, Austria, Belgium, Brunei, Chile, Czech Republic, Denmark, Estonia, Finland, France, Germany, Greece, Hungary, Iceland, Ireland, Italy, Japan, Latvia, Liechtenstein, Lithuania, Luxembourg, Malta, Monaco, Netherlands, New Zealand, Norway, Poland, Portugal, San Marino, Singapore, Slovakia, Slovenia, South Korea, Spain, Sweden, Switzerland, Taiwan, and the United Kingdom.

The main requirements of these countries are a biometric passport and an ESTA, which is valid for two years or until the passport expires. It will allow you to stay in Puerto Rico for three months. To qualify as a resident, you must be present in the country at least 183 days in a year, must spend at least 549 days in a 3-year period, and should not have any other tax home other than Puerto Rico.

Another alternative is finding a job in the USA or trying to migrate to the USA first. After seven years, you can get a green card that will make you eligible to also stay in Puerto Rico.

Work

You are not allowed to work under an ESTA. What you can do is find work in advance before moving to Puerto Rico. Besides, seeing nature all around you, would you even think about work? Thinking of investing instead? This might be the fastest option to get a green card – at least AUD 678,610 is accepted as an investment in target employment areas.

Tax*

Puerto Ricans are taxed on their worldwide incomes no matter where it comes from, while non-residents are taxed on their Puerto Rico-source income only. If one offers a personal service within Puerto Rico under AUD 4,072 or less, while being present in the country for 90 days or less, it will not be taxed as well. Otherwise, here's a quick guide for you:

Taxable Income	Tax Rate
Not over USD 9,000	0%
USD 9,001 – USD 25,000	7% of the excess over USD 9,000
USD 25,001 – USD 41,500	USD 1,120 + 14% of the excess over USD 25,000
USD 41,501 – USD 61,500	USD 3,430 + 25% of the excess over USD 41,500
USD 61,501+	USD 8,430 + 33% of the excess over USD 61,500

* USD has been retained as default currency for all tax figures in this article. Currency exchange rate USD1 = AUD1.36.

Food

The culinary tradition and practices trace their roots to Europe — particularly Spain, Africa, and the native Tainos — promising rich and flavorful food that will keep you coming back for more. At first look, it may seem similar to Spanish and other Latin American countries, but look closely and you will find a unique blend of influences.

The diet of Taino, since they are related with the Maya, involves lots of tropical roots such as yuca or cassava, cachucha pepper or a mild chili, avocado, peanuts, guavas, pineapples, and varieties of beans. The Spanish brought over wheat, cumin, onion, garlic, eggplant, chicken, beef, pork, lamb, and goat. Meanwhile, the African influences include coconuts, coffee, okra, tamarind, yams, sesame seeds, banana, and guinea hen. Insert the influence of the United States that includes bacon and Latin America with cocoa, tomatoes, bell peppers, and passionfruit, and you got a satisfying meal from all parts of the world. Here's the ultimate list of dishes that you should not miss out on while you are in Puerto Rico:

★ **Mofongo** is mashed plantains. Once mashed, it is combined with pork skin, onion, and garlic. This is then fried, boosting the flavor.

★ **Arroz con gandules** is a Boricua staple and probably a signature dish in the country that is perfect throughout the year. Pigeon peas are cooked with rice in a large pot, along with salted pork, olive oil, sofrito, bay leaves, and tomato paste.

★ **Sofrito** plays an important role in Puerto Rican dishes. It is a sauce whose main ingredients include tomatoes, red and green peppers, onion, and ajies dulces peppers. It makes a tasty sauce that makes a great base for a variety of dishes.

★ **Pernil** is slow-roasted pork and is typically reserved for big celebrations or family functions. Seasoned with garlic, oregano, and pepper, the pork is then cooked for a long time until it is so tender that the meat slides right off the bone.

★ **Pastelon** is the way to go if you love eating lasagna. Instead of using pasta sheets, the locals use plantains and ground beef. The best part remains in the cheese with beef seasoned in cumin and oregano, mixed with tomato sauce, olives, and sofrito.

★ **Empanadilla** is the Puerto Ricans' version of empanada. It literally means little empanada and is a deep-fried meat pie filled with either beef, chicken, or cheese. It is a savory pastry that has a thinner crust.

★ **Arroz y habichuelas** or rice and beans are essentials in a Puerto Rican side dish. The beans are stewed with onion, garlic, pepper, ham hock, squash, and sofrito. It is served with white, medium-grain rice.

★ **Pasteles** are traditionally made with green bananas stuffed with stewed pork meat. Add yuca and other root vegetables, then press it onto a plantain leaf before boiling it.

★ **Flan** is a combination of crème brulee and cheesecake. The most popular flavor is flan de queso and flan de naranja or flan flavored with oranges.

★ **Arroz con dulce** is a sweet coconut-rice pudding that is made of rice, coconut milk, sugar, cloves, nutmeg, and cinnamon. Garnish it with raisins and cinnamon sticks and you'll get an amazing rice dessert!

If the above is not enough for you and if you ever find yourself craving for something different, a variety of international restaurants are available in Puerto Rico and you'll find something that will suit your taste.

Recommended Cities in Puerto Rico

Central Mountains

If you prefer to live somewhere cooler, the towns in the Central Mountains are for you. Known as the City of Fog, you can have all of Puerto Rico's benefits with less of the heat. It is located four hundred meters in the mountainous region of the island so the temperature is a lot more comfortable at 21 – 30 degrees Celsius. It can even go down during wintertime.

The Central Mountain is also a perfect place for nature lovers with winding roads offering dramatic perspectives at every turn.

With a small population of not more than 45,000, it offers a sparse suburban feel. The history and culture of the region are rooted in agriculture, where you can find diverse vegetation and, of course, coffee!

The Central Mountains consist of fifteen regions – all not meant to be rushed. There is so much to explore, from humid patches of the jungle to cliff-edge vistas, from the island's highest peak to the haciendas, and from the agricultural towns to the thrilling adventure parks. No wonder many retirees call it their home.

Essentials in Central Mountains:

★ **Healthcare:** In the rural areas and small towns in the interior mountain zone of Puerto Rico, there is an inadequate supply of healthcare professionals. You may consider traveling an hour or two away to get to San Juan's hospitals.
   ★ Cayey Menonite Medical Center
   ★ CDT Cayey
   ★ 24/7 Emergency Room Menonita
   ★ Hospital General Menonita de Aibonito

* **Accessibility:** The Cordillera is only 1.5 hrs. drive from San Juan Airport and the city itself.

Things You Can Do in Central Mountains

The Central Region is not always visited by most tourists unless they are outdoor enthusiasts. Because it has fewer tourists, retirees enjoy the authentic feel Puerto Rico can offer. There may be no beach close by, but the rugged mountains are always ready to entertain you with the countless hiking routes you can take part in and where you can enjoy the exceptional natural vistas. Living in the Cordilleras will give you plenty of chances to explore the following must-see places. And if ever you miss the beach, remember, it is only a couple of hours away.

* Toro Verde Nature Adventure Park
* Tanama River
* Hacienda Tres Angeles
* Cañón de San Cristóbal
* Gozalandia
* Hacienda Pomarrosa
* Hacienda San Pedro
* Pitorico Rum Distillery
* La Piedra Escrita
* Hacienda Tres Angeles
* Bosque Estatal de Guajataca
* Bosque Estatal de Maricao
* Cerro de Punta
* Bosque Estatal de Guilarte
* Casa Museo Canales
* Lago Guajataca
* Festival de las Flores
* Mirador La Piedra Degetau
* Centro de Bellas Artes de Caguas

West Coast

Do you know why the West Coast is also known as Porta del Sol of the Gate of the Sun? It is because it is brimming with gorgeous beaches where you can view the best sunsets in the country. It has a laid-back surfer vibe, so much different from the hustle and bustle of the metropolitan area. No wonder why people from the city visit on the weekend for surfing, snorkeling, and diving.

With its rocky coast, made up of protected lagoons and big swells, it has become a mecca for surfers. And even if you are not a surfer, the region has enough going on and yet it is far enough from the metropolitan to have a relaxed ambiance, which attracts retirees from in and out of the country.

Aguadilla and Aguada are two lovely seaside towns with a running rivalry with Columbus's first landing in the country. Then there's Rincon, with its community made of farmers and fishermen who have called this village their home for generations.

It is a home for the creatives too, with art galleries spread across the town. Walking around here, you'll find locals performing music, food trucks, and handicrafts for sale — a total Caribbean experience. Mayaguez, a colonial gem and the third-largest city in Puerto Rico is also nearby.

Essentials on the West Coast:

* **Healthcare:** There is a sufficient number of hospitals for every need on the West Coast, particularly in Mayaguez. Here is a list of hospitals to choose from:
    * Doctor Juan Sanchez Montano
    * Costa Salud Community Health Centers
    * Mayaguez Medical Center

- ★ Hospital Perea
- ★ Hospital Bella Vista
- ★ Hospital San Antonio

★ **Accessibility:** Eugenio Maria de Hostos Airport serves the West Coast but with limited domestic commercial service. Only Cape Air Airlines fly to San Juan. There is always the option of driving 2.5 hrs. to San Juan.

Things You Can Do on the West Coast

The West Coast is a popular destination in Puerto Rico for both locals and foreign tourists. It may not be as popular as its eastern counterpart, but if you prefer a relaxed island lifestyle, spending your days surfing and swimming in the beautiful beaches, then the towns of Rincon, Aguada, and Aguadilla might be the choice for you. Here are the points of interest you can spend your retirement days in:

- ★ La Parguera Nature Reserve
- ★ Los Morillos Lighthouse
- ★ Gilligan's Island
- ★ Punta Higuero Lighthouse
- ★ Nature Pools of Isabela
- ★ Guajataca Tunnel
- ★ Plaza de Colon in Mayaguez
- ★ The Guanica State Forest and Biosphere Reserve
- ★ Natural Bridge
- ★ Porta Coeli Convent Museum
- ★ La Playuela
- ★ Las Salinas

Ponce

Ponce is the country's second-largest city, with two hundred thousand in population, located at the southern coast of Puerto Rico. It is known for its interesting architecture and rich history, which earned the name Ciudad Señorial or the Noble City.

It has become a famous retiree choice because of its cultural attractions and festivals. It was once the capital of the country while it was under Spain until it fell to the United States in 1898. Plazas, churches, and colonial homes dotted the city, and up to today, money is poured in to preserve its colonial core.

Living here is also cheaper than the capital, with the median home price at about AUD 162,867. The traffic is also not as busy as San Juan even if it is an important trading and distribution center. Playa de Ponce Port is one of the busiest Ports in the Caribbean and it handles different products from tropical fruits, coffee, and tobacco to rum.

Essentials in Ponce:

★ **Healthcare:** Several clinics and hospitals are serving the city. It has comprehensive care hospitals, with mental and cancer specializations. Here are the hospitals that made it on our list:
- ★ Hospital San Cristóbal
- ★ Hospital Dr. Pula
- ★ Hospital de Damas
- ★ Hospital San Lucas

★ **Accessibility:** Ponce is only 1.5 hrs. drive from San Juan. It also has its own small commercial airport, The Mercedita, which receives a handful of domestic flights from the United States.

Things You Can Do in Ponce

The city has a vibrant art scene, culture, and live music. You will never get bored of the ambiance – it is not too big and not too small. There is an abundance of festivals and the list of things to see is so diverse. Outside the city, you can soak up its beautiful beaches, but in the city you can easily drown yourself in museums, castles, and plazas.

- ★ Plaza de las Delicias
- ★ Parque de Bombas
- ★ Casa Armstrong-Poventud
- ★ Cathedral de la Guadalupe
- ★ Teatro la Perla
- ★ Casa Alcaldia
- ★ Central Mercedita
- ★ Museum of Puerto Rican Music
- ★ Ponce School of Fine Arts
- ★ Art Museum of Frame Masters
- ★ Ponce Museum of Art
- ★ Casa Paoli
- ★ House of the Ponce Massacre
- ★ La Guancha Paseo Tablado
- ★ El Vigil Hill
- ★ La Cruceta del Vigia
- ★ Castillo Serralles
- ★ Tibes Indian Ceremonial Center
- ★ Museo de la Historia de Ponce
- ★ Hacienda Buena Vista

Is Puerto Rico LGBT-friendly?

The LGTB community has the same protections and rights as heterosexual people in Puerto Rico. Same-sex marriage has been legal since July 2015. They are also allowed to legally change their gender, join the military, adopt and foster a child. Domestic violence protection is also extended regardless of sexual orientation and gender.

The above has made Puerto Rico one of the most LGBT-friendly islands in the Caribbean, if not in the world. Retiring here or living here, you can be as open as you can whichever part of the island you may be, whether it's in the city or in the rural areas.

Senior Discounts

Senior citizens in Puerto Rico enjoy a wide range of discounts from retail, grocery, leisure activities to travel. When you reach the age of 65, you can officially claim Medicare and Social Security benefits. In fact, you can already enroll in AARP or Associations of Mature American Citizens on your 50th birthday to start getting senior discounts. When in doubt, don't hesitate to ask so you can save some bucks.

Living in Puerto Rico: What to Watch Out For

Before packing your bags for your move to Puerto Rico, be reminded of the following warnings first:

★ **Devastating Hurricanes**
The last most devastating hurricane that affected Puerto Rico was in 2017 with Hurricane Maria. It uprooted trees, drowned weather stations, and ripped wooden houses apart. Electricity was cut off across the island and the residents had struggles in accessing clean water and food. Therefore, it is essential to find the sturdiest home should you decide to live here.

★ **Watch Out for Critters**
Mosquitoes, scorpions, sand fleas – you name it, Puerto Rico has it. These critters can bite and spread disease. After Hurricane Maria, sanitation is not as rigorous anymore so it is better not to drink the tap water.

★ **Unhealthy Economy**
There is an ongoing economic crisis in Puerto Rico and it has suffered through a recession, housing crisis, population loss, and major hurricanes. The recession has also resulted in unemployment that even if the crime rate is generally low, you may have to watch out for petty crimes such as theft.

Summary

Puerto Rico has a lot of advantages that made it stick to our list. Colonial towns – check. Sunsets and beaches – check. Culture and the resilience of its people – a big check. The country has a lot of potential, that hopefully in the future, it can improve its response to hurricanes and retirement visa issues.

Healthcare: ★★★
Culture: ★★★★★
Cost of Living: ★★★
Housing: ★★★
Accessibility: ★★★★
Safety: ★★★

TOTAL STARS: 21 ★

EUROPE

Dubrovnik, Croatia

Retire in Croatia

Reasons to Retire in Croatia

Croatia is as enchanting a country as its name suggests — a long strip of Mediterranean coastline facing west that brings amazing sunsets over the blue sea. Sunshine is aplenty with winter temperatures rarely dropping below freezing point, and snow is not so frequent.

Croatians are also some of the nicest people you'll meet and you won't struggle with the language because a big percentage of the population speaks English. Plus, it's also one of the safest countries in the world, ranking at 28th, compared to the USA which ranks at 128. Their lifestyle is arguably among the most enviable in the world because they know how to relax, relish a good cup of coffee, and enjoy quality time with family and friends.

The cost of living in Croatia is also an advantage. It still depends on where you choose to live, but there are cheaper options available. If you go to the market instead of eating at restaurants, you can save a lot of money. The medical system also offers universal coverage for the entire population.

The landscape is rich and fertile, which makes it the perfect place to produce wine and olive oil. Retiring in Croatia provides you with over a thousand islands to explore, with a variety of things to do, from wine tasting to hiking, sailing, snorkelling and diving. In the warmer months, Croatia offers easy access to European countries.

Why Retire in Croatia:

★ Life moves at a relaxed pace.
★ One of the safest countries in the world.
★ The majority of the population speaks English.
★ There are a thousand islands to explore.
★ Fresh and delicious food and wine.

Culture

Only four million people are living in Croatia, but they are consistently friendly. They are always happy to help, armed with a smile and a can-do attitude most of the time. Croatians are also known to be cultured people – they are well-read and well-educated. You can talk to them about anything, from theatres to contemporary culture. Thus, it is easy to make friends with the locals.

Try speaking with a Croatian and you'll find how they're the funniest! They will probably tone it down with foreigners but expect to hear a funny remark or two to break the ice. You'll know that you've reached their inner circle once they say more jokes than usual. At the start they may come across as uninterested and rude but only because they don't prefer any false pleasantries.

They are also proficient in English so it is not necessary to study the local language, which can be difficult. As long as the locals are under the age of 50, you'll find they have a good grasp of English.

Croatians tend to operate at a relaxed pace especially in the Mediterranean side, but not quite as the Spanish. There is no pressure, and things still run on time. This more relaxed mode is common among Istrians, who bear strong influences from Italy. Meanwhile, places like Zagreb, Zagorje, and Slavonia have a strong interest in personal advancement over pleasure. So, if you want a faster pace of life with more hardworking people, you may want to live in these latter areas.

Climate

Croatia has two climate regions: Continental and Mediterranean, which are good considerations when choosing your retirement location. The country is marked by a variety of geographical characteristics, including mountains, plains, coast, and forests.

The coasts and islands in the north, covering Istria, Kvarner, all the way to Dalmatia, are influenced by the Mediterranean climate. It means the summer temperature is between 24 to 26 degrees Celsius, while wintertime experiences somewhere between 2 to 9 degrees Celsius. The summer season is dry, while rain pours over the winter season. Dubrovnik receives most of the rain, averaging 952 mm for the whole year. It rarely snows along the coast, rather it receives plenty of sunshine from Split, Vela Luka to Dubrovnik.

The Continental climate influences the interior of the country such as Zagreb and Slavonia which are separated from the country by mountains. Snow is common in this area and the temperature is much colder, with winter ranging from -2 to -4 degrees Celsius, and summer goes between 10 to 18 degrees Celsius, making it a great escape from the summer heat.

Cost of Living

Croatia is one of the youngest countries in Europe, gaining its independence just around thirty years ago. Although it is a part of the European Union, the country has its own currency called the Kuna (HRK) where AUD 1 is equivalent to HRK 4.64. When you speak to a local, they may tell you that it's expensive to live here, but upon doing the comparison, groceries and products are about the same price as in France and Spain.

Eating in a restaurant will cost at least AUD 12.30, while fast food costs about AUD 8.20. Utility cost is 30% higher than other European countries. Housing will depend on where you choose to

live. The more expensive area refers to those closer to tourist destinations. Transportation in Croatia is reliable and if you are commuting, you can buy a monthly pass of AUD 74.

To cover the basic necessities while living in Croatia, a single person needs AUD 2,051, and a couple needs AUD 2,735 per month. Here are some figures to look at:

Expenses	Prices
Housing rent (average area)	AUD 752
High-speed internet	AUD 44
Electricity and water	AUD 274
Phone with basic data plan	AUD 21
Loaf of white bread	AUD 2
A dozen eggs	AUD 3.40
Local beer	AUD 4.25
Taxi per kilometre	AUD 2.75

Housing

Owning a property in Croatia is affordable. A 60 sqm apartment in Trogir costs AUD 201,645, while an old stone house of 100 sqm is AUD 411,355. However, keep in mind that you have to obtain permission from the Ministry of Foreign Affairs before purchasing, and it may take some time and a bit of inconvenience before finally getting it.

Rent is pricey in places like Dubrovnik and Zagreb, where you can expect to pay AUD 1,162 a month for an 85 sqm, while an average property area like Trogir and Pula will cost around AUD 752 a month.

Nursing homes and retirement villages are available in Croatia too. They are modernly equipped, offering 24-hour welfare and medical care. Individual housing is also possible with recreational activities, where you may expect to pay around at least AUD 821 for private ones. There are a lot of options in different counties, so it should not be difficult to find what's right for you.

Healthcare in Croatia

With Croatia's landscape, there's no doubt that the locals live healthier here because they are more active. People walk a lot, making use of their parks and natural pathways or along the coasts. Because its residents are healthier, Croatia has become a world leader for organ transplants ratio-wise, with 400 organ transplants per year.

Upon applying for a residency in the country, you will be required to register and pay for the state's health system called HZZO. This will provide you with access to free public doctors. Before you can use the system, you are also required to pay at least a year of back-payment before using the system, which is approximately AUD 1,095 for a couple.

Croatia's healthcare system offers decent healthcare facilities. Doctors are English-speaking so it is easy to ask around. The government is also promoting medical tourism in Croatia so there's no surprise why foreigners travel here for dental and cosmetic surgery. Procedures are offered at a cheaper price here because of the government support. Another advantage of the HZZO policy is it also covers the rest of the EU.

If you prefer going to private doctors, it is also available at competitive prices so that it can compete with the state's health system. Nevertheless, the safest way is to get private insurance just in case.

How to Retire in Croatia (Retirement Visa)?

The country has been a popular destination for retirees because of its good quality of life and low cost of living. Clean air? Clean water? Croatia is the ideal place. However, the country does not offer a permanent retirement visa yet. If you want to stay more than 90 days, you have to apply for a temporary residency permit, otherwise, if you still plan to work or start a business, then it is better to get a work or a business permit.

A temporary residence permit can be applied for in the embassies of Croatia, where you have to submit documents and a reason why you want to live in the country. A valid reason can be related to investment, business, family, employment, studies, or purchasing real estate, which is considered the best reason. Having a yacht moored in the marina counts as a valid reason, too.

Whether you will be granted a yearly extension will be subject to approval, but if you manage to extend for a consecutive five years, you will be considered for a permanent residency. With Croatia's bureaucracy, we recommend getting a lawyer with connections within immigration.

Work

The temporary yearly visa does not permit retirees to work in Croatia. You have to apply for a working permit or a business permit if you prefer to do otherwise.

Tax*

With a visa, you are only allowed to pay taxes if you are earning money from Croatia. A temporary visa meant for retirement does not permit you to work so you don't have to pay any taxes. Your pensions coming from other countries will not affect the tax you pay here, so that's good news for you and less of a worry.

If you decide to get a work permit to stay in Croatia, then your personal income will be taxed as follows:

Income	Tax Rate
HRK 360,000 HRK and below	24%
HRK 361,000 and above	36%

* HRK has been retained as default currency for all tax figures in this article. Currency exchange rate HRK1 = AUD0.22.

Food

Croatian cuisine is influenced by Greek, Roman, and Mediterranean cuisine, particularly Italian. Along the coast, you'll find coastal cuisine using more olive oil, herbs and spices, lemon and orange rind, while the mainland is characterized by Slavic, Hungarian and Turkish cuisine. The latter uses lard for cooking, and spices from pepper, paprika to garlic. Yes, that's a lot of variety!

The culinary tradition varies in every region: Dalmatia, Dubrovnik, Gorski Kotar, Istria, Lika, Medimurje, Podravina, Slavonija and Zagorje. The country has two main wine regions: Kontinentalna and Primorka, with more than 300 wine-producing areas in Croatia, both

serving red and white. If you are a wine lover, then you should try Malvazija and Teran, Istria's signature wine.

Croatia is also a coffee-drinking country, with the average person consuming 5 kg of coffee annually. Across the country, you'll find plenty of cafes, also because of the Ottoman Empire influences. Living in Croatia? Here are the top cuisines that will surely delight you every day:

- ★ **Black risotto** is locally known as crni riZot is made with squid (or cuttlefish), olive oil, garlic, red wine and squid ink, giving out the wonderful aroma and seafood flavour. It is a very popular cuisine along the coast.

- ★ **Strukli** refers to a delicious pastry filled with all the goodness of cottage cheese and sour cream. Although it originates from Slovenia, Strukli is one of the most popular foods especially in Zagreb.

- ★ **Brodetto** is fisherman's stew coming from Italy's Marche region. It is traditionally cooked in an open fire with the catch of the day, adding vinegar to the pot preserving the stew for a few days. Tomato base is also used like in Italy.

- ★ **Buzara** refers to a simple dish of mussels cooked in garlic, breadcrumbs and wine broth. The name itself means 'stew', while the preparation can be compared to how the French makes moules mariniere.

- ★ **Istrian Ham** often comes on a platter with cheese. It is skinned pork leg, dry-rubbed with sea salt and seasoned with pepper, garlic, bay leaves, and rosemary. The Istrians smoke their ham and age it for twelve months at least, resulting in a special aroma.

- ★ **Peka** is your tender meat and vegetable dish cooked under an iron lid over burning embers. It consists of either octopus, lamb, or chicken and potatoes.

- ★ **Truffles** from Croatia may not be as well-known as Italy, but the Istrian's Motovun forests have some of the highest truffles in the world! Plus, they are a lot less expensive.

- ★ **Rozata** is a typical custard pudding in Dubrovnik that is similar to crème caramel custard, but with a special taste of rose liqueur. It is very common in the summer months in the country.

There are limited choices of international restaurants in Croatia, and most often available in the big cities of Zagreb, Split, and Dubrovnik. Cuisine from all over the world, from South America to Asia, is sufficient to satisfy your cravings.

Recommended Cities in Croatia

Zagreb

Welcome to the country's capital, Zagreb, where 25% of its population live. It is a vibrant city boasting a charming medieval feel in its architecture and cobbled streets, similar to that of Vienna, Budapest, and Prague. The cost of living is significantly lower compared to other European cities and is characterized by reasonable house prices with a safe environment, so that you can feel secure while walking even at night.

Zagreb also offers culturally interesting neighbourhoods, so even if you can't work here, you will find plenty of things to do and explore. Many foreigners who choose the centre to live in enjoy the wide boulevards, the Austro-Hungarian vibe, and its gardens. There are art-nouveau buildings, trams and streets you can walk for hours. Then there's the other part of Zagreb, which features Soviet-style buildings.

There are plenty of apartments to choose from in the centre, and some can be quite affordable. There is a train available, which has a beautiful construction, however, it is only good for accessing the city itself – not any of the tourist destinations. Zagreb, after all, is not often on the top of the list for tourists, which is a good thing for retirees. If you prefer urban living, then Zagreb is the perfect place for you in Croatia. Aside from museums, whose subjects range from classic to the most bizarre, there are also tons of interesting restaurants and cafes to choose from. Want to go on a hike? The jaw-dropping Plitvice National Park is only a couple of hours away!

Essentials in Zagreb:

- ★ **Healthcare:** Hospitals and clinics in the capital are sufficient. With its European quality standard, the feedback has always been positive. Here are some of the best hospitals/clinics in Zagreb:
    - ★ University Hospital Centre Zagreb
    - ★ Sisters of Charity Hospital, Zagreb
    - ★ Klinicki Bolnicki Centar Zagreb

- ★ **Accessibility:** Zagreb Airport offers flights to most European countries, such as Madrid, Amsterdam, and Munich. It also connects to Middle East cities, such as Doha and Dubai, which then connects to other countries around the world.

Things You Can Do in Zagreb

Zagreb is a flat-planed and vibrant city, making it a perfect place for long strolls and cycling. It is small compared to other European capitals, but it features a lot of parks and forests from the upper town to downtown, or you can also travel to nearby villages for lunch. Here are things you can do and see as you spend your retirement days in Zagreb:

- ★ Museum of Broken Relationships
- ★ Zagreb's Farmer's Market

- ★ Lake Jarun
- ★ Medvednica Mountain
- ★ Zagreb Cathedral
- ★ Plitvice Lakes
- ★ Drive to nearby Slovenia and visit Ljubljana
- ★ Samobor
- ★ Lotrscak Tower
- ★ Mestrovic Atelier
- ★ Klovicevi Dvori Gallery

Pula

Pula is the largest city in Istria County in Croatia. It is situated in the northwestern part of the country, a working city featuring ancient Roman architecture. Residents of Pula celebrate the city's Roman heritage with a special event called Days of Antiquity. The small city also has a vibrant market called Trznica, a commercial centre dating back to the early 20th century. Strolling around here, you'll find lots of colourful produce and bottles of its specialty, Istrian olive oil.

Living in Istria is like living separately from Croatia. It is the largest peninsula in the country and, given its geographical location, you are closest to the warm sea of Central Europe. You can have both the continent and the sea in a small area.

If you love trekking, Istria offers lots of trekking paths. In autumn, you can spend your time in the forests in the search for mushrooms including truffles. A month after, you can then spend your time picking up olive oil or making your homemade wine.

Making Pula your home base allows you to explore other nearby Istrian destinations, such as Rovinj with its pastel-coloured buildings, and Motovun, a hilltop village similar to those in Tuscany, where they host the annual film festival.

Essentials in Pula

- ★ **Healthcare:** When choosing a place to live in Istria, choose an apartment closer to the hospitals. Here are some of Istria's best hospitals and clinics:
  - ★ Pula General Hospital
  - ★ Clinica Cukon
  - ★ Bolnica Hospital
  - ★ Izola General Hospital
  - ★ Health Center Umag Ambulance
- ★ **Accessibility:** Pula has a small international airport serving a few airlines that connect to other parts of Croatia and some cities in Europe. Otherwise, decent bus connections are also good options.

Things You Can Do in Pula

The region is a popular destination for history lovers, foodies, and cyclists. In summer time, the towns of Pula, Rovinj, and Porec are also the place to be if you are looking for beach fun or any other sun and beach activities. These towns and beaches are not meant to be rushed, so retiring in any of the towns in the region allows you plenty of opportunity to slow down and breathe in the atmosphere it offers. Here's a list of things you can see and do:

- ★ Bale
- ★ Hum
- ★ Cave Baredine
- ★ Verudela
- ★ Motovun

- ★ Groznjan
- ★ Oprtalj
- ★ Buje
- ★ Zavrsje
- ★ Labin
- ★ Buzet
- ★ Rabac
- ★ Brijuni National Park
- ★ Učka mountain range
- ★ The Roman Arena
- ★ Porec
- ★ Rovinj Bell Tower
- ★ St. Andrew's Island
- ★ Glavani Adventure Park

Dubrovnik

Dubrovnik is well known today for serving the backdrop of a popular HBO show called Game of Thrones. With its magnificent walled old town, sandwiched between mountains and the Adriatic Sea, Dubrovnik creates a dramatic ambiance filled with churches, monasteries, and fountains. Compared to other Mediterranean hotspots, Dubrovnik offers an affordable cost of living.

From here, you can also hop to the islands of Korcula, Lokrum, and Mljet, with ferry connections also to the Italian city of Bari. The city of Dubrovnik is also near the borders of Montenegro and Bosnia-Herzegovina so you can easily take a day trip to Kotor and see its fantastic fortress.

Traveling north of Dubrovnik, you can find the town of Ston with its walls surrounding the city. It is also known for its amazing oysters and sea salt production. Recently, American magazine Forbes ranked Dubrovnik as one of the best 20 places to live in, which is not a surprising accomplishment.

Essentials in Dubrovnik

- ★ **Healthcare:** With only one general hospital in the centre of Dubrovnik, severe cases are usually transferred to Split or Zagreb. Here is a list of hospitals/clinics in case you decide to retire here:
  - ★ Dubrovnik General Hospital
  - ★ Polyclinic Marin Med
  - ★ Polyclinic Glavic
  - ★ Sveti Vlaho
- ★ **Accessibility:** Dubrovnik Airport is the third busiest airport in Croatia, following Zagreb and Split. Seasonal flights to major European cities are available, connecting the country to nearby countries such as Ireland, Italy, Israel, Austria, Dubai, and Moscow.

Things You Can Do in Dubrovnik

With its old-world charm, retirees can soak up all the history and culture Dubrovnik has to offer. The city of Dubrovnik may be touristy but it does not mean you cannot enjoy them yourself especially once you call it your home. Your daily activities can include any of the following activities:

- ★ Old town
- ★ Lokrum
- ★ The Red History Museum
- ★ Old Pharmacy Museum
- ★ Rector's Palace
- ★ Troubadour
- ★ Dubrovnik Brewery
- ★ Banje beach

- Gunduliceva Poljana Square
- Konavle
- Lazareti
- Dominican Monastery

Zadar

With Split and Dubrovnik often the stars of Croatian tourism, Zadar tends to be missed out. This city on the Dalmatian coast is popular for its Roman and Venetian ruins, as well as for having an amazing view of the sunset, a claim supported by Alfred Hitchcock when he visited the country in 1964. It had been a part of the Republic of Venice, so you'll find remnants of that heritage in its Land Gate and Lion of St. Mark. Similar to the one in Pula, you will also find a well-preserved Roman forum with views of the Adriatic Sea. Even outside summer, the city remains beautiful and dynamic.

Five of Croatia's national parks can be found here, including Kornati, Northern Velebit, Krka, Plitvice. and Paklenica, where you can hike, boat, swim or cycle. The city is a perfect size with only 70,000 inhabitants, and some are the friendliest people in the Balkans.

Essentials in Zadar

- **Healthcare:** There are a few hospitals serving the center of Zadar. Aside from the following options, there are also options to travel two hours to Zagreb to access more hospitals if necessary.
    - Zadar General Hospital
    - Polyclinic Zadar
    - Poliklinika Therapia
    - Department of Emergency Medicine Zadar
- **Accessibility:** Zadar international airport, the 4th largest airport, has become a Ryanair base serving eight European destinations. Otherwise, Zagreb and Split airport are also available with more flight connections.

Things You Can Do in Zadar

Zadar is steeped in history but still leads a vibrant and dynamic cultural life. Retiring here offers plenty of things to fill your time with. It is located between Split and Zagreb so you can easily drive 2 hrs. to explore these cities. The cost of living here is also cheaper and your dollar will surely go a long way. Meanwhile, here are the places you can fill up your time with while in Zadar:

- The Riva
- Anastasia's Cathedral
- Pillar of Shame
- Zeleni Trg
- St. Donatus' Church
- The Forum
- Zadar Markets
- Saharun, Zaton, Kolovare, Nin's Lagoon beaches
- Sea Organ
- Barkajoli
- Museum of Ancient Glass
- Museum Church of Art
- St Donat Church
- The Garden
- Kraljevski Vineyard
- Nin Salt Works
- Ugljan Island
- Pag Island
- Plitvice Lake National Park

- Kornati Islands
- Krka Waterfalls

Is Croatia LGBT-friendly?

The rights of LGBT in Croatia have improved in recent years. With the Life Partnership Act of 2014, same-sex couples can now enjoy rights equal to heterosexual married couples, covering the aspects of adoption.

The country has also banned all kinds of discrimination on grounds of gender identity, sexual expression, and sexual orientation. Members of the LGBT community are also permitted to serve in the military.

It is also good to keep in mind Croatians are still conservative about this, and the constitution has banned same-sex marriage since 2013. When the public was asked about their opinion, 50% believe that LGBT must enjoy the same rights, while the rest are either still uncomfortable or feel indifferent. If you are a couple who wants to move to Croatia, you may want to consider the bigger cities, which are generally more friendly to the LGBT.

Senior Discounts

Most public transportation companies provide a discount for seniors aged 65 and above. This includes the use of trams and regular busses. Some museums offer a little discount, too. Other benefits also include a two-year government funded housing, only if you don't have enough means to cover your living needs.

Living in Croatia: What to Watch Out For

Croatia is one of our favorite places to travel to, but living here is another story. If you want to adjust well, you have to keep in mind the following nuisances:

- **Emergency services may be slow.**
  The country has many inhabited areas, especially on its islands. This results in delays in emergency service responses in some parts of the country. Also, Croatia is situated in an earthquake-prone region so it sometimes experiences intense seismic activity.

- **Lots of activities are shut down during winter.**
  Croatians live for the summer – that being said, a lot of establishments close down during the winter months. The country relies on tourism so although the environment is lively during summer, you might want to think of what to do and where to go during winter time. This also means that flights tend to be limited so you may have to drive to the next airport to get proper accessibility.

★ **Croatia has cumbersome bureaucracy.**
And that's frustrating! Any kind of task, even if it's a very simple one, as long as it involves a government office, can be turned into a multi-hour-long exercise. Even visa applications can take weeks or, sometimes, months.

Summary

Croatia is a beautiful country that offers good quality living for retirement. It's still a young country with a small population which can be both a good and a bad thing. The positive thing is it has a lot of growth potential and developments in the future, we just have to be a little patient. Here's our overall rating for Croatia:

Healthcare: ★ ★ ★
Culture: ★ ★ ★ ★ ★
Cost of Living: ★ ★ ★
Housing: ★ ★ ★
Accessibility: ★ ★ ★
Safety: ★ ★ ★ ★ ★

TOTAL STARS: 22 ★

Nice, France

Retire in France

Reasons to Retire in France

If you are aiming to have a great quality of life that comes with modern comforts available in Australia, France should be on the top of your list. Undeniably, it is one of the most beautiful countries in Europe with a long history, fascinating culture and fantastic food. The country is also famed for its natural beauty—alpine scenery, cliffs, nature reserves, mountains and rivers. Travelers from all around the world flock to the country to see their famous man-made landmarks such as the Eiffel Tower and over thirty palaces.

If you enjoy cheese, baguettes, wine and beer, you can get them all in great quality and good prices in France. Paris can be one of the most expensive cities in the world, but other areas in France offer a significantly lower cost of living. With careful planning, you can enjoy all France has to offer.

Accessing different countries around the world from France, as well as navigating around the country, will not be a problem. It has easy access to trains, well-maintained roads, and well-connected domestic and international flights. Plus, you'll never have to buy bottled water again because you can drink the water straight from the tap.

Why Retire in France:

- ★ Slower pace of life.
- ★ Easy access and convenience of urban transportation.
- ★ Fresh food and great wine.
- ★ An existing and thriving expatriate population.
- ★ Healthcare is the best in the world.

Culture

French people can be a little uptight, but they can be welcoming, especially if you learn a few words and phrases in French. You may survive in Paris by speaking mostly in English, but not in other areas. The French people will show you more respect if they see that you are making an effort and that you're trying your hardest.

Should you kiss on both cheeks or shake hands? In getting to know French people, it is better to let them lead. Are they a little older than you? It does not really matter – just refer to them as "vous" or the formal way to address someone who is older or has authority. They'll appreciate it and will be more likely to give you what you want.

You will find most French people to be well rounded. At such a young age, they study beyond reading, writing and counting. They also take theater, music, art appreciation and philosophy seriously. All these flavor the French way of life. Nevertheless, you'll also find them to be polite, friendly and with a good sense of humor.

Climate

France enjoys a temperate climate with a few regional differences. The locals get cool winters and mild summers except in the Mediterranean, where winters are mild and summers are hot. The most pleasant period is springtime, when the temperature is mild and sunshine offsets the frequent precipitation. Autumn is usually damp.

The north and central regions, where Paris is, get rainy winters with the lowest temperatures at around 1 degree Celsius.

The central and eastern region that includes the Alps, the Pyrenees and the Massif Central have a continental climate—abundant snow and a lot of rain throughout the year.

The southern region has a Mediterranean climate where summers are hot and winters are mostly dry. Autumn brings heavy rain that may cause some flooding.

Cost of Living

If you are looking for a place where you can stretch your dollars, France may not be the first country that comes to mind. Yes, Paris is famed to be one of the most expensive cities in the world – for tourists. But once you adjust your lifestyle or escape the city, it can be a different story. A Coke in Champs Elysse is equivalent to a lunch in a nice bistro away from the tourist's trail.

Cheap real estate is also sprouting everywhere in France. In the rural areas, you can get a great bargain with the cost of villas starting from AUD 164,114. Meanwhile, if you want to enjoy the good things in France, the starting monthly amount for a couple is AUD 3,419, which covers the utilities, basic groceries and rent.

Expenses	Prices
Rent (one-bedroom apartment in the city centre)	AUD 1,094
High-speed internet	AUD 44
Electricity and water	AUD 137
Phone with basic data plan	AUD 41
Loaf of white bread	AUD 1.80
A dozen eggs	AUD 4.90
Local beer	AUD 3.40
Taxi per kilometre	AUD 4.80

Housing

The cost of living in France and the US can be similar but France's rent is a lot cheaper. The average cost of a one-bedroom apartment in the centre of Paris is around AUD 1,778. Other places such as Montpellier or Sarlat-la-Caneda, can start from AUD 957.

Anyone can buy a house in France – even the non-residents. As long as you have a French bank account and a valid ID, you can make your purchase. A villa in Montpellier will cost you around AUD 717,855, while an apartment will be around AUD 322,631.

Retirement villages in France are quite common. These are usually gated communities with individual houses. While rent to be paid per month may increase because of inflation, most of the maintenance is well taken care of, from water, septic tank system, to the village communal area.

Healthcare in France

The French are known for their healthy lifestyles and a huge part of it was because the country has one of the best healthcare systems in the world. Life expectancy in the country is 80 for men and 85 for women. Having regular check-ups has become a residents' habit.

The country offers universal coverage for all its citizens whatever their age, financial status or regardless of whether they have pre-existing conditions. Everyone in the country and foreign retirees in France are eligible to have the coverage. If you have been living in France for 183 consecutive days, then you can get 70–100% healthcare treatments.

The universal healthcare system of France is called Protection Universelle Maladie, which grants an automatic right to healthcare for legal residents. If you are not eligible yet, then having medical insurance is a mandatory requisite before moving to France. Visits to the doctor will cost EUR 25, while a specialist visit EUR 50.

Once you are a legal resident, you need to pay at least 8% of your declared income into the French Social Security System. If you are earning EUR 25,000 a year, then you need to contribute EUR 2,000 yearly. This will cover at least 70% of your visits to the doctor and 80% of your hospital visits. Qualifying drugs are 100% covered. Most residents sign up for private insurance in case there is any shortfall.

How to Retire in France (Retirement Visa)

France does not offer a retirement visa. However, the process of the alternative is pretty simple. First, you will need to get a long-term visa at the nearest French consulate, where you can also obtain a permit called a Carte de Séjour. You cannot obtain the latter in France – you must apply for it beforehand in your home country.

You also must provide financial proof which can either be your bank account or your pension plan. Other requirements include a passport, application forms, passport photos, medical insurance and proof of where you plan to live in France.

The whole process might take you around two months, inclusive of an interview. Once you arrive in France, you only need to reapply for your Carte de Séjour yearly. After three years, you may proceed to apply for a residency card, valid for ten years. The residency card will allow you to work and can be renewed automatically.

Work

It is not permitted to work while you are under the Carte de Séjour permit. You can only work once you receive your 10-year residency card. Once you have the residency card, you can work, invest and start a business in France.

Tax*

France has high social contributions, which is one of the reasons why the country offers a high standard of living. All residents are subject to be taxed for their worldwide income. If you have a pension coming from Australia and you declare France as your permanent residence, you will be taxed at 10%, capped at EUR 3,660 per household.

Once your 10-year residency card is approved, you will be taxed like the locals. The French tax system is calculated depending on how many members are there in a family. For example, for a couple without children, the income will be divided by two and the tax rate will be based on the quotient.

Here is the rate of income tax for your reference:

Taxable Income	Tax Rate
Lower than EUR 9,964	Exempted
EUR 9,964 – EUR 25,405	11%
EUR 25405 – EUR 72,643	30%
EUR 72,643 – EUR 156,244	41%
Over EUR 156,244	45%

Those high earners or those who earn over EUR 250,000 pay an additional tax of 3–4%. There are also social charges in all types of income, such as 9.7% for employment or self-employment income and 17.2% for investment income.

*EUR has been retained as default currency for all tax figures in this article. Currency exchange rate EUR1 = AUD1.61.

Food

French food? As much as we want to dedicate a whole chapter to it, we'll simply cover what you need to know. Moving to France means having to eat the French way, too. The first thing you'll notice is that bread is present in every meal: croissants and pain au chocolate for breakfast, sandwiches for lunch and rolls for dinner. If there's any nation in the world that takes their bread seriously, that will be the French.

Time to ditch the soda. You'll either drink water or wine when you eat in the restaurants which will be served perfectly with cheese and meat. Sometimes you'll also get to eat snails, beets and organ meats.

Whether you eat in restaurants or visit a French person's home, you will eat multiple courses, which means group meals can be long. Keep in mind that regardless of the length of time they spend on meals, the French don't binge. Instead, they eat their food in small portions and in good moderation. Here are the some of the foods that you'll find in your daily meal:

★ **Boeuf** bourguignon refers to French beef stew made with bacon, mushrooms, onions and red wine. The iconic dish, which comes from Burgundy, applies an ultra-slow cooking method to tenderize the meat.

- **Cassoulet** is a hearty, slow-cooked casserole that consists of sausage, confit, pork and white beans. It is cooked for hours until the meat and beans blend into perfection. It is preferred especially on cold winter nights.

- **Foie gras** is a famous delicacy in French cuisine because of its rich and buttery flavour. The fattened liver is ten times more expensive than the bird itself, and France is its largest producer.

- **Escargot** is a well-loved appetizer in the country. The snails are first removed from their shells and cooked with garlic butter and chicken stock. Afterwards, they are placed back into their shells and served with herb-infused butter filled with garlic, thyme and parsley.

- **Cheese souffle** is a classic specialty, prepared with cheese, béchamel and eggs. It is often referred to as the king of all souffles that perfectly reflects French artistic performance—the dish must be golden, airy and fluffy as a cloud.

If you ever get tired of French cuisine and would want to try something else, there are international restaurants serving Chinese, Thai, Japanese and Indian cuisine which you can find easily in the city centres.

Recommended Cities in France

Lyon

Lyon is France's third-largest city, with a population of half a million. It has all the offerings of a large city, from museums, theatres and festivals, as well as an extensive transportation system. You can also find farmers' markets and plenty of restaurants that will satisfy all kinds of palates.

Lyon is favoured by retirees because it does not have the skyscrapers, nor the terrible traffic. Instead, you'll find a serene city filled with beautiful buildings matching the hues of the Mediterranean. There are also two rivers, the Saône and the Rhône, cutting through the town – where the locals go for picnics or a stroll.

The city is also known for being the capital of French gastronomy. You can expect the highest quality of local ingredients served in over 2,000 restaurants. Good news for the connoisseur because around 22 of them have earned a Michelin star.

There are expat groups already thriving in the city, which means you will find more opportunities to speak in English. Lyon is not as expensive as Paris, plus it has the best healthcare with a wide enough choice of doctors and pharmacies.

Essentials in Lyon:

- **Healthcare:** With 74 hospitals in Lyon's list, you will be in good hands with a wide range of highly specialized private and public healthcare. It has one of the most ideal healthcare systems in the world, which may be why the city is called the healthiest in France. Here is a list of our recommended hospitals:

- Hôpital Edouard Herriot
- Center Léon Bérard:
- Hospital Center Saint Joseph-Saint Luc
- Hôpital Louis Pradel
- Hôpital de la Croix-Rousse
- Hôpital Renée Sabran
- Hôpital Henry Gabrielle
- Hôpital Pierre Wertheimer

★ **Accessibility:** Public transportation in the city is efficient and you can also walk pretty much everywhere. It is also a two-hour drive away from the French alps where the locals flock whether it's summer or winter. Its international airport serves both domestic and international destinations. From Lyon, you can fly to many places, such as Dublin, Montreal, London and Istanbul.

Things You Can Do in Lyon

As a UNESCO World Heritage city, Lyon's list of things to do would be very long. It is a vibrant city that you can never get bored of. With its combination of modern and old-world charm, it offers an interesting contrast that will continue to stimulate a retiree's mind. Here are some of the things you can see in your first few years:

- La Place Bellecour
- Funicular to Fourviere Hill
- Notre-Dame de Fourvière
- Gallo-Roman Amphitheatre
- Parc de la Tête d'Or
- Les Quais du Rhône
- Croix Rousse
- Les Pentes
- Hotel de Ville
- Bartholdi Fountain
- Viex Lyon
- Les Bouchons Lyonnais
- Les Traboules
- Confluence
- Le Crayon Tower
- Les Peniches
- La Cité International
- Musee de Beaux Arts
- La Fete des Lumieres
- Opéra de Lyon
- Cathedrale de St-Jean
- Musees Gadagne
- Les Marches
- La Halle de Lyon
- Part-Dieu
- La Fresque des Lyonnais

Montpellier

A historic university town, Montpellier has attracted its fair share of foreign retirees over the years. Its location along the Mediterranean coast, its medieval streets, cafes and the tranquillity of the village atmosphere are some of the reasons why. From here, you can easily access Spain and Italy.

It is also the home to several universities, including the world's oldest medical school. Remember Nostradamus? Yes, that's where he studied. Montpellier is also one of the most affordable cities in the country, so most of the essentials here are reasonably priced.

One of the fastest growing metropolises in France, Montpellier is currently going through a

booming economy with a dynamic social scene. The price of real estate here is also very attractive. Plus, there's the Mediterranean climate that brings more sunshine than anywhere else in the country. If you want to have the finer things in life for less, Montpellier would be the perfect setting for you.

Essentials in Montpellier:

- **Healthcare:** Montpellier has great access to excellent healthcare. The hospital network of Centre Hospitalier Universitaire is made up of six different hospitals, two clinics and a medical institute. It houses one of the top medical universities, guaranteeing competent medical staff and modern equipment. Here is a list of recommended hospitals in Montpellier:
    - Centre Hospitalier Universitaire Chu Chru de Montpellier
    - Clinique Champeau Béziers
    - Centre Hospitalier Mas Careiron
    - Groupe Oc Sante
    - Hospital Local de Pezenas
    - Clinique du Parc Castelnau le Lez
    - Centre Hospitalier Universitaire de Nîmes
    - Polyclinique Grand Sud
    - Polyclinique Saint Privat
    - Centre Hospitalier Beziers
    - Clinique du Docteur Jean Causse
- **Accessibility:** Montpellier airport is located on the outskirts of the city with direct flights to a lot of European countries such as Italy, Portugal, Spain, Holland, Greece, the UK and even Morocco. There are flights to the US and even to Paris.

Things You Can Do in Montpellier

Montpellier may be one of the largest cities in France, but it has its own charm and soul. It is characterised by gorgeous buildings and multicultural communities. Living here, retirees can spend their time chatting with friends in a café while playing a game of petanque.

Because of the city's wine production, it has become a wealthy port city. The top universities have given it a great youthful energy. Here are the things you can see while you spend your retirement days here:

- Place Royale du Peyrou
- Ecusson
- Jardin des Plantes
- Montpellier markets
- Fabre Museum
- Cathedrale Saint-Pierre
- Porte du Peyrou
- La Panacee
- Esplanade Charles de Gaulle
- Place Jean-Jaurès
- Montpellier Cathedral
- Park of Meric Estate
- Odysseum
- Castle of Flaugergues
- Church Saint-Roch of Montpellier
- Carré Saint Anne
- Pavillon Populaire

Bordeaux

The French town of Bordeaux is known for its beautiful surroundings and high standard of living. It is in one of the most picturesque parts of France, blessed with warm summers and mild winters. Retirees who choose this city can enjoy ancient streets and beloved vineyards.

Just recently, technology and communications have been added to its growing economy, along with its reputation for wine and aeronautics. Wine is still the biggest thing, with more than 7,000 wineries and vineyards in Bordeaux. That's 960 million bottles produced every year.

If you are not keen on visiting a different vineyard every day, there are 350 buildings dating back to the 18th century that can keep you occupied. Museums, galleries and concert halls never come short as well. These are the reasons why tourists keep on coming back to this beautiful city. But don't worry, it is also the ninth biggest town in the country, so it won't get overcrowded.

Essentials in Bordeaux

- **Healthcare:** Remember to keep your records because doctors don't keep a health file for you. Like in all parts of France, residents are satisfied with the skill and competency of medical staff here. Here are the most recommended hospitals in Bordeaux:
    - Hospital Saint-Andre
    - Groupe Hospitalier Pellegrin
    - Polyclinique Bordeaux-Nord Aquitaine
- **Accessibility:** Bordeaux is well-connected because of its international airport and train station. The Bordeaux-Merignac Airport operates regular direct flights to many European cities such as Amsterdam, Berline, Catania, Geneva, Tel Aviv, Glasgow and Hamburg. The train is also reliable and can connect to cities across France.

Things You Can Do in Bordeaux

Bordeaux is the Mecca for wine lovers, but aside from drinking wine, there are other things you can spend your days with as a retiree of this lovely city. Here are the places recommended by the locals:

- La Cité du Vin
- Bassins de Lumières
- Saint-Seurin Basilica
- Château Les Carmes Haut-Brion
- Moon Harbour Distillery
- Patinoire Meriadeck for ice karting
- Miroir d'Eau
- Jardin Public
- Librairie Mollat
- Bassin a Flot
- Saint Michel bell tower
- Port Cailhau
- Gallo-Roman Bordeaux
- Bordeaux markets
- Marche des Capucins
- Marche des Quais

Sarlat-la-Caneda

If you are a fan of old medieval towns, love to wander through a maze of narrow streets, gothic and renaissance mansions, then you may consider retiring in Sarlat-la-Caneda. It is located in the Black Perigord and has a long history dating back to 1081. It was one of the few regions not raided by the Vikings, so it managed to preserve some of 14th century France.

What does it mean to retire here? You'll find plenty of plump birds, the official mascot of the area, adorning the shop windows. With a population of only around 11,000, it offers convenience and activities in a smaller setting. You can spend your days canoeing the rivers or biking country roads. The Wednesday and Saturday markets are filled with people and wonderful aromas.

Sarlat-la-Canéda is positioned far enough from the large cities that it can provide you a retiree's quiet small-town life. Still, it is an easy 2-hour drive to major cities of the southwest.

Essentials in Sarlat-la-Caneda

- **Healthcare:** Despite having only two hospitals, Sarlat-la-Caneda prides itself for having the best healthcare professionals and the latest medical equipment. It offers a good range of medical treatment from cardiology, endocrinology, gastroenterology, nephrology, urology, ophthalmology, to cancer care, gynaecology, and even plastic surgeries.
    - Centre Hospitalier J. Leclaire
    - Salles du Centre Colombiers
- **Accessibility:** The nearest domestic airport to Sarlat-la-Canada is 35 km away, located at Brive. An international airport is about 150 km away located in Bordeaux. From here you can also access the train to major parts of the country.

Things You Can Do in Sarlat-la-Canéda

Living in this part of France will give you a chance to explore the most beautiful villages of Dordogne Valley, either by car or by bike. Camping cars are also common. Here are the places you can keep on coming back to while you spend your retirement days in and around Sarlat-la-Caneda:

- Saint-Sacerdos cathedral
- Chapel Recollects
- Castle of La Boetie
- Castle Campagnac
- The Episcopal castle
- Jardin des Enfeus
- The Tower Executioner
- Manor Gisson
- La bastide de Domme
- Roque Gageac
- Castelnaud la Chapelle
- Marqueyssac Hanging Gardens
- Beynac et Cazenac
- Puymartin Castle
- Limeuil
- Cloister de Cadouin
- Belves
- Bastide de Monpazier
- Maison Forte de Reignac
- La Roque St Christophe
- St-Leon-sur-Vezere
- Hautefort Castle
- Saint-Jean-de-Côle

Is France LGBT-friendly?

Fortunately, France has some of the most advanced lesbian, gay, bisexual and transgender (LGBT) rights in the world, making it one of the most gay-friendly countries in the world. Same-sex marriage was legalized in 2013, and it is one of the first countries in the world to de-list transgender identification as a mental illness. There are also laws that prohibit discrimination based on sexual orientation.

Generally, Parisians are open-minded. That means retiring in Paris as a gay couple is convenient. There are not a lot of problems related to homophobia. The gay scene is very much alive, with Le Marais as the epicentre, along with Pigalle and Champs-Elysees.

Senior Discounts

Seniors benefit from discounted transportation in France, from flights to trains. There are also museums, attractions, concerts and activities that can provide a cheaper price if you mention that you are a senior. If you are unsure, just remember this phrase, "Y a-t-il une réduction sénior s'il vous plaît?", the polite way to ask for a senior discount.

Living in France: What to Watch Out For

Like almost any country in the world, France has its share of drawbacks. Before packing your bags and applying for a visa, you may want to keep the following in mind:

- ★ **Be careful of old housing in France.**
  The real estate market might be booming in France, but it can also come with a price. Most apartments in the country, while charming, are quite old. This means they may have smaller rooms and lack proper insulation. Make sure to check the apartments properly before moving in.

- ★ **You really have to learn French.**
  Yes, you can survive in France by speaking only English, but French people are protective of their language. It is considered rude to speak in English to locals while assuming that you will be understood. If you want to have a harmonious relationship with your neighbour, learning to speak the language is the first step.

- ★ **Crime in the big cities.**
  For the last few years, France has been baffled by numerous terrorist attacks, so you may find military units patrolling important landmarks. Other problems such as pickpockets and petty theft are common in big cities like Paris. Apart from this concern, a few suburbs are completely safe at all hours.

Summary

There is no doubt that the French know how to live the good life, from work-life balance to its divine food and wine, for a lot less. France remains to be one of our favourite places to retire in Europe.

Healthcare: ★★★★★
Culture: ★★★★★
Cost of Living: ★★★
Housing: ★★★
Accessibility: ★★★★★
Safety: ★★★

TOTAL STARS: 24 ★

Rialto Bridge, Venezia, Italy

Reasons to Retire in Italy

Many people think that living in Italy is expensive – that's the impression tourists get, especially when they go to tourist areas such as St. Mark's Square in Venice. But beyond these spots, say, for example, in the south, you can get a bottle of local wine for as cheap as AUD 5.50, while a nice meal in a restaurant will cost around AUD 27.50. Thus, it is possible to stretch your dollar by choosing where and how to live in Italy.

If you want to enjoy the sweet life (la dolce vita), especially in retirement, start with the food. Without a doubt, Italian food is the best in the world, from pizza, pasta, to gelato. The freshness of food is unbelievable. You can sip your wine while enjoying the Mediterranean climate. There is a diverse landscape, whether you prefer skiing in the Italian Alps or cruising along the Amalfi Coast.

Italy has plenty of rich architectural and historical sites – you can explore something new every day. Imagine half of the world's art treasures at your doorstep. Most important are the people that you can surround yourself with. Having an Italian as a friend is golden; they'll do anything for you even if you don't ask. Once you have an Italian friend, you have them for life.

Having great access to excellent healthcare is a must in our senior life and living in Italy guarantees you that. Fortunately, the World Health Organization ranks Italy as the second-best in the world!

Why Retire in Italy:

- ★ Excellent and cheap healthcare
- ★ Stunning scenery with enough cultural and historical sites
- ★ It has the finest cuisine in the world
- ★ The cost living is not bad – including real estate

Culture

Italians are concerned about fashion. They take care of their appearance and make sure to dress up in style. The stronger and more colourful, the better. They also give importance to exercising. Since Italian cuisine is composed of a lot of carbohydrates, they balance it out with a lot of exercising, from walking in the park to riding a bike.

Italians are also an emotional people, thus you may have to be careful with what you share with them, as things may escalate quickly. Notice how expressive they are in communication through their gestures and facial expressions.

Because the country is heavily influenced by Catholic tradition, family always comes first. Italians are used to having a strong support system. The household is very traditional, and women do most of the household chores, so yes, gender equality still has a long way to go in this country.

Don't expect them to be punctual either. It is acceptable and 'elegant' to be ten to fifteen minutes late. To socialize with Italians, you must learn to love their food – probably the easiest thing to do. They love to talk about food, what they want to eat, and how to prepare it, so you have to adjust the conversations around this. Otherwise, you can also talk about football as Italians are fanatics.

Generally, Italians are polite, kind and helpful and will likely appreciate it if you speak their language. Not a lot of people speak English in the smaller cities, so you will have to learn the basics, at least, before moving here.

Climate

Italy experiences a Mediterranean climate: cool, wet winters and hot, dry summers. The weather varies because Italy is quite a big country so you may expect to experience different weather in different parts of the country.

In the north and the mountainous zone, winters are both cool and humid, with cold air from northern Europe spreading down into Italy. Summertime in Italy is hot, particularly in the south of the peninsula, with temperatures reaching 28-40 degrees Celsius, while the northern regions are characterised by some rainy days and thunderstorms in the afternoons and evenings.

Travelling to the east coast, you'll notice that it is not as wet as the west coast. It is also colder in the winter. In the Alps, snow falls more during autumn and spring, while winter is marked with cold and dry periods. While choosing where to retire in Italy, it is important to know your weather preference to avoid getting stuck in a place where you don't like the weather.

Cost of Living

The cost of living in Italy is flexible to your preference. If you want to enjoy all the cultural offerings, you may opt for the convenience of living in the big cities. However, living a low-key lifestyle in small towns can save you a lot of money. Housing costs in the former are always higher, but going for the latter is also not a bad option and does not mean a compromise in quality of life.

Other than the housing costs, the living expenses are pretty much consistent in the country. Utilities are operated by public-private partnerships and are usually charged with the rent, with bills issued every couple of months. Meanwhile, gas is used for both cooking and heating, and so is cost-efficient.

AUD 2,600 is sufficient for a couple to live for a month. This covers all the essentials in smaller cities. Here is the breakdown of some expenses you need to deal with as you retire in Italy:

Expenses	Prices
Housing rent (Palermo, Sicily)	AUD 781
High-speed internet	AUD 45.25
Electricity and water	AUD 274
Phone with basic data plan	AUD 21
Loaf of white bread	AUD 2
A dozen eggs	AUD 2.75
Local beer	AUD 2.75
Taxi per kilometre	AUD 2.75

Housing

The property market in Italy is still struggling, so you can take advantage of it and get a house at a reasonable price. For instance, in Palermo, one of the most beautiful cities in southern Italy, will cost you EUR 1,250 per sqm. A two-bedroom apartment at 80 sqm costs EUR 240,000, while a detached house at 75 sqm is at EUR 130,000. If you look long enough, you'll find something as little as AUD 27,400.

Meanwhile, rent for furnished apartments in provincial cities will cost between AUD 548 and AUD 959. In smaller towns, it can even go down to AUD 411. Should you decide to go for the bigger cities such as Rome, you may expect to pay at least AUD 1,370 monthly.

There are lots of choices for nursing homes with 24-hour professional assistance. Facilities such as common areas, libraries and gyms are available. If you would prefer to have a more independent lifestyle, retirement homes are an option too.

Healthcare in Italy

There are 3.8 doctors per thousand people in Italy, which is among the highest rates around the world. Italy also has a high life expectancy, 79.4 years for men and 84.8 years for women. These are the reasons why Italy ranks second in the World Health Organization when it comes to healthcare.

Even mid-sized cities in Italy have good facilities and shorter queues. Each town has a doctor available and also a guardia medica on weekends and for holiday emergencies provided by public hospitals. There are private hospitals available that accommodate patients covered by their medical insurance or those who can pay out of pocket.

In every provincial city, there are many options for private doctors and medical facilities. But even private hospitals would only charge around EUR 75, which is a fraction of what it would be in other First World countries. Keep in mind however, that hospitals don't accept credit cards as payment, though most of them will only bill the patient after discharge. There are also a good number of private clinics that usually charge higher.

For foreign retirees who became legal residents of Italy, healthcare is considered a right within the National Health Plan. All you have to do is obtain a certificato di residenza issued by the Italian consulate abroad, along with your stay permit from the local police station and your registry of self from the Registrar of Vital Statistics, which you can get at the local town hall.

If your application is approved, you will get a medical registration card, which you need to show every time you make an appointment. What's great about this is you can choose a family physician from the list of participating doctors. We still recommend getting private health insurance because not all treatments are covered by the National Health Plan. Travel insurance for a couple costs about AUD 343 per year.

How to Retire in Italy (Retirement Visa)

Expatriates who want to retire in Italy must apply for an Elective Residence Visa. It is a straightforward visa application and is mostly used by foreign non-EU nationals who have the financial means to support themselves without working. The conditions include the following:

- ★ Must be at least eighteen years old
- ★ Must prove to have sufficient funds to support oneself by means of savings, investments or pensions
- ★ Proof that passive income can be generated while staying in Italy
- ★ Health insurance
- ★ Rental contract during stay
- ★ Police clearance from home country

The elective residence visa is valid for a year and can be renewed at the police headquarters. One you reach five years of residence in Italy, it is possible to request for a permanent residence permit.

Work

Having an Elective Residency Visa does not permit you to apply for any kind of work in Italy. If you intend to do other types of activities such as studying, then you must apply for a student permit. If you prefer to work, then you must get a working visa.

Tax*

Recently, Italian law has extended a 7% flat tax for foreign pensioners living in the country. To benefit from the flat tax, the pensioner must have stayed in Italy for at least five years. The pensioner must also be a resident of one of the municipalities with a population not exceeding 20,000 – examples of these places include Sicily, Calabria, Abruzzo and Puglia.

If you are working in Italy as a foreign resident, you will only be taxed based on what you earn in the country, while if you are an Italian resident who spends more than 183 days a year in the country, then your worldwide income is subjected to IRPEF (L'imposta sul Reddito delle Persone Fisiche). Once the allowance is taken into account, the progressive income tax is charged as follows:

Expenses	Prices
USD 36,000	23%
USD 36,001 – USD 39,300	33%
USD 39,301 – USD 119,200	39%
USD 119,201+	45%

* USD has been retained as default currency for all tax figures. Currency exchange rate USD1 = AUD1.36.

Food

Italian food relies mostly on the freshness and quality of the ingredients. Enjoying it is more experiential, not intellectual – words from Michael Chiarello which ring true. What is typical of Italian cuisine is how they use the most basic ingredients and yet still come out as flavourful.

Olive oil is present in every meal whether for braising, frying or drizzling. Onion and garlic, too, mixed with the intensity of green vegetables. The Italians also love to preserve their pork as sausages and salami, as well as their olives into extra-virgin olive oil. Their techniques have been developed since antiquity and later spread around the world.

With the country's vast area, each region has developed its own specialties. In Abruzzo and Molise, using chili peppers is typical. Apulia is known for its desserts called zeppola and cartellate. If you want to try pasta dishes that use guanciale, then proceed to Lazio, which is famous for its pasta alla carbonara and pasta all'amatriciana. Sardinian cuisine often includes roasted suckling pig and wild boar.

Just this year, 371 restaurants in Italy have been awarded Michelin stars – the second country in the world to have the most Michelin restaurants. Beyond pasta and pizza, Italy offers a great variety that you won't ever get tired of, should you choose to eat one specific cuisine for the rest of your life.

- ★ **Arancini** is a dish of crispy, golden brown stuffed rice balls. It is filled with ragu, tomato sauce and mozzarella. Each region in Italy has its own version of Arancini.

- ★ **Lasagne** is a flat pasta noodle, baked in layers in the oven. Did you know that originally, lasagne was not made with tomatoes? Even today, only a tiny bit of tomato sauce is used in traditional ragu, unlike in most American versions of the dish.

- ★ **Risotto** is rice cooked with broth until it reaches a creamy consistency, that came from northern Italy, Originally, saffron is used for flavouring, resulting in its signature yellow colour.

- ★ **Prosciutto** is another Italian favourite, referring to dry-cured ham or an Italian-style bacon. It is salty, thinly sliced and served uncooked with pasta or wrapped around a chunk of mozzarella.

- ★ **Ribollita** refers to a hearty, vegetable soup and is considered to be a 'poor man's food'. It was said that servants created this soup by collecting unfinished food such as bread and vegetables, which also explains why its name translates to 're-boiled'.

- ★ **Gelato** is a frozen dessert made with 3.25% butterfat, whole milk and sugar. It is also lower in fat and has 70% less air. There are many flavours to choose from, from vanilla, chocolate, pistachio to stracciatella.

- ★ **Tiramisu** is a coffee-flavoured dessert that consists of ladyfingers, coffee, eggs, cocoa and mascarpone cheese. It's the most sought-after dessert for its lightness and creaminess.

Don't worry if you're suddenly craving other types of cuisine while living in Italy. There is a good variety of international restaurants you can enjoy, with Japanese, Chinese, American, and Indian cuisines.

Recommended Regions in Italy

Abruzzo

Abruzzo is an undiscovered gem. If you are looking to retire surrounded by inland hills, medieval towns, alpine peaks and an amazing sea coast, then Abruzzo is for you. It is in the centre of Italy, around 31 miles from Rome. The region is appealing with its vibrant weekly market, stone-built buildings and tidy lanes.

Life in Abruzzo offers a wide range of activities that can easily fill up your schedule. It can be a simple bocce ball game, watching medieval palio or horse racing events, or a food festival where you will find a myriad of pasta dishes.

Retirees who love the outdoors will find Abruzzo the best sanctuary for them as it is the home of the largest national park in the country – the Gran Sasso d'Italia . There are options to do mountain biking, horseback riding, hiking, skiing and fishing. Otherwise, there are mineral hot springs and spas if you simply want to relax. You can also explore the coastline with plenty of beaches to choose from.

Compared to its neighbouring cities, Abruzzo is a bargain. You can get the best quality of life at a cheaper price. Imagine, a three-story townhouse can be as cheap as AUD 86,310. You can even find a village home at AUD 40,250. Rental for the meantime can be at least AUD 274 a month. With inexpensive rental, you can have lots of affordable fun.

Essentials in The Abruzzo:

- ★ **Healthcare:** Like the rest of Italy, healthcare in Abruzzo is reliable. Here are some hospitals we recommend:
  - ★ San Salvatore Hospital, L'Aquila
  - ★ San Fillipo and Nicola, L'Aquila
  - ★ Castel di Sangro Hospital, L'Aquila
  - ★ SS. Annunziata Hospital, L'Aquila

- ★ **Accessibility:** Rome is only a two-hour drive by car, making Abruzzo accessible to the rest of the world. Abruzzo also has its own airport, which connects it to local places such as Palermo and other European cities like Malta, Prague and Warsaw.

Things You Can Do in Abruzzo

With its diverse scenery, relaxed lifestyle and low cost of living, Abruzzo can be a haven to retirees. Tourists don't usually reach this part of the country because of its countless mountains – but isn't that a good thing? You can have all this paradise to yourself! Here are places you can explore while spending your retirement days here:

- ★ Museo Archeologico Nazionale d'Abruzzo
- ★ Ristorante Gino
- ★ Eremo di Sant'Onofrio al Morrone
- ★ Santuario di Ercole Curino

- ★ Locanda Sotto gli Archi
- ★ Basilica di Santa Maria di Collemaggio
- ★ Lake Scanno
- ★ The Calanchi di Atri Nature Reserve
- ★ The Stiffe Caves
- ★ National Park of Abruzzo, Lazio and Molise
- ★ Abbey of San Giovanni in Venere
- ★ The Majella National Park
- ★ The Gran sasso and Monti della Laga National Park
- ★ The Fortress of Civitella del Tronto

Puglia

Its southern peninsular position may seem isolated, but it is not at all remote with two airports serving the area. The number of retirees in Puglia has been growing annually, especially those who seek a laidback and yet intriguing place to retire. With only 63 days of rain annually, you're guaranteed plenty of sunshine where you can enjoy loads of activities all year round. It also blends Greek, Arab, Roman, Byzantine and Baroque influences together wherever you look.

Even in the winter months, you can enjoy horseback riding and going to seafood restaurants. Summer is hot and dry, making it the best time to enjoy a myriad of water sports and a great line-up of festivals. If you prefer a slower pace of life, where lunches are followed by siesta or evening strolls with friends, then Puglia is the place for you.

Another thing retirees love is the variety of golf clubs available here. You can also swim, snorkel or windsurf in its beaches with low reefs and rocky shorelines. In addition to that are the wineries where you can take your own jug and fill up directly from the barrels at a very cheap price.

Essentials in Puglia

- ★ **Healthcare:** With a population of 4 million, the number of hospitals in Puglia also ensures that everyone will be taken care of. Check out our list of some recommended hospitals:
    - ★ Casa di Cura Salus Brindisi
    - ★ Azienda Ospedaliera Specializzata
    - ★ Ospedale Generale Regionale F Miulli
    - ★ Puglia Sanita
    - ★ Casa di Cura Madonna del Buoncammino
- ★ **Accessibility:** The two airports, Bari and Brindisi and a rail line running up at the Adriatic coast, makes Puglia accessible. Bari airport connects the region to tons of European cities from Munich, Vienna, Madrid to Moscow. Brindisi is also another good airport that provides flights to other parts of Italy and some parts of Europe such as Geneva and Rotterdam.

Things You Can Do in Puglia

Relocating in Puglia will allow you to explore hundreds of attractive towns in the region and the myriad charms in its ancient landscape. It runs along a 500-mile coastline where you can experience the real Italy. If you appreciate antique churches built in the 11th century, enjoy the traditional way of life or enjoy losing yourself in twisting streets, then look no further. Puglia will keep you busy in your retirement days. Here are the things you should not miss:

- ★ Bari

- ★ Valle d'Itria
- ★ Alberobello
- ★ Martina Franca
- ★ Locorotondo
- ★ Cisternino
- ★ Ostuni
- ★ Ceglie Messapica
- ★ Adriatic Coast
- ★ Monopoli
- ★ Lecce
- ★ Casarano
- ★ Gallipoli
- ★ Otranto
- ★ Gargano National Park
- ★ Castel del Monte
- ★ Trani
- ★ Matera

Tuscany

Travellers who reach this part of the world find it easy to fall in love with Tuscany – what else would you ask for? The culture is rich, the landscape is stunning and the food is heaven itself. There's a sense of perfection to Tuscany, plus the feeling that there is no need to look further, especially if you aim for a lifestyle 'under the Tuscan sun.'

The majority of the region is filled with bucolic hills, wild mountains, river valleys, canyons and a 250-mile stretch of Mediterranean waterfront. Florence, the heart of Tuscany and where the Renaissance started, may be the priciest city, but travel a little further to the rustic country retreat and you'll get better value for your money.

If you love history, Tuscany is dotted with art cities, cultural events and outdoor activities. If you are keen to get active after retirement,

there is never a shortage of walking trails, bike routes and golf courses. There is also a rich array of churches, private galleries, museums and churches. It also contains a wealth of UNESCO heritage sites, opera theaters and music venues. You won't get bored!

If you are planning to settle here, it is not necessary to learn Italian because there is a solid English-speaking population in every town.

Essentials in Tuscany

- ★ **Healthcare:** Italian healthcare is excellent, and hospitals are pretty much everywhere in Tuscany, operating 24/7. Here are the best hospitals in Tuscany:
  - ★ Azienda Ospedaliero Universitaria Careggi
  - ★ Servizio Sanitario della Toscana
  - ★ Casa di Cura Villa Donatello
  - ★ Clinica Neurochirurgica dell'Università degli Studi di Firenze
  - ★ Azienda Unita Sanitaria Locale Lucca
  - ★ Azienda Sanitaria di Firenze

- ★ **Accessibility:** Tuscany has two international airports: Galileo Galilei International Airport in Pisa and Amerigo Vespucci Airport in Florence. It also sits between Rome and Milan – both 3 hours away.

Things You Can Do in Tuscany

Tuscany is one of the most visited places in Italy. This does not mean that you can't do anything not-touristy. You may visit Da Vinci's hometown and indulge yourself with testaments to his genius. Or you may soak in its hot springs, followed by visiting its wineries. If you are looking for something more unusual, hitting the beach may be the solution for you. The list goes on and on. Here are other things you can do while spending your retirement days in Tuscany:

- ★ Piazza del Duomo and Renaissance Florence
- ★ Uffizi Gallery, Florence
- ★ Pisa's Leaning Tower and Campo dei Miracoli
- ★ Cathedral of Santa Maria Assunta in Siena
- ★ Lucca's Walls and Centro Storico
- ★ The Towers of San Gimignano
- ★ Piazzale Michelangiolo and San Miniato
- ★ Etruscan and Roman Volterra
- ★ Accademia Gallery
- ★ Arezzo
- ★ Elba
- ★ Montepulciano
- ★ Medici Villas and Gardens
- ★ Viareggio Carnevale

Lazio

To Italy's central peninsular section, Lazio sits with the second most populated region of Italy. It is a long, narrow region that runs alongside the Tyrrhenian Sea, located at the southern end of central Italy. Its landscape is superb because of its volcanic terrain, numerous lakes and sandy coast.

Its capital Rome is also the capital and the largest city of the country. What makes it attractive are its towns and hamlets filled with history, hidden gems, nature reserves, archaeological sites, lakes and beaches. The Vatican, the smallest country in the world, is also within reach.

Some of the localities you may explore are Ostia Antica with its beautiful archaeological parks or the Pontine Islands, an archipelago consisting of six volcanic islands. Or why not explore Tarquinia, an art city that remains a symbol of the Etruscan culture. There's also Tivoli that's host to magnificent villas such as Villa di Adriano and Villa D'Este.

Rome also has an excellent coffee culture, so you will find many cafes such as the oldest café, Caffe Greco, near the Spanish steps. Lazio probably has it all, and there will never be a dull moment if you choose to live here in your retirement days.

Essentials in Lazio

- **Healthcare:** Lazio has some of the best hospitals in the country. Here is a list of our recommended hospitals:
  - Machiavelli Medical House
  - Casa di Cura Marco Polo
  - UPMC San Pietro FBF
  - Laboratorio Casella
  - Guardia Medica
  - Villa Fulvia

- **Accessibility:** A few airports serve the region of Lazio. The airport in Rome serves both international and domestic flights. There's also the Perugia San Francesco D'Assisi in Umbria, Pescara and Naples.

Things You Can Do in Lazio

Rome alone will surely keep you busy. The good news is, as you retire here, you can choose to go through these places at your own pace. You may take advantage of its rich cultural and architectural offerings. Here are places you should not miss out:

- Vatican Museums
- Roman Forum
- St. Peter's Basilica

- ★ Palatino
- ★ Colosseum
- ★ Museo e Galleria Borghese
- ★ Capitoline Museums
- ★ Pantheon
- ★ Sistine Chapel
- ★ Museo Nazionale Romano: Palazzo Massimo alle Terme
- ★ Basilica di San Giovanni in Laterano
- ★ Villa Adriana
- ★ Piazza Navona
- ★ Trevi Fountain
- ★ Necropoli di Tarquinia
- ★ Monastero di San Benedetto
- ★ Necropoli di Banditaccia

Is Italy LGBT-friendly?

The country largely accepts and welcomes the lesbian, gay, bisexual and transgender (LGBT) community. Same-sex relationships are legal with civil unions in the law since 2006, with anti-discrimination protections in place. The LGBT community can openly serve in the army, and transgender people can change their gender.

As of this writing, Italy still has not allowed same-sex marriage. It is also essential to keep in mind that smaller towns are more conservative and less accepting of the community. If you intend to retire here as an LGBT couple, it is best to live in the north.

Senior Discounts

People aged 65 years old and above can enjoy senior discounts for as high as 50% for public transportation. If you are a resident in Portugal, you are entitled to many benefits such as exemptions on certain medical bills. There are also huge reductions to utilities such as electricity and gas.

Living in Italy: What to Watch Out For

While Italy promises good wine, good friends and good life, there are still things you have to watch out for. Here are the things you have to deal with upon moving here:

★ **Unemployment is high.**
If you intend to work in Italy while you are sort of 'retired,' your best bet is being self-employed. The unemployment rate in the country is high compared to other parts of Europe. Because of this, thousands of graduating university students may have to wait for a year before securing something stable.

★ **Beware of the language barrier.**
If you want to save money by living in a rural area, you'll find fewer English speakers. You may not find this a problem if you choose to live in cities like Rome, Venice or Milan but in other parts of Italy, you'll have to travel far before meeting someone who can understand you. Retiring in Italy? Start learning the language now.

★ **Beware of grime.**
Grime is very common in Italy. There is a serious problem with cleanliness in the country with the overcrowding of tourists, plus issues of trash collection. You'll find dirty streets, and graffiti everywhere that you'll have to learn to ignore.

★ **The driving culture is a little aggressive.**
Most Italian movies show driving along an open road with vineyards and rolling hills. However, that only exists in the movies. Italian drivers can be quite aggressive and not patient enough when stuck in traffic. Plus, they drive fast. Before driving in Italy, you may want to familiarize yourself first with what is waiting for you.

Summary

There is no doubt that Italy is the epitome of the perfect haven, not only for retirees, but also to the younger folks who are looking for a new place to live a meaningful life. It may not be the cheapest place in the world, but Italy makes sure that it's worth every cent.

Healthcare: ★ ★ ★ ★ ★
Culture: ★ ★ ★ ★ ★
Cost of Living: ★ ★ ★
Housing: ★ ★ ★
Accessibility: ★ ★ ★ ★ ★
Safety: ★ ★ ★

TOTAL STARS: 24 ★

Marsaxlokk, Malta

Retire in Malta

Reasons to Retire in Malta

Locating Malta on the world map is not difficult. You only have to look for an archipelago between Sicily and the North African coast. Though small in size, it boasts numerous historic sites, fortresses and megalithic temples from the Romans, Moors, the Knights of Saint John, the French and the British.

How small is Malta? Here's a quick comparison: Estonia is 143 times its size, while New Zealand, 848 times. It is the size of a big city – it is, after all, the fifth smallest country in the world, after Vatican City, Monaco, San Marino and Liechtenstein.

Malta offers one of the easiest retirement visa schemes for non-Europeans who wish to live and retire on its islands. This visa can be extended indefinitely, which you can apply while you are on a regular tourist visa. There are plenty of benefits for those who are living here. Firstly, it is convenient to get around without owning a car. The whole country is so well-connected that you can easily take the bus.

Secondly, the community is also well-connected and densely packed. There are other retirees with whom you can socialise. If you are looking for a quiet, slower pace of life and want to be closer to nature while also being close to all essential amenities such as the hospital, shopping malls and restaurants, then Malta is for you.

The country offers an affordable retirement, with rent listings going as low as AUD 342. The price of real estate is also not bad for European standards. Going out to eat in a restaurant is reasonable, with three- to four-course menus starting at AUD 34. Otherwise, everyday life is affordable.

Why Retire in Malta:

- ★ Three hundred days of sunshine in a year
- ★ It is an extremely safe country
- ★ English is the official language
- ★ Because it is a small country, most areas are connected by public transportation
- ★ The visa process is straightforward even for non-Europeans

Culture

Malta's culture is influenced by its neighbouring countries, as well as by nations who ruled the country for long centuries. So, who are the Maltese people? Five hundred thousand Maltese live in the country. They are considered Latin European with British and Arab influences. If you look at their diet, you'll find it is mostly Mediterranean.

The main religion in the country is Roman Catholic. The Maltese participate in religious services. Catholicism is taught in school although it is not compulsory. It also has English as its official language along with Maltese, which is the national language. Because of its entry to the European Union, Maltese has become one of the EU's official languages. This means that laws and official documents should also be translated into Maltese. The country has always had a multilingual nature and it's been one of their strengths ever since.

With more foreigners coming into the country for work, or as asylum seekers or refugees, the number of languages being spoken in the country has increased. More schools have developed English courses in recent years aimed at helping non-English speakers. It is also good to keep in mind that most Maltese can speak Italian, which is the third most spoken language here.

Attitude-wise, they can be seen as conservative because of their religion. They dress modestly and tend to be light-hearted as long as no profanities are spoken regarding their country. The Maltese are also hard working, which is one of the reasons why they were awarded the George Cross after World War II. You will also find them to be loud and bubbly, so expect to hear conversations from a nearby table when you're dining. They love to have fun, which explains their festas that are associated with car and stereo tunes.

Climate

Because of its size, the climate is the same throughout the country, and is mostly influenced by the sea. It has Mediterranean weather, pleasantly sunny where the locals enjoy around twelve hours of sunshine in summer and down to six hours by mid-winter.

Winter brings mild rain and wind lasting from December to February. Cold days are still rare. The coldest night of the year usually ranges around 4–5 degrees Celsius. It does not snow, although it did once in December 2014 – very light snowfall in some areas, particularly in the highest part of the island.

Springtime promises less rain. And by April the sun shines more and more. Keep in mind that during this period, Malta may experience Sirocco, the hot and dry wind that comes from the Saharan desert during spring and autumn.

Summer lasts from June to August. It is hot, dry and sunny. From July to October, everyone can enjoy swimming in the warm waters. The wind from Africa also helps in bringing in very hot periods that sometimes reaches up to 40 degrees Celsius.

Cost of Living

Thinking of moving to Europe? Malta is one of the most affordable countries you may consider. Surprisingly, your dollar can go far in this country, given that you're in the middle of the Mediterranean islands. Of course, the cost of living varies depending on where you want to live or the kind of lifestyle that you prefer, but generally, the expenses are still reasonable.

The groceries are affordable. Basic items such as bread only cost AUD 0.48. You can safely allocate a budget of AUD 684 for groceries every month. Transportation-wise, a full-day bus ticket will cost you AUD 5.47, while a one-month bus ticket is AUD 38.29. You don't have to own a car, nor allocate money for gasoline because the transportation system is well-connected.

AUD 2,051 is sufficient for a single person per month, while a couple will require AUD 3009 per month to cover the necessities. Dining out tends to be expensive, so you may want to limit that to once a week. To minimize your rent, you may want to avoid the main island of Malta and instead go for Gozo, a more laid back and cheaper place to live.

Expenses	Prices
Housing rent (average area)	AUD 726
High-speed internet	AUD 52
Electricity and water	AUD 99
Phone with basic data plan	AUD 21
Loaf of white bread	AUD 1.58
A dozen eggs	AUD 3
Local beer	AUD 2.75
Taxi per kilometre	AUD 3.45

Housing

Before purchasing a property in Malta, keep in mind that, if you are a non-EU citizen, you'll need to obtain an acquisition of immovable property (AIP) permit from the Ministry of Finance, and the entire process can take up to three months. With this permit, you are only allowed to purchase one residential property with the intention to use it only for yourself and your family. Expect to pay AUD 322631 for a two-bedroom apartment in Gozo.

Renting an apartment is also not a bad idea. It can start at AUD 726 a month. If you want something bigger, then prepare AUD 1,129 for a two-bedroom house per month.

Nursing homes are available in the country, but the choices are limited. They offer sufficient services such as everyday meals and personal care and organise various activities such as bible stories, bingo and cooking sessions.

Healthcare in Malta

Malta may be small but did you know that it has been ranked the world's fifth for overall healthcare services? The country has a strong public healthcare system that provides free services to all of its citizens, as well as EU residents who have the European Health Insurance Card (EHIC).

Malta has several public hospitals with a huge one on the island of Gozo. The size of the country makes its healthcare accessible to everyone. There are two private hospitals that offer a range of services and boast the latest in medical technology. A network of health clinics and pharmacies are also present.

For those who are non-EU citizens, you must obtain private healthcare insurance. Prices vary depending on your age, health and needs. Getting private health insurance in Malta is relatively cheaper compared to that in the USA. You can check out Laferla and Bupa which also cover CT and MRI scans. Medical costs are affordable. A visit to the doctor costs approximately AUD 27 while consulting a specialist, AUD 89. You can check for packages, for example, there is a package that includes a mammogram, a bone density test and blood work analysis for only AUD 230.

How to Retire in Malta (Retirement Visa)*

The best visa to get if you want to call Malta your home for retirement is the permanent residence permit. It allows you to live in the country but not work, and instead live off your pension or retirement fund. There are three main requirements to obtain it:

★ You must have a net worth of at least USD 39,5130 or earn an annual income of at least USD 26,100.

★ You must have a clean criminal record.

★ You have to go through an interview process.

Upon receiving the permanent resident permit, you should either purchase a house worth USD 132,463 or an apartment at least USD 80,000. Otherwise, you need to provide proof that you paid at least USD 4,700 in annual rent. This is also required to open a Maltese bank account.

This permit can be renewed annually and once you've lived in Malta for five years, you may apply for permanent residence. This will afford you all the same rights as before, but this time, you only need to renew your permit or card every five years.

If you are married to an EU national, you and your spouse can live in Malta without the need of a visa. All you need to do is apply for an e-residence card upon arrival.

* **USD has been retained as default currency for all immigration investment figures. Currency exchange rate USD1 = AUD1.36.**

Work*

The residence permit does not allow you to work while living in Malta. If you intend to work instead, then you must apply for a single work permit. You may choose to invest USD 700,000 in the country and get citizenship automatically.

* **USD has been retained as default currency for all immigration investment figures. Currency exchange rate USD1 = AUD1.36.**

Tax**

With the permanent visa, you will be subject to taxes on capital gains and income you earn from Maltese sources. That includes selling your property for gain. Since you are not permitted to work in Malta, you won't be subjected to any income tax. Do check with your respective countries if you still need to file your taxes there.

Should you, in any case, decide to get a working permit instead, here is a quick guide for married resident taxpayers:

Taxable Income	Tax Rate
0 – EUR 12,700	0%
EUR 12,701 – EUR 21,200	15%
EUR 21,201 – EUR 28,700	25%
EUR 28,701 – EUR 60,000	25%
EUR 60,001+	35%

** **EUR has been retained as default currency for all tax figures. Currency exchange rate EUR1 = AUD1.61.**

Food

The influences on the Maltese food scene come from all of its neighbours as well as from the civilizations that have occupied the islands for centuries. It is an eclectic combination of Mediterranean cooking. Food is a big deal in the country, and the Maltese are big fans of their cuisine.

Maltese food is rustic and based on seasons. This is obvious in their lampuki pie (fish pie), bragioli (beef olives), and kapunata (Maltese ratatouille). Try going to the Marsaxlokk fish market on a Sunday morning and it will show you the variety of seafood caught in its waters which vary in its seasons too.

Their food is so full of flavour and healthy, but it can also be calorie dense. Meals served at home are aplenty with savory dishes, making it the largest part of Maltese cuisine. These qualities of Maltese food are cause for high figures on the weighing scale, so you might want to watch what you eat and make sure to balance it with exercise. Here are the best Maltese dishes to get used to when you live here:

- **Stuffat tal-fenek** is a traditional rabbit stew, considered to be the national dish of Malta. It is slow cooked so that the meat falls off the bone. It blends perfectly with tomato, garlic sauce and red wine.

- **Kapunata** is a popular summer dish in Malta, made of tomatoes, capers, aubergines and green peppers. This is their version of ratatouille.

- **Minestra** refers to thick vegetable soup, with vegetables cut to large pieces or mashed. It is always served with rustic bread and olive oil.

- **Pastizzi** is the most popular snack in the country. It is savory pastry filled with mushy peas or ricotta and you'll find it across the country, so it is easy to spot and try one.

- **Ħobż tal-Malti** is another Maltese bread with a crusty exterior and a soft inside. It is based in wood ovens and eaten with olive oil. The bread is usually spread with tomato paste with olive oil and a choice or mix of capers, tuna, olives, onion, bigilla and gbejna.

- **Timpana** is a baked macaroni pie made with a variety of meat, vegetables, cheese, shortcrust pastry and bolognaise sauce. It is similar to the Italian timpano which is an encasing of tubular pasta.

- **Qagħaq tal-għasel** refers to the Maltese traditional Christmas biscuit. It is literally translated as honey rings. It is made with cloves, treacle, star anise, all spice and blackstrap molasses.

- **Cassata** is a colourful cake originating from Sicily. It is made of almond paste, sweet ricotta and marzipan.

- **Lampuki** pie is a result of Maltese people making good use of Malta's abundance of fish. Lampuki is a type of fish that is commonly caught around the island. In this pie, it is perfectly combined with potatoes, spinach, capers mint and olive oil.

There is no shortage of restaurants in Malta so if you are craving for international cuisine, whether Asian, Russian or South American, you can have them all here.

Recommended Cities in Malta

Sliema

This is probably one of the liveliest parts of the Maltese islands. With a population of 15,000, countless restaurants, bars, shops, cafes and hotels as well as its thriving dining and nightlife scene, there are plenty of things to do, explore and eat. The locals call it the shopping capital of the country. Because it is so popular, parking spaces here can be a big problem. Living in Sliema offers all the amenities you will need from schools, supermarkets, churches to pharmacies.

It is in the centre of the mainland, which means it is very well-connected. You will find people of all sorts of nationalities in this area of Malta, from British, Swedish, Eastern European and American. The ambiance is very international, and you will not have a hard time adjusting.

Furthermore, the coastal town has recently enjoyed a huge cultural revival. It wants to be the next big place for young entrepreneurs as well as working expatriates. A lot of people assume that it is expensive to live here, given the high quality of life it offers, but as long as you're patient enough to look closer, you'll find rent as cheap as AUD 1,095.

Essentials in Sliema:

- **Healthcare:** With the size of Malta, it is surprising to find plenty of hospitals easily accessible to everyone in the mainland. Here are some hospitals in and around Sliema.
  - Mater Dei Hospital
  - St. Luke's Hospital
  - Sir Paul Boffa Hospital
- **Accessibility:** Sliema is only 20 minutes away from the International Airport of Malta. The international airport connects the Maltese to cities around the world such as Athens, London, Madrid, Copenhagen and Doha.

Things You Can Do in Sliema

The Maltese definitely know how to live the ideal island life, from taking a stroll along the promenade, cheering the country's most successful football team to celebrating its annual parish feasts. With the rising expat community in Sliema, particularly young, techie entrepreneurs (some lured by the online gaming industry), you will surely feel forever young as you spend your retirement days here. Here are some points of interest in this tiny city:

- Tigne Point Beach
- Sliema Promenade
- Fort Tigne
- Manoel Island
- Fond Ghadir
- The Point Shopping Mall
- Parish Church of Sacro Cuor

St. Julian

This is one of the most sought-after regions in the main island, and is locally known as San Giljan. It is a vibrant seaside town, right in the centre of action and filled with activities. The town was originally a fishing village that was briefly occupied by the French. It is filled with ancient Latin architecture such as the Spinola Palace. The Portomaso Marina, full of luxury yachts and high-end restaurants and bars, is frequented by tourists in the summer.

The cost of living here is higher compared to other areas, but it also means you will be close to amenities such as local food shops, a large cinema, bowling alley, and shopping malls that sell everything you need. You will also find the nightlife to be lively. Currently, it has about 8,000 residents breathing life into the town, creating a community spirit. St. Julian has different developed areas in which to live. Some of the popular areas are Paceville, Portomaso, Pender Gardens, Swieqi, Madliena and Spinola Bay. Regular bus routes link these villages to the rest of the mainland.

Essentials in St. Julian

- **Healthcare:** Being in the mainland has its advantages, including having several hospitals and clinics surrounding St. Julian. Here are some of them:
  - Saint Thomas Hospital
  - Mount Carmel Hospital
  - Saint James Hospital
- **Accessibility:** St. Julian is 30 minutes away from Malta International Airport. Its location makes it the perfect place to be if you want to travel outside the country. Malta Airport offers flight to most parts of Europe.

Things You Can Do in St. Julian

There are things to do beyond clubbing in St. Julian. After all, this is where you'll feel the hustle and bustle of a European Mediterranean city. It is a modern town that has developed rapidly since 1960. Its accessibility to the airport – being located at the northern coastline of Malta, adjacent to Sliema, with a few miles away the capital city of Valletta – means St. Julian is at the centre of it all. Here are places of interest that you can explore should you decide to stay in this busy city:

- Lapsi Church
- Spinola Palace
- St. Julian's Parish Church
- Portomaso Tower
- Palazzo Parisio
- Vineyards
- St. George's Bay
- Paceville
- Dragonara Casino
- Balluta Square
- Parish Church of Our Lady of Mount Carmel
- Bay Street Shopping Centre

Gozo

Imagine walking along a beautiful coast in the middle of January with the warm sun on your skin and gentle breeze on your face. Retiring in Gozo means you can enjoy majestic coastal walks every day.

Now imagine, waking up every morning to the sound of nature, while the aroma of fresh bread and dried herbs enters your window. This is a common sight in Gozo, a small island in Malta as big as 26 square miles in the Mediterranean, just a little south of Sicily. This is also the second largest island in the archipelago, with about 37,000 in population. Many say the island is what Malta used to be like. The island is quiet and rural, and is known for gbejniet, or mild goat cheese (similar to mozzarella).

Living here means you can save a lot of money from the rent alone. You can rent a one-bedroom apartment for as cheap as AUD 342 a month. A bus ticket only costs AUD 1.36 for the whole day, with 50% off if you're a senior.

You'll also have access to fresh, local food and quiet areas. The locals are also approachable and will find time for you.

Essentials in Gozo:

- ★ **Healthcare:** There is only one hospital, called Gozo General Hospital. It provides both inpatient and outpatient medical and surgical services. It is also equipped with an emergency service that can connect you to the hospitals on the mainland. An air ambulance is also available if necessary. The hospital has a capacity of about 270 beds with services ranging from radiology, maternity, paediatric, dentistry, psychiatry, acupuncture to chemotherapy.

- ★ **Accessibility:** With the Gozo ferry sailing 74 times a day, every day, the island is very accessible to the main island of Malta, which is an hour away. Crossing onto the next island guarantees beautiful views so make sure to prepare your camera. The ticket is also as cheap as AUD 8.07 per way.

Things You Can Do in Gozo

The much quieter sister of Malta is less urbanized and provides a more laid back experience. Even in winter, you'll find it a greener island that guarantees pleasant, long walks in the countryside. In summer, the alluring beaches and clear waters are something to remember. Sandy beaches are quite limited in Gozo but the few that are there are really stunning. Here are places you can explore and re-explore as you spend your retirement in this tiny island:

- ★ Calypso's Cave
- ★ Qbajjar
- ★ Tal-Merzuq Hill
- ★ Wied l-Ghasri
- ★ Carnival in Gozo
- ★ Borg l-Imramma
- ★ Ras il-Wardija Nymphaeum
- ★ Ggantija Temple
- ★ The Gozo Museum of Archeology
- ★ Cittadella Cathedral

Is Malta LGBT-friendly?

Malta enjoys the high standards of lesbian, gay, bisexual and transgender (LGBT) rights compared to other European countries. It is one of the few countries in the world that made LGBT rights equal at a constitutional level. It is a safe environment for foreign LGBT couples who decide to call Malta their home.

Any kind of discrimination on the basis of sexual orientation has been banned since 2004. LGBT

people can serve in the military and transgenders are allowed to change their legal gender without any medical intervention.

Same-sex marriage has been legal here since September 2017. A couple can form a civil union which allows them to adopt children. The country is also the first European state to add gender identity to their constitution as a protected category.

In recent years, the living conditions for the LGBT community have continuously improved. Same-sex relationships are widely accepted in the public.

Senior Discounts

Foreign residents in Malta who are between 75 and 79 years old will benefit from the Senior Citizen Grand Discount which is a one-time payment every year. The amount is EUR 300 (AUD 484). For those who are 90 years old and above, the amount of EUR 350 (AUD 564) is granted. Local transportation cost is also offered at 50% off.

Living in Malta: What to Watch Out For

No place is paradise. Like anywhere else in the world, there are some things you have to factor in before you decide that Malta is for you. Here are some things to watch out for:

★ **Non-violent crimes are increasing.**
This includes pickpocketing and burglaries. Although it is nowhere near EU-average levels, it is bothering the locals who are used to leaving their houses and cars unlocked. The police have been successful at catching criminals, but living here still requires vigilance.

★ **Lack of natural diversity.**
Malta only consists of seven islands, three of which are inhabited. There are beaches but they tend to get overcrowded, especially during summertime. There are a few nature reserves but if you've been there and done that, you may crave to see more, which will require you to travel out of the country.

★ **Lack of space.**
If you prefer to have plenty of space with not so many people, then Malta is not for you. It is one of the most densely populated places in the world and its population just keeps on expanding year after year.

Summary

Malta's charm and offer of an easy life keeps the country on our list. It may be small, but other essentials such as healthcare, cost of living, available entertainment, attractive property prices, tax incentives and accessibility make it an ideal place for foreign retirees. The country has a British feel to it, minus the rain and, of course, the prices.

Healthcare: ★★★★★
Culture: ★★★★
Cost of Living: ★★★
Housing: ★★★
Accessibility: ★★★★
Safety: ★★★★

TOTAL STARS: 23 ★

Lisbon, Portugal

Reasons to Retire in Portugal

Portugal has been attracting more foreign retirees for years now, and there are great reasons for it. The cost of living is lower compared to France and Germany. Lisbon is the only European capital where you can get coffee for only 50 cents. Food is cheap even in restaurants, where you can expect to pay AUD 16 for a full menu. Real estate is also enjoying a 'golden age' in the country. You can get good property away from the tourist areas at a cheaper price.

Additionally, there is a variety of landscapes you can enjoy despite it being a small country. It may be six times smaller than France, but each region has something different to offer. You'll find the northern part of Portugal to be mountainous with lots of green natural parks. When you reach the Douro and Tagus Rivers, you can admire Serra de Estrela, the highest point of the country at 2,351 meters. Onto the south of the Tagus River, you will be greeted by wide plains filled with Mediterranean species.

Another advantage of living here is Portuguese gastronomy. It is hearty and of good quality. Fresh vegetables and seafood filled the market and retiring here will allow you the time to explore them all. Aside from the food, the Portuguese are known for having a good life expectancy because of the good private health system.

Why Retire in Portugal:

- ★ Blessed with sunshine, with over 300 days of sun especially in the southern part
- ★ Has some of the best beaches in Europe
- ★ Vibrant cities packed with restaurants, cafes, museums and art
- ★ Portuguese food is fresh and delicious

Culture

There are both positives and negatives in Portuguese culture. Let's take a look at the former first. Portuguese people are some of the kindest and most compassionate people you'll meet. They are hospitable and know how to welcome retirees from all parts of the world. Just don't be gullible to well-crafted scams and you'll be fine.

Portuguese people value their friends and family. They are also open-minded and tend to get talkative. Still, making friends in Portugal for non-Portuguese is hard especially if you don't try to speak the language. It is not essential to learn the language, but the locals will assume that expatriates don't prefer to integrate. A good number of Portuguese can speak English, learning from American TV shows, however they simply won't speak it. Thus, to get by, learning at least the basic Portuguese is recommended. Alternatively, talk about the things they care about, such as football. Everybody loves football so much that whenever the team plays, the whole country watches it.

Now, for the negative traits: Don't be surprised if you find old people staring at you for no apparent reason. It is common for them to stare from their balconies or windows or from their car. The Portuguese can be nosey people, but they do not mean disrespect. They are simply surprised or curious. Punctuality is not seen as important in the country. It is normal to arrive five minutes or even thirty minutes late.

Climate

Portugal offers one of the most ideal climates for retirees, with its position in the south-western tip of Europe by the Atlantic Ocean and Mediterranean. It is neither too cold nor too hot, with an average temperature of 15 degrees Celsius in the north and 18 degrees Celsius in the south.

The country, with its Mediterranean climate, gets warm and dry summers while winter remains cool and wet. What people enjoy the most in Portugal is the amount of sunshine it gets, especially in Algarve. Amareleja is one of the hottest places, having recorded 47 degrees Celsius during summer.

There is higher rainfall in the northwest part of the country. Snow is only common in the mountainous regions of the north which includes Serra de Estrela, its highest peak.

Cost of Living

The low cost of living in Portugal attracts many retirees to the country, given the western European way of living. Everything from rent to groceries is affordable compared to its neighbours, Spain, France and Italy.

Food costs are low. Luxury items that are expensive elsewhere such as wine or olive only cost AUD 5 a bottle here. Restaurant meals are not expensive which will cost approximately AUD 13 – 18. Dinner for two with wine included costs about AUD 40.25. Utilities will not exceed AUD 161. However, you need to find ways to heat your apartment during the mild winter.

A lot of locals in Portugal live for only AUD 1,208 a month. With AUD 3,220 for couples, you can enjoy an excellent lifestyle in Portugal. City-wise, Lisbon is the most expensive city in the country, followed by Cascais, Porto and Coimbra. Here's what your monthly expenses will look like in Mafra (near the Lisbon coast):

Expenses	Prices
Housing rent	AUD 685
High-speed internet	AUD 55
Electricity and water	AUD 192
Phone with basic data plan	AUD 21
Loaf of white bread	AUD 1.90
A dozen eggs	AUD 3.15
Local beer	AUD 3.43
Taxi per kilometre	AUD 5.75

Housing

Renting a humble city apartment in the capital or in Algarve will cost around AUD 966. If you are fine with living in other areas of Portugal, you can still lower your rental expense down to AUD 725 and if the space is unfurnished, it can be cheaper still. If you prefer something more spacious and with more rooms, then be prepared to pay AUD 1,610 a month.

It is possible to own property in Portugal. For instance, a two-bedroom apartment in Algarve will cost about AUD 241,5000 – AUD 290,000. The price is even better in Coimbra and Cascais where it can get to AUD 241,500 for a three-bedroom apartment. Go to rural areas and you can even find properties as low as AUD 161,000.

Retirement villages are available too. For example, there is a site by Senior Living Portugal, nestled in Tavira town, in Eastern Algarve, there are facilities that offer preferred care solutions where experienced staff can assist you in whatever you need. The monthly rates include all meals, care and a range of services and activities. If you think you can manage independently, the retirement village can just rent out an apartment for you, whether you prefer to face the sea or the city centre.

Healthcare in Portugal

The country has some of the finest doctors in the world. Portugal ranks in the top 12 of the World Health Organization for its global healthcare system, compared to Canada which is at 30th place and the USA at 37th.

Staff speak English because many graduated from the finest universities in the UK and other European countries. You can also find them in smaller towns in rural areas.

Public healthcare is accessible to both temporary and permanent residents. For foreign retirees, you must have a Portuguese número de contribuinte, or social security number, to access state facilities. Upon entering the country, you still need to get medical insurance, but this will not be asked for again when you renew.

Private healthcare is more popular for expatriates. Private clinics and hospitals are available throughout the country and their number continues to grow daily. The good news is it only costs AUD 8 – 16 to consult with a doctor in the public sector, while a private clinic charges AUD 81. Dental cleaning is free in public clinics and costs AUD 40 in private clinics.

There are as many pharmacies as there are cafes in Portugal. You'll distinguish them by their flashing green neon cross on all four corners. You can choose between a traditional pharmacy or an "American-style" drugstore. The latter allows you to buy drugs without prescription.

How to Retire in Portugal (Retirement Visa)*

There are two visa routes if you decide Portugal is your retirement place.

* The Retirement Visa (D7 or Passive Income visa) is for those who don't desire to work in Portugal but have a steady income from pension or savings. The application procedure is straightforward; it includes proof of monthly income of at least EUR 1,000, accommodation, health insurance and criminal background clearance.

* The application can be done at your local Portugal embassy which will be valid for a year. You can then renew it twice each time for two years, and once you reach the fifth year, you may apply for permanent residency in Portugal. Keep in mind that you must spend at least six months in the country each year to get a permanent residence permit.

* The Golden Visa program is for those who can purchase a property of at least EUR 500,000, invest at least EUR 350,000 in an urban regeneration area or donate EUR 350,000 for research activities.

With this type of visa, you and your family members can live and work in Portugal and have access to the health and education system. You can also have visa-free access to Schengen and, five years later, get a Portuguese passport. To start with your application, find the ARI portal and create an account. Having this visa option does not require you to actually live in Portugal to get a permanent residency. Seven days in one year is the minimum amount of time you need to be in Portugal.

Between the two, getting the retirement visa is easy enough so it is not necessary to invest on the latter. Both offer the options to have your family members join you while living in Portugal.

* EUR has been retained as default currency for all tax and immigration investment figures in this article. Currency exchange rate EUR1 = AUD1.61.

Work

The D7 visa's flexibility permits retirees to work and study in Portugal. You can also work as a freelancer or as an employee without any additional authorization.

Portugal also welcomes expatriates who want to start their business, but in this case, you have to apply for the start-up visa (D2). This visa is suitable for entrepreneurs, freelancers and people who intend to open or buy a company in Portugal. An additional requirement for this visa is a business plan as proof of your initiative.

Tax**

Residents of Portugal get taxed on their worldwide income, but by applying as a non-habitual resident (NHR), foreigners are entitled to favourable tax arrangements for the next ten years. The scheme was approved in 2009 and was consistently promoted by the country to expats to attract foreign pensioners. For ten years, any income from wealth, capital gain, inheritance, gift from close relatives, will not be subject to tax. After ten years, however, foreign pension is going to be taxable by 10%.

Meanwhile, any type of income earned in the country is subject to a progressive rate. You may refer to the table:

Income	Tax Rate
Lower than EUR 7,112	14.5%
EUR 7,113 – EUR 10,732	23%
EUR 10,733 – EUR 20,322	28.5%
EUR 20,323 – 25,075	35%
EUR 25,076 – EUR 39,967	37%
EUR 39,968 – EUR 80,882	45%
EUR 80,883+	48%

* EUR has been retained as default currency for all tax and immigration investment figures in this article. Currency exchange rate EUR1 = AUD1.61.

Food

One common myth about Portuguese cuisine is that it is similar to Spanish cuisine. Yes, both countries have tomato and bean-based stews, as well as paella, but there is more to Portuguese cuisine, and it goes beyond Port wine and bacalhau.

The influences from former colonies of Portugal are notable in the cuisine. There is a wide variety of spices used in dishes, from small, fiery chili peppers, cumin to nutmeg, that are used in multiple savory dishes. Garlic and onions are widely used, as well as thyme, mint, rosemary and coriander. Olive oil is also one of the bases of the cuisine. Another distinctive characteristic is the presence of bread in every meal.

Portugal is full of specialty seafood restaurants where you'll often find lobsters, shrimp, oysters displayed artistically. The traditional breakfast only consists of coffee and bread rolls, while lunch remains to be a big affair that can last for a couple of hours. Dinner is often late with three courses. Retiring in Portugal means having more opportunity to explore its cuisine that varies by the region:

- ★ **Caldo Verde** is a hearty, comfort soup. It is cooked with cabbage, particularly Couve Galega, onion, garlic, potato and chorizo.

- ★ **Bacalhau** is cod that although not native in Portuguese waters, became a national obsession, so much that the Portuguese have 365 ways of preparing it, from grilled, baked, canned to fried.

- ★ **Alheira** is a smoked sausage that is made of poultry (not pork). While chorizo does not need to be cooked, Alheira has to be fried for a few minutes. The Portuguese often eat it as snacks or even as the main meal, served with fried eggs and fries.

- ★ **Bifanas** are sandwiches containing slides of pork that are marinated and simmered in a sauce of garlic, paprika and white wine, and served on soft bread rolls with mustard and piri-piri sauce.

- ★ **Chicken Piri-Piri** (also known as Frango Churrasco) refers to the roasted chicken seasoned with Piri-Piri sauce. If you've been to Nando's or Oporto in Australia, you've probably tried it. This amazing dish came all the way from Mozambique, a former colony of Portugal, and because the Portuguese love it so much, they opened lots of Piri-Piri restaurants everywhere.

- ★ **Bifana** is a pork steak sandwich filled with garlic and spicy sauce, originating from Vendas Novas. Between the North and South of Portugal, it is served differently. In the former, the pork steak is cut into thin pieces and comes with a big pot of spicy sauce, while in the latter they do not cut the meat and the sauce is not as spicy.

* **Arroz de Marisco**, or seafood rice, is appreciated by many locals. It is usually eaten at a festival or important day in Portugal. It is a combination of different seafood such as mussels, shrimps and lobsters while the rice is slowly cooked in seafood broth.

* **Grilled Sardines** are served during saints' festivals in summertime. Portugal has an abundance of fish in its coast so sardines is a typical dish, served with cornbread and roasted red peppers.

* **Carne de Porco** a Alentejana, actually from Algarve even if it mentions Alentejo, is made with pork meat, clams, garlic, paprika, red wine, bay leaf and coriander.

* **Pastel de Nata** is the most famous dessert in the country originated from Jeronimos Monastery's monks in Lisbon. People around the world love its crunchy tart filled with delicious egg cream, roasted in the oven, toppled with cinnamon.

If you suddenly find yourself craving for international cuisine, there are Asian and other Western restaurants you may indulge in in the city centre.

Recommended Cities in Portugal

The Algarve

A retiree's life in the Algarve will never be dull because there are plenty of things to do. There's sunbathing, golfing, tennis, horseback riding and hiking to name a few. You can walk the cobbled streets and climb the castle ramparts where you can view the Great White Stork.

The Algarve is the most popular choice in the country to retire because of its lovely weather, which makes it easy to explore around. There is also a variety of geological formations and a wide stretch of beach.

There are more people speaking English in this part of Portugal so it will be easier to adjust.

We recommend three locations where you can settle in the region: Alvor, Olhão and Vilamoura.

Alvor is a traditional fishing village with nice beaches and a small marina. The narrow streets are filled with cafes and restaurants. If you want to experience the essence of the country, Olhão is the way to go; it is Algarve's largest port. Its old quarter has a Moorish character filled with whitewashed houses. If you want to have an upscale kind of living, then choose Vilamoura where there are elegant hotels and fine restaurants.

Algarve is not the cheapest place to be in Portugal, but it is possible to find apartments that cost AUD 685 a month.

Essentials in The Algarve:

* **Healthcare:** There are plenty of hospitals and clinics to choose from in Algarve. The three main hospitals (the first three mentioned below) can provide serious medical assistance as well as emergency care.
  * Hospital of Faro
  * Hospital of Portimao
  * Hospital of Lagos
  * Hospital Particular do Algarve – Gambelas – Faro
  * Hospital Particular do Algarve – Alvor
  * Clínica Particular do Algarve
  * International Health Centres

* **Accessibility:** Faro Airport is the major airport in Algarve, only 4 km outside the city of Faro, the largest city in the region. Direct flights to Lisbon only take about 45 minutes. Driving, which will only take 3 hours, is also an option.

Things You Can Do in The Algarve

Algarve has earned its reputation for having a resort feel, while keeping its authenticity. Easy to award-winning golf courses can be found on the coastline. The restaurant culture here is amazing with dining scenes ranging from local food to small cafes, to Michelin-starred restaurants. Here are the top places to explore while spending your days here:

* Faro
* Vila Real de Santo Antonio
* Alcoutim
* Tavira
* Olhão
* Loule
* Vilamoura
* Albufeira
* Silves
* Portimão
* Serra de Monchique
* Lagos
* Sagres
* The West Coast

Porto

The second largest city in Portugal, after the capital, Lisbon is found in the Douro River. The vibrant city has lots happening all year round, where you can step back in history and tradition. With a small city's feel, around 240,000 people call it home. International businesses surely thrive here, which makes it easy for expats to find the amenities they need.

There is no need to own a car in Porto because it boasts an extensive bus network and a tramway. The town, anyway, is best explored by foot. You can witness the beautiful architecture such as the São Bento train station, the church of São Francisco and Café Majestic.

The lifestyle in Porto is interwoven with their love for food and wine. After all, its fortified wine has made the city famous. It fits well with their love for parties. In midsummer, you can participate in Festa de São João, or the festival of St. John, when thousands of people flood the streets.

Essentials in Porto

* **Healthcare:** Second to Lisbon, Porto has some of the best hospitals in the country. Here is a list of our recommended hospitals:

- Geral de Santo Antônio Central Hospital
- Clinica Central do Bonfim LDA
- Hospital CUF
- Hospital Central Especializado de Crianças Maria Pia
- Julio Dinis Maternity Hospital
- Instituto CUF
- Lusiadas Saude

★ **Accessibility:** Porto Airport connects the city to other European cities such as Madrid, Paris, London, Brussels, Luxembourg, and Istanbul. Meanwhile, Lisbon is only a 3-hour drive from Porto.

Things You Can Do in Porto

With the famous Douro River as the ultimate backdrop of the city, it is impossible not to fall in love with Porto's colours and charms. One minute, you'll find cobblestone laneways, the next, a beautiful landscape of beaches greeting you. If you enjoy history and culture, you're sure to frequent the Porto Cathedral and the Stock Exchange Palace. If you love arts, you can hang out at the National Museum or at the Contemporary Art Museum. Here are the places you can explore while you're here:

- Dom Luis Bridge
- Se do Porto
- Jardins do Palácio de Cristal
- Avenida dos Aliados
- Parque de Cidade do Porto
- Estação de São Bento
- Capela das Almas
- Mercado do Bolhão
- Porto beaches
- Igreja de São Francisco
- Livraria Lello & Irmão
- Palacio da Bolsa
- Fundação de Serralves
- Dragão Stadium
- Clerigos Church
- Cais da Ribeira
- Igreja do Carmo
- Porto Bridge Climb
- Casa da Musica
- Mosteiro da Serra do Pilar
- Igreja dos Carmelitas

Coimbra

With a population of 144,000, Coimbra can be both a busy and mellow metropolis. It was Portugal's former capital and home to the oldest universities in Europe. One is situated high on a hill, and as you descend the steep and narrow streets of Baixa you will find a series of alleys filled with shops and cafes.

It has a youthful vibe to it, so it is possible to get by speaking only in English. It is a city with lots of history and culture to offer, starting from the National Museum of Machado de Castro on Largo Doutor José Rodrigues to the galleries where art collections thrive.

If you want to enjoy listening to Fado, the traditional music form of Portugal, there is no better place to hear it than here. Surprisingly, the real estate prices here are affordable. The same thing goes with rental places where you can get the best stretch of your money.

Essentials in Coimbra

★ **Healthcare:** Coimbra has some of the hospitals with the highest quality standards with a broader medical

therapy. There are also medical clinics that offer first-class treatment for each health issue. Here are some of the top hospitals in the region:

- ★ Centro Cirúrgico de Coimbra
- ★ Coimbra University Hospital
- ★ IdealMed Unidade Hospitalar de Coimbra

★ **Accessibility:** There is no airport in Coimbra, but its proximity to Lisbon of only a two-hour drive makes it accessible.

Things You Can Do in Coimbra

Your day in this medieval university town between Lisbon and Porto can start with a stroll along the ribbon of the River Mondego running through the city, followed by a lunch at the riverfront café, then a walk around the alleys of shops. Its youthful population can easily influence your retirement days. Here are the places to see in Coimbra:

- ★ Velha Universidade de Coimbra
- ★ Igreja de Santa Cruz
- ★ Se Velha
- ★ Se Nova
- ★ Machado de Castro National Museum
- ★ Mosteiro de Santa Clara-a-Velha
- ★ Mosteiro de Santa Clara-a-Nova
- ★ Arco de Almedina
- ★ Jardim Botânico
- ★ Portugal dos Pequenitos
- ★ Jardins da Quinta das Lágrimas
- ★ Praca do Comercio

Is Portugal LGBT-friendly?

Portugal's lesbian, gay, bisexual and transgender (LGBT) rights have improved in the last two decades and are considered to be the best in the world. Homosexuality was first decriminalized in 1982 after the Carnation Revolution. Portugal is also the eighth country in the world to recognize same-sex marriage.

Although the country is strongly influenced by Roman Catholicism, the country has embraced homosexuality, with 80% of the population believing that the LGBT community should have the same rights as heterosexuals. This is obvious in Lisbon and Porto where you'll find several gay bars and nightclubs. Under Portuguese law, the adoption of children by same-sex couples has been allowed.

Senior Discounts

People aged 65 years old and above can enjoy senior discounts for as high as 50% on public transportation. If you are a resident of Portugal, you are entitled to many benefits such as exemption on certain medical bills. There are also huge reductions on utilities such as electricity and gas.

Living in Portugal: What to Watch Out For

Nowhere is perfect. While Portugal offers a lot of pros to living here, there are also downsides. Go through the following before deciding if Portugal is right for you:

- ★ **Portuguese Houses tend to be cold during winter.**
  This is because most properties don't have central heating, which means you may have to wear your winter jacket (and gloves) inside. Warm properties are also available, but you have to look carefully and ask the right questions. Even if Portugal is enjoying sunshine, you still need to watch out for winter which is cold, grey and damp in some places.

- ★ **Portugal is not a place to find a job.**
  Although Portugal attracts a lot of retirees, it is not a place to find a job with a great salary. Compared to other Western European countries, Portugal still has a long way to catch up salary-wise. By European standards, there are a limited number of jobs here and salaries are low. If you are going to choose to retire in Portugal, you can forget about finding a job, or consider starting a business instead.

- ★ **The ocean is cold.**
  Yes, there are plenty of beaches in Portugal and that's good news, especially if you love being in the water. However, keep in mind that it is the Atlantic Ocean, not the Mediterranean Sea. In the region, this is unique to Portugal; other countries such as Spain and Greece enjoy warmer waters.

- ★ **Bureaucracy in Portugal is overwhelming.**
  Bureaucracy is common in most countries, but it's not only because of it that makes living in Portugal difficult. It can be difficult to know which person you need to speak to, or which form you have to fill up. You have to figure these things out yourself. If you can pay someone else to do the paperwork for you, whether it concerns visas or taxes. There are companies that can make things go faster. Alternatively, you may join Facebook groups and forums to find people who have encountered the same thing.

Summary

Portugal remains to be an attractive destination for retirees around the world. The country is stunningly beautiful, rich in history and culture, serves delicious cuisine and on top of the safety index. The low cost of living is just icing on the cake.

Healthcare: ★★★★
Culture: ★★★★
Cost of Living: ★★★★
Housing: ★★★
Accessibility: ★★★★★
Safety: ★★★

TOTAL STARS: 23 ★

Plaza Mayor, Madrid, Spain

Reasons to Retire in Spain

Spain is one of the most famous locations for both tourists and retirees from all over the world. Every year, there are over thousands of expatriates choosing the country to be their new home. Who wouldn't fall in love with its warm climate and beaches? Plus, you'll have easy access to all parts of Europe.

Living here means you will get a good combination of both the old and the new. Spain boasts a long and rich history, world-class infrastructure and good quality of living at a cheaper price. Outside Madrid and Barcelona, you'll find better value for your money. You can explore its diverse terrain across regions. Each region in Spain offers a distinct gastronomy and culture that will enrich your life.

Spanish people also tend to be more active. They busy themselves with activities such as sailing, art classes, language learning – you name it. They love to organize social events, from a simple meal to a trip around the country. If you love a laid-back and family-oriented culture, then retiring in Spain will be the best option for you.

As it is a part of the European Union, you can enjoy the benefits of traveling to different countries from the Schengen area. The bonus of it all? Spain has a great public health system, one of the best in the world. Healthcare in Spain is affordable and offers a good level of service.

Why Retire in Spain:

- ★ A European country where you can enjoy the sun all year-round
- ★ 5,000 miles of coastline, most of it with beach access
- ★ Fresh food and great wine
- ★ Modern infrastructures for retiree's convenience
- ★ Healthcare is one of the best in the world

Culture

You probably have heard of the famous mañana habit. If you decide to live in Spain, you'll also have to adjust your expectations because you can't get something done as quickly as you would prefer. Sure, it will still get done, but because of the slower pace of life, you'll need to wait. There's less stress and people opt to enjoy their afternoon siestas after lunch. Shops also tend to close between 2 to 5 pm.

You will have to bid goodbye to rush hour at 6 or 7 am because things don't start until nine in the morning. Lunch doesn't start until 1:30 pm, and dinner until around 9 pm. Dinner at 10 pm on the weekend is also common.

Spanish people are also friendly, hospitable and welcoming. Physical contact during a conversation is well-accepted. 65% of them are Catholic so you will find plenty of Spanish churches. However, the younger generation choose not to follow the Church's teachings anymore, from morals to sexuality.

If you are planning to stay in Spain for a short time, you may get by with just speaking in English. Younger people under thirty will likely know English. But if you plan to retire and live here, learning the language can take you a long way, especially if you need to deal with the bureaucracy or simply for socialising with your neighbours.

Climate

Because of Spain's size, the country features three different climate zones. Generally, it has a Mediterranean climate, with hot, dry summers and mild, rainy winters. The north of the Cantabrian mountain, which includes the Basque Country, Asturias and Galicia, has a maritime climate where it's often cloudy and frequented by rainfall.

Meanwhile, in its Mediterranean coast, you'll find a moderate climate with rain only coming in spring and autumn. The area of Murcia gets an African climate where rainfall is low and temperature is high, especially in summer. Spain's Atlantic coast experiences a cooler summer with heavier rainfall in winter.

Central Spain has a continental climate with a baking hot summer and a cold winter. Still, Spain has one of the most envied climates in Europe. In summer, the temperature rises as high as 40 degrees Celsius while the average winter is around 5 degrees Celsius.

Cost of Living

Many retirees in Spain manage to live comfortably with a low budget. It is also true that the cost of living in Spain is one of the lowest in Western Europe. Costs will still depend on where you live. If you want to have better value for your money, you may want to escape Madrid and Barcelona.

Nevertheless, you can get a local beer with free tapas anywhere in Spain at around AUD 2.75. Some tapas are generous in size so it can be a filling meal. A classic restaurant with wine can cost at least AUD 62.

Grocery bills can be difficult to predict, but allocating AUD 137 per week should be sufficient. The warm climate in Spain helps a lot for many basic food items. You'll find reasonably priced fruits and vegetables. Transportation-wise, a car is optional because many shopping centres are accessible by walking. You can also use the monthly transportation pass which offers a good discount. A comfortable budget is AUD 2,740 –

3,425 per month for a couple. Here's what the monthly expenses look like:

Expenses	Prices
Rent (one-bedroom apartment in the city centre)	AUD 959
High-speed internet	AUD 69
Electricity and water	AUD 137
Phone with basic data plan	AUD 41
Loaf of white bread	AUD 1.65
A dozen of eggs	AUD 3.10
Local beer	AUD 1.43
Taxi per kilometer	AUD 5.75

Housing

Rental prices for small apartments in Spain, even in a popular expat area outside Madrid and Barcelona, costs about AUD 685 per month.

If you plan to buy a newly built property, expect to pay VAT, which is around 10% of the price. You also need to incur the levied tax, called ITP which is between 7% and 10%. Keep in mind that there is also annual property tax from the local authority that varies for each region, which is another 0.4% and 1.1% of the property value.

Here's the good news for retirees — Spain's real estate is still recovering, so you'll more likely to find a great house or condo in a great location at a good price. For instance, a four-bedroom town house is at AUD 805,000, while a one-bedroom apartment costs around AUD 161,000 - 322,000.

Retirement villages have sprouted all over Spain. One example is Ciudad Patricia, a senior resort located in a quiet residential area that comes with all kinds of amenities including a rehabilitation centre. Medical services are also available 24 hours a day.

Healthcare in Spain

Spain offers high-quality healthcare guaranteeing universal coverage for all its residents. There are both public and private healthcare systems in the country. The former provides basic healthcare to those residents who are contributing to the social security system.

Even retirees from EU countries can enjoy the benefits. For example, the UK government will pay a yearly sum for every pensioner to cover the health costs. If you are not a retiree or a pensioner, then you are not qualified to get free medical treatment in the public system. Once you arrive in Spain, you must register for a seguridad social so you can enjoy the benefits. In case of emergency, you only need to go straight to the hospital and show your social security card or proof of insurance.

Ninety percent of Spaniards prefer the public healthcare system in Spain which is deemed sufficient. Private healthcare runs alongside the public system. If you are not yet eligible for the public system, be sure to have health insurance which can cover your private healthcare needs. Insurance costs at least AUD 81 a month.

How to Retire in Spain (Retirement Visa)*

There is an option of getting a long-stay visa that can allow you to work, study, retire or even live in the country indefinitely. First, you may live in Spain for at least six months. Afterwards, you can renew your visa annually.

To get approved for the visa, you need to prove that you have at least USD 2,500 of income per month. If you have a dependent with you, then that's an additional USD 532 per month. The visa application is straightforward and can be accomplished in any Spanish embassy or consulate, which will cost around USD 200.

Alternatively, you may get the Spain retirement visa if you are 65 years old and above. You can take your pension in Spain. Keep in mind that by the year 2027, Spain is planning to raise the age limit to 67. In this case, you don't need to have at least USD 2,500 per month in the bank. The process will take two to three months and you will not be allowed to take part in any employment.

If you are planning to invest in Spain, you can automatically get a residence permit, along with your family members. You are eligible for a Golden Visa if you purchase real estate in Spain worth EUR 500,000 or invest at least EUR 2,000,000 in the Spanish public debt. If you buy shares in a company, make a deposit of at least EUR 1,000,000 or invest in a new business that offers employment opportunities, you can also get in. The golden visa is valid for a year, which is enough time to apply for a Spain residence permit.

* USD and EUR have been retained as default currency for all immigration investment figures in this article. Currency exchange rate USD 1 = AUD 1.36; EUR 1 = AUD1.61.

Work

While you are not permitted to work with a retirement visa, you can always get the long-term visa which allows you to live and work in the country. There are possibilities of starting a business in Spain too with any of the above-mentioned visa options.

Tax**

Spanish tax can be quite complicated, and it comes with penalties for anyone who fails to declare and pay correctly. For example, a foreigner with assets in the UK in excess of EUR 50,000 is required to declare those assets.

Spanish residents are taxed for their worldwide income. If you are getting a salary, pension, rental income, then you will be taxed once your personal allowances have been taken into consideration. The basic personal allowance for those under the age of 65 is EUR 5,550. Once you reach 65, that allowance rises to EUR 6,700.

Here is the rate of income tax in Spain:

Income	Tax Rate
Lower than EUR 12,450	19%
EUR 12,451 – EUR 20,200	24%
EUR 20,201 – EUR 35,200	30%
EUR 35,201 – EUR 60,000	37%
EUR 60,000	45%

** EUR has been retained as default currency for all tax figures in this article. Currency exchange rate EUR 1 = AUD1.61.

Food

Spanish cuisine comes across as all kinds of surprises. There's so much variety, flavours and colour! Each region offers a different style of

cuisine. It's not as spicy but the amazing flavours are bursting in every plate as they make use of spices, seafood, meat and vegetables.

Spain's geography, being surrounded with endless coastlines means that there is an abundance of seafood. You'll find fish, squid, shrimp, clams, mussels – and a lot more, and all of them fresh! Another distinctive feature of Spanish cuisine is its family-style size, that you can share them with everyone, and you can also have the opportunity to try a little bit of everything.

Spanish food is famous around the world, but eating it in Spain has a more authentic flavour and experience. Here are the foods that you'll expect to eat everyday should you choose Spain as your home:

- ★ **Paella** is hard to miss because it is the most famous dish in the country, and also available in every restaurant in the country. Originating in Valencia, paella comes in different styles and flavours. Paella Valenciana comes with white rice, meat and vegetables, while seafood paella has all the seafood goodness. Arroz Negro is filled with squid ink giving it a black hue.

- ★ **Tortilla Española** is a Spanish omelette that you'll often find in a tapas menu. It comes thick and fluffy with potatoes and onions inside.

- ★ **Jamon Iberico** shops with full legs of jamon hanging are available along almost every street in the country, as well as in bars, meat shops and restaurants. Spain is the largest producer of dry-cured ham. Iberico comes from black Iberian pigs which have a distinctive flavour.

- ★ **Chorizo** is a fermented pork sausage seasoned with heavy paprika. It is either spicy or sweet or both. Because it is cured (aged for several weeks), then smoked, it has a deep, smoky flavour.

- ★ **Croquetas** refer to crispy balls filled with bechamel sauce. Its ingredients consist of jamon, seafood and vegetables. Its creamy and rich taste is perfect as tapas to share with family and friends.

- ★ **Gazpacho** originated in Andalusia. It refers to cold soup made of tomatoes, cucumber, onion, garlic and olive oil, with a bit of vinegar and salt. Warm gazpacho is also available and is served with more vegetables and croutons.

- ★ **Churros Con Chocolate** is the perfect dessert in every Spanish meal. Or you can have it for breakfast or any time of the day as well. Dipped in chocolate sauce, it is crispy on the outside, doughy on the inside and rolled in cinnamon and sugar.

- ★ **Sangria**, from the word 'sagre', meaning blood, is red wine mixed with brandy, chopped fruit, and/ or more! This is Spain's signature drink in Andalucia.

International restaurants don't come short in Spain. Western and Asian cuisine are also available.

Recommended Cities in Spain

Costa del Sol

An ideal place for retirees is Costa del Sol, which literally means 'sunshine coast'. A Mediterranean paradise, it provides a laid-back lifestyle with at least 300 days of sun, a friendly community and a delicious choice of Andalusian cuisine.

Costa del Sol's sun-drenched lifestyle is suitable for those who want to live luxuriously or have more affordable living. English is widely spoken in Costa del Sol, considered an expat haven and popular amongst Europeans and the Brits. Its terrain and weather can be compared to Southern California.

Stretching at 180 miles starting from the Strait of Gibraltar to Granada, Costa del Sol is dotted with former fishing villages and sanded beaches. Out of eight stunning coasts, our top three go to Malaga, Marbella and Estepona. While Malaga is a vibrant cosmopolitan city with everything you can ask for, from restaurants, museums to architecture, Marbella reigns as the beach resort destination. The latter has a unique charm with bougainvillea and whitewashed buildings in the old quarter. Estepona, at the western end, is a less touristy smaller town that holds on to its traditions.

Essentials in Costa del Sol:

- **Healthcare:** Northern Spain's healthcare is world class so you will have nothing to worry about, whether you get into an accident or have long-term health conditions. Hospitals here are well-staffed and have advanced equipment. Here are the hospitals we recommend:
  - Hospital Costa Del Sol
  - Hospital Maritimo
  - Hospital Valle del Guadalhorce
  - Malaga General Hospital
  - Vithas Xanit International Hospital
  - Hospital Quirónsalud
  - Hospiten Estepona

- **Accessibility:** Malaga Airport is the only airport in Costa del Sol, which is sufficient if you want to travel domestically and internationally. The international airport has a wide reach, extending from China to Dubai. All kinds of transportation are available such as buses, taxis and trains. The high-speed rail connects Malaga to Madrid in three hours.

Things You Can Do in Costa del Sol

The main reason why retirees choose Costa del Sol is the beach. The second reason? The golf courses. You can easily spend a day with these two, but we've listed others that can fill your retirement days as well:

- Alcazaba
- Marbella old town
- Puerto Marina Benalmadena
- La Carihuela
- Bioparc

- ★ Cueva de Nerja
- ★ Benalmadena Pueblo
- ★ Balcony of Europe
- ★ Centro Historico de Estepona
- ★ Parque De La Paloma
- ★ Rio Chillar
- ★ Mercado Central de Atarazanas
- ★ Los Boliches
- ★ Plaza de Toros de Mijas
- ★ Malaga Cathedral
- ★ Castillo de Gibralfaro
- ★ Paseo Maritimo

Bilbao

If you prefer to stay in the city but prefer to avoid the crowded capital, then Bilbao is for you. It is a great city with classic architecture and art. You can find the famous Guggenheim Museum here. It is also the second-cleanest city in the country.

In contrast to Costa del Sol, Bilbao enjoys a cooler climate in the north of Spain. Summer is milder here so you can avoid the suffocating humidity. The cost of living compared to the quality of life you get is a lot better than the rest of Spain, although its charm, rich and unique history is often overlooked by tourists and retirees.

The Basque Country has its own language and culture too so you might feel like you are not in Spain anymore. English is widely spoken here so you won't have any issues adjusting. In case you miss the beaches, you'll have them here too, and it's known for its first-class waves. The city is built against the lush green mountain backdrop.

Essentials in Bilbao

- ★ **Healthcare:** Bilbao has 12 Acute Care Hospitals, 7 healthcare districts and 5 psychiatric units. With its extensive healthcare system, it can meet every citizens' needs. Here is a list of hospitals and clinics just in case:
  - ★ Hospitalde Basurto
  - ★ Hospital de Cruces
  - ★ Clinica Indautxu
  - ★ Clinica San Francisco Javier
  - ★ Sanatorio Bilbaino
- ★ **Accessibility:** The Bilbao Airport is a minor international airport that operates flights to some European cities such as Dublin, London, Lisbon and Frankfurt. It also connects to Madrid via train for five hours or an hour flight.

Things You Can Do in Bilbao

Although formerly known as an industrial centre, the city became more vibrant probably because of the Guggenheim effect. After the construction of the Guggenheim museum, designed by Frank Gehry, the city transformed into a cultural hub. Retiring in Bilbao means you'll have plenty of chances to experience all of them. Here are things you should not miss:

- ★ Guggenheim Museum
- ★ Museo de Bellas Artes de Bilbao
- ★ Casco Viejo
- ★ La Salve Bridge
- ★ Plaza Nueva
- ★ Euskal Museoa Bilbao
- ★ Catedral de Santiago
- ★ Bizkaia Museum of Archaeology
- ★ Parque Doña Casilda de Iturrizar
- ★ Basílica de Begoña
- ★ Museo Marítimo Ría de Bilbao
- ★ Palacio Euskalduna

- Mercado de la Ribera
- Gran Via

Granada

Situated at the confluence of two mountain streams, Granada has so much to offer for retirees in Spain. For years, it was the epicenter of the last Moorish Kingdom in Spain, until it became under Spanish control in 1492. The king and queen at that time acknowledged its beauty so instead of destroying Granada, it was preserved instead.

Walking around Granada, you'll find a romantic ambiance in its 500-year-old churches and ancient quarters.

Granada is conveniently set at the foot of Sierra Nevada mountains; thus, humidity is low making it more comfortable to walk around. Winters are colder but the snow rarely lasts a day. Meanwhile, summers in this part of Spain remain dry and humidity-free. Around 235,000 people call it home, with access to the convenience of the regular transit system. The buses too are great ways to travel in and around the city.

Essentials in Granada

- **Healthcare:** Like the rest of the country, Andalucia boasts a high standard of healthcare. With highly-trained staff and latest equipment, you will surely be in good hands as you spend your retirement days. Here is a list of hospital that can take care of you:
  - Hospital Virgen de las Nieves
  - Hospital Provincial de San Juan de Dios
  - Comunidad Terapeautica Area Norte
  - Hospital de San Rafael
  - Hospital Universitario San Cecilio
  - Clinica Inmaculada Concepcion

- **Accessibility:** The small airport of Granada connects the city to other parts of the country such as Madrid and Barcelona. Otherwise, the next airport of choice would be Malaga that can fly into different European cities. Alternatively, one can drive to Madrid for 4.5 hours.

Things You Can Do in Granada

The city of Granada is built for people who love the outdoors. Beyond learning its fascinating history and culture while walking along the streets filled with art and tapas bars, Granada is also a hiker's paradise. Its valleys are surrounded by rolling foothills and mountain streams, as well as 5,000-year-old villages. Here are things you can fill your time with as you spend retirement in Granada:

- The Alhambra palace
- Albaicin neighborhood
- Grananda Miradors
- Sacromonte
- Granada Cathedral
- Carmen de los Mártires garden
- San Juan de Dios Basílica
- Bib-Rambla Square
- Alcaiceria Market
- Granada ancient Arab baths
- Cartuja Monastery

San Sebastian

If you want a deep-dive into Basque culture, then San Sebastian is another place to explore. You can forget everything you knew about Spain, including the word for tapas, which are called pintxos here.

You'll find a stylish, seaside city of San Sebastian along Spain's north Atlantic coast, just ten minutes by car from the French border. From glorious beaches to old-world glamour, its charm and picture-perfect views of one of the world's most beautiful urban beachfronts.

San Sebastian is also one of the most visited cities in Spain because of its world-renowned cuisine. There are eleven Michelin-starred restaurants in the city – and that tells a lot about its restaurant scene.

Essentials in San Sebastian

- **Healthcare:** Hospitals do not come short in San Sebastian. Here are our top hospital choices in the city:
    - Quironsalud
    - Hospital Donostia
    - Centre Hospitalier Côte Basque
    - Centre Hospitalier de la Côte Basque
    - Hospital San Juan de Dios
    - Clinica San Miguel
- **Accessibility:** San Sebastian's small airport connects the city to Madrid and Barcelona with an hour flight. There are plans to operate a flight to London in the near future. Alternatively, you can also drive to Madrid, which is five hours away.

Things You Can Do in San Sebastian

It's easy to fall in love with the Basque charm of San Sebastian. But charm and culinary excellence aside, it also features beautiful landscapes from the mountain to its coast. If you are not checking out the restaurants in the city, you may fill up your time with the following sights:

- Ayuntamiento de San Sebastián
- Museo de San Telmo
- Monte Igueldo
- La Catedral del Buen Pastor
- Playa de la Concha
- Palacio de Miramar
- Monte Urgull
- Santa Clara Island
- Plaza de la Constitución
- Mercado de La Bretxa

Is Spain LGBT-friendly?

Spain nearly tops the list of countries that are most friendly to the lesbian, gay, bisexual and transgender (LGBT) community. In fact, it is the third country to have legalised same-sex marriage. LGBT rights in the country, including adoption rights, are also some of the most advanced in the world.

Transgenders are permitted to change their legal gender without the need for sterilization. About 88 percent of the population accepts homosexuality, and discrimination in employment due to sexual orientation has been banned since 1995. LGBTs people are permitted to serve in the military.

Senior Discounts

Once you reach the age of 65, you can enjoy senior benefits such as 50% discount on bus travel, 55% for glasses and hearing aids, hotels, cinemas, museums, monuments and theme parks. There are also subsidies for home improvements.

The Spanish train company RENFE features a travel discount card entitling seniors over age of 60 up to 40% discount. When eating out, you may want to check with the restaurant as sometimes, they offer a 10% discount.

Living in Spain: What to Watch Out For

Living in Spain has both advantages and disadvantages. Relocating here means you have to embrace both the good and the bad. Here are the things you need to watch out for:

- ★ **Jobs are scarce in Spain**
  Spain has one of the highest unemployment rates in Europe because of the economic and financial crisis of the 1980s. Also, if you ever find one, the salary you'll get will be much lower compared to other European countries like the UK and Germany. Because of siesta time, the hours of work may be very long.

- ★ **Crime in Spain**
  There is a low rate of murder in this part of the world, however, robberies are very common. As a foreigner, you can be an easy target especially in the big cities of Madrid and Barcelona. Pickpockets frequent tourist places and train stations. Retiring in Spain will require you to take necessary precautions such as avoiding carrying big sums of cash.

- ★ **The very laid back culture in Spain**
  The laid back culture of Spain does not mix well with its bureaucracy. Getting the simplest thing done will take you countless trips to the municipal hall and multiple copies of forms.

Summary

As the largest country in Southern Europe, Spain has less population density compared to its neighbours. With a democratic government, dependable infrastructure and nice people, there's no doubt that Spain will continue to rise as a retiree's destination in the years to come.

Healthcare: ★ ★ ★ ★ ★
Culture: ★ ★ ★ ★ ★
Cost of Living: ★ ★ ★
Housing: ★ ★ ★
Accessibility: ★ ★ ★ ★ ★
Safety: ★ ★ ★

TOTAL STARS: 24 ★

AFRICA and WESTERN ASIA

Camps Bay, Cape Town, South Africa

Reasons to Retire in South Africa

South Africa is one of the most overlooked countries when it comes to retirement destinations. There are commonly held but otherwise egregious misconceptions about South Africa, but the list of reasons why anyone would want to retire here is a longer list.

Let's start with its unparalleled beauty. If you are looking for the widest beaches on the planet, lush forests, and elevated mountain ranges, South Africa has it all. The country also does not have any recurrent natural disasters – that means, no earthquakes, cyclone storms, or hurricanes. You can instead focus on making unforgettable experiences, such as diving with sharks, whale watching, seeing the tallest waterfall in Africa, just to name a few.

Love to explore the flora and fauna? If seeing the big five is on your bucket list, South Africa's national parks can offer it to you. You can experience nature at its finest with the best infrastructures too. With the low cost of living, you can enjoy an excellent lifestyle. Just imagine going wine-tasting in the morning, visiting the galleries after, and hiking the mountains in the afternoon.

You can easily find a South African friend too, as the people are known as among the friendliest in the world. South Africans will always greet you with a smile and a helping hand. Do you know that it is also named as the third most inclusive country in the world, right after Canada and the US? That means whatever your religion, sexual orientation, political views, or wherever you came from, you will be socially accepted. English is also widely spoken so you do not have to adjust big time here. Plus, you will barely miss home because there's sound WiFi, modern shops, and water you can drink straight from the tap.

Why Retire in South Africa:

★ The food and the wine are amazing, and yet still underappreciated outside the country.
★ The weather is good all year round and suited for an outdoorsy lifestyle.
★ There are no recurrent natural disasters.
★ Because the rand is so weak, your dollar can go far!

Culture

South Africa is one of the most multicultural countries in the world, gaining the name "The Rainbow Natio." Its population of 58 million is made up of ethnic groups, indigenous black people, immigrants from Europe, India, China, and many more. Thus, it will be difficult to generalize South Africans altogether. It even has eleven official languages, but at least English is widely spoken so you do not have to spend the time studying each and every language there is.

The black population makes up 79% of the population. They are warm, patient, and charismatic people, and consist of multiple tribal groups. Each of the tribe groups has their own beliefs, language, and cultural practices.

The white population makes up 9%. These are the descendants of French, Dutch, and German settlers. Then there's the Asian population at 2.5%, which are descendants of Chinese and Malay immigrants. There is no official state religion, but the majority are identified as Christian; the religion was first introduced by missionaries from the Netherlands in the 1600s.

Keep in mind that some may take offence when they are referred by race or ethnicity so be careful with descriptors.

Etiquette-wise, there are a few things to know, such as removing your shoes when entering a home, or avoiding openly criticizing the country or its government. There are sensitive topics, such as the Apartheid, racism, violence, and inequality.

Climate

For travelers around the world, South Africa is a year-round destination. You can enjoy all of its seasons that offer abundant sunshine and blue skies. In its location in the Southern Hemisphere, between the Atlantic and Indian Oceans, South Africa experiences the dry season or winter from May to September and wet season or summer in October to April.

South Africa has plenty of sunny and dry days but the temperature is still bearable, ranging from 15 – 28 degrees Celsius. The summer rain usually comes in the afternoon, but its average annual rainfall only comes up to 464 mm (compared to the global average of 786 mm). The winter period is also still pleasant at 6 – 25 degrees Celsius, and virtually does not include any rainfall.

Cost of Living

Compared to all the cities in the world, Pretoria, which is Africa's most expensive city, ranks 252, meaning it is an affordable place to live.

The South African Rand has remained weak for years, so your dollar can be stretched here. You can enjoy the perks of lower-cost housing, food, and utilities even in the most populated locations of Johannesburg, Pretoria, Bloemfontein, and Cape Town. Living in South Africa with a budget of AUD 1,370 a month is considered comfortable.

If you have extra budget, we recommend purchasing a car, as the transportation system in this part of the world can be unreliable. Here's a quick look at the basic costs in South Africa:

Expenses	Prices
Housing rent (one-bedroom in Cape Town)	AUD 754
High-speed internet	AUD 79
Electricity and water	AUD 159
Phone with basic data plan	AUD 14
Loaf of white bread	AUD 1.40
A dozen eggs	AUD 3
Local beer	AUD 2
Taxi per kilometer	AUD 1.20

Housing

Foreigners are allowed to purchase and own properties in South Africa without any restrictions. As long as you live in South Africa legally, you will not encounter any issues in purchasing. You may expect to pay AUD 127 per square foot for an apartment in Johannesburg, or AUD 164,400 for a two-bedroom apartment in Cape Town.

The cost of rent is also reasonable. A one-bedroom apartment in the suburbs of Cape Town is AUD 685 a month.

Retirement villages are available in South Africa. These are upscale villages that cater for seniors with on-site healthcare facilities. Some of the top retirement villages include Waterfall Hills, Helderberg Village, Onrus Manor, and Evergreen Val de Vie.

Healthcare in South Africa

The good news is, this country featured the world's first heart transplant and, ever since, has always been proud of its medical care. However, keep in mind that most of the hospitals in South Africa are public, and are usually overcrowded and struggling with being under-resourced and overburdened. They also don't have the most updated equipment and facilities.

Therefore, expatriates and foreign retirees in the country would opt for private hospitals and practitioners that are available in the urban areas. There are well-established hospitals that offer a high standard of care. It has even become one of the countries to go to for plastic surgeries. You also won't encounter any problem with the language because most of them can speak English. The services can be expensive so it is best to purchase private health insurance.

How to Retire in South Africa (Retirement Visa)*

Foreign retirees can take two routes upon retiring in South Africa.

★ **Retired permit**
This is valid for up to four years with a minimum income per month to be proven. The amount is USD 2,700 a month, which can come from a pension fund or an irrevocable retirement annuity or a combination of assets. There are no age restrictions, and one can exit and

re-enter the country freely. It is also a pathway to permanent residency. Keep in mind, however, that this type of permit does not allow you to work in South Africa. The application will take typically between 4 – 12 weeks.

★ **Independent financial person permit**
This option allows anyone to work, study and start a business in South Africa. This will require a minimum net worth of USD 800,000, and a fee of USD 8,000. This is also ideal for people of any age and nationality. If the amount is too high for you, you can always go for the retired permit option. The downsides of this option are it will take a processing time of eight months, and your spouse can't be included in the application.

Work

Having a retired permit does not allow you to work in South Africa. If you intend to find work, study, or manage a business, then it will be better to apply for an independent financial person permit. It can be tough to find work unless you have specific skills needed in the country.

* USD has been retained as default currency for all immigration investment figures. Currency exchange rate USD1 = AUD1.36.

Tax**

Because of the wealth disparity in South Africa, taxes are only collected from a small percentage of the population. If you are not a resident yet, then you are only subject to pay for taxes made in the country. However, if you are present in the country for more than 91 days, you are considered as a resident so you are subject to pay a progressive income tax ranging from 18% - 45%. Here's a quick glance:

Taxable Income	Rates of Tax
0 – ZAR 205,900	18%
ZAR 205,901 – ZAR 321,600	ZAR 37,062 + 26% of taxable income above R205,900
ZAR 321,601 – ZAR 445,100	ZAR 67,144 + 31% of taxable income above ZAR 321,600
ZAR445,101 – ZAR584,200	ZAR 105,429 + 36% of taxable income above ZAR 445,100
ZAR584,201 – ZAR744,800	ZAR 155,505 + 39% of taxable income above ZAR 584,200
ZAR744,801 – ZAR1,577,300	ZAR 218,139 + 41% of taxable income above ZAR 744,800
ZAR1,577,301 and above	ZAR 559,464 + 45% of taxable income above ZAR 1,577,300

** ZAR has been retained as default currency for all tax in this article. Currency exchange rate ZAR1 = AUD0.093.

Food

The traditions from the various communities that inhabit South Africa are reflected in the country's cuisine. One of the indigenous peoples is the Khoisan that foraged over 300 species of food plants. During the British colonial rule, there were also immigrants from Asia that enriched South African cuisine. One example is the Indian South Africans who brought an abundance of spices and seasonings with them.

By the 17th century, the Dutch and British also brought their food elements resulting in a further culinary diffusion. Another distinctive regional style came from the Cape Malay influence who brought over spicy curries, sambals, and pickled fish. Later on, French refugees also brought wine which is one of the most celebrated beverages in the country. These factors influenced the evolution of South African cuisine.

South African wine has a history that dates back to 1659. Nowadays, the production is concentrated around Cape Town, Constantia, Stellenbosch, Paarl, and Worcester. The soil type and climate are perfect in these areas. Grape varieties include Chenin blanc, Riesling, and Palomino.

A typical breakfast is the same as the English breakfast: eggs, bacon, tomato and onion. Other households would serve mielie pap or maize meal porridge. It is boiled and eaten with milk and sugar. For the rest of the day? Here are the top choices:

- ★ **Bobotie**, is pronounced ba-bo-tea, refers to minced meat spiced with curry, turmeric, garlic, lemon zest, and herbs. It is baked until well cooked, then topped with an egg and milk mixture.

- ★ **Potjiekos** which literally translates to "food made in a pot" is a flavorful dish made with vegetables and meat. It is then cooked in low heat, usually outside on a small fire.

- ★ **Boerewors** or farmer sausage is traditionally barbecued. It contains 90% meat, either beef, lamb, pork, or a mixture, while the rest are spices and other ingredients.

- ★ **Vetkoek** is South Africa's version of a burger bun. It may be an unhealthy meal considering how crispy and golden it is on the outside, while the inside is filled with curried mince or chicken mayo, but it is one of the locals' favourites.

- ★ **Sosatie**s, also known as kebab is a dish that also came from Malay origin. These are skewered meat marinated in spicy sauce and then barbecued, resulting in a smoky flavor.

- ★ **Koeksisters** is a sweet snack of twisted dough, fried until it is crunchy. It is dunked into honey that will result in a slightly hard crust, while keeping the softness inside.

- ★ **Amanqina** tastes nicer than it looks. It is a slow-cooked stew with cow heel, pig feet, lamb feet, or chicken feet, and cooked with herbs such as thyme, rosemary, garlic, and Benny spice.

- ★ **Biltong** is dried, cured meat that is common in Southern African households. It can be beef or game meats like ostrich, cut in fillets, spiced and dried. It is similar to beef jerky but the African ingredients vary.

- ★ **Biryani** is a mixed rice dish that originates from India. Usually, the South African version is mixed together after the cooking and not while cooking.

- **Melktert** or milk tart is probably the most famous dessert in South Africa. It is made with a sweet pastry crust with a light cheesecake filling, topped with powdered cinnamon.

South Africa has an "eating out" culture, serving traditional cuisine to international cuisines from Chinese, Japan, Moroccan, and many more. International food restaurants are also easy to find, but they are facing competition with home chains such as Nando's Galito's and Steers.

Recommended Cities in South Africa

Cape Town

Also called the Mother City, Cape Town is the largest city in the Western Cape Province and the second-most populous city in the country. It is also known for its harbor, and location by the shore of Table Bay Mountain. Living in Cape Town means you are never from what nature has to offer. However, it is not just its natural beauty that keeps people coming back for more.

Firstly, the infrastructures in Cape Town are of a much higher standard compared to anywhere else in South Africa. There are industries that thrive in Cape Town from manufacturing to IT, plus it offers growing opportunities for work and investment.

It is a dynamic African city that offers the frills of both European and African feeling — an international city where you can have breakfast from a German bakery, lunch at a Chinese restaurant, and have Italian cuisine for dinner. There is no other place in the world where you can enjoy an outdoor Cape Town lifestyle. Choose between leisurely strolls by the Camps Bay beach or hardcore mountain climbing. Or why not kayak with dolphins?

Essentials in Cape Town:

- **Healthcare:** Foreign retirees have several options for private hospitals in Cape Town. Generally, the consultation costs are affordable but can escalate quickly so it is recommended to always have insurance with you. Here are the top private hospitals in the city:
  - Christian Barnard Memorial Hospital
  - Vincent Pallotti Hospital
  - Cape Town Medi Clinic
  - Life Kingsbury Hospital
- **Accessibility:** The Cape Town International Airport is the second-busiest airport in the country and the third in the whole of Africa. It connects South Africa to several destinations in the continent, Europe, and Asia.

Things You Can Do in Cape Town

For the past two decades, Cape Town has emerged as one of the world's greatest capitals that thrives with dramatic scenery, diversity, and thrill. It has tons of restaurants to delight your

senses, art galleries, theatres, museums, events, and festivals all year round that can keep your retirement days busy. No wonder it is ranked among the world's top holiday destinations and has a high return visitor rate. The city has something for everyone so whether you prefer diving with the sharks or have a getaway trip to the Winelands, you are in the best place.

Another good thing to know is the swanky jazz tunes that would absolutely get your hips moving. Here, you can enjoy late-night jazz in the oldest cathedral to street musicians playing even on rainy days. Here are some more things to explore while spending your retirement days in South Africa:

- ★ The Cape Wheel
- ★ Cape Town Diamond Museum
- ★ Heart of Cape Town Museum
- ★ The Old Biscuit Mill
- ★ St. George's Cathedral
- ★ Canal Walk Shopping Centre
- ★ Cape Point Ostrich Farm
- ★ Castle of Good Hope
- ★ Table Mountain
- ★ Kirstenbosch
- ★ Zeitz Museum of Contemporary African Art
- ★ Boulders Beach
- ★ Robben Island
- ★ Neighbourgoods Market
- ★ Norval Foundation
- ★ Woodstock Street Art
- ★ Lion's Head

Stellenbosch

The town of Stellenbosch was founded in 1679 by Governor Simon van der Stel who named it after himself. It grew quickly and became an independent local authority, and fast forward to today, it now has around 200,000 in population. Stellenbosch has become known as the city of Oaks of Eikestad because of the huge number of oak trees that grace the streets and homesteads.

With its location about 50 km east of Cape Town, living in this historic town is the perfect escape from the bustle of the mother city. Stellenbosch is also the home of the Stellenbosch University, Technopark, and Stellenbosch Golf Course. The region has a Mediterranean climate, which means hot and dry summer and cool wet winters. With its location lying at the foot of the Cape Fold mountain range, Stellenbosch is one of the favorable areas for wine production.

Spending your retirement days guarantees a lush mountain range of the western cape with lots of activities aside from wine-tasting, of course. You cannot live here and not go for the Stellenbosch Wine Route, which is the most popular wine route in the country. There are also sidewalk cafes, student pubs, and gastronomic restaurants that will satisfy your tastebuds. Stellenbosch also boasts a solid infrastructure to serve its vibrant community.

Essentials in Stellenbosch:

- ★ **Healthcare:** With the size of Stellenbosch, there are a fewer number of private hospitals in the area. For more hospital options, it will be best to travel an hour away to Cape Town. Meanwhile, here are some hospitals in the area in case of emergency:
    - ★ Mediclinic Stellenbosch
    - ★ Mediclinic Vergelegen
    - ★ StellDOC Medical Centre

- **Accessibility:** The town of Stellenbosch is only 45 mins away from Cape Town city centre and only 30 mins away from the airport.

Things You Can Do in Stellenbosch

Stellenbosch is a food and wine haven! However, there is more to Stellenbosch beyond its beautiful wine estates offering the best of the best food, wine, and chocolate, there are other activities you can enjoy too. As South Africa's second-oldest town, the whole town is a living museum itself with its vibrant street culture. Locals often organize lively events that highlight the country's art, music, history, and outdoor pursuits. An ideal retirement day will probably include a visit to one of its museums, shops, restaurants, distilleries, and galleries. Here are some of the points of interest that you should not miss:

- Waterford Estate
- Spier Wine Farm
- Delaire Graff Estate
- Jordan Wine Estate
- Stellenbosch University Botanical Garden
- Jonkershoek Nature Reserve
- Vergenoegd Low the Wine Estate
- Dylan Lewis Sculpture Garden
- Tokara Wine Estate
- House of J.C. Le Roux
- Giraffe House Wildlife Centre
- Stellenbosch Village Museum
- Rupert Museum
- Oude Libertas Amphitheatre
- MOK Gallery

The Garden Route District

The district is a 300-kilometre stretch of the south-eastern coast. It extends from Witsand to the border of Tsitsikamma Storms River in the Eastern Cape. The Garden Route District includes the towns of Knysna, Plettenberg Bay, Mossel Bay, Nature's Valley, and George. Its location by the coast gives it an oceanic climate with moderate summers and winters. In 2017, the route was added to UNESCO's World Network of Biosphere Reserves. The good news? It is still often overlooked by holiday-goers so you don't find many tourists in this area. No wonder it has attracted many retirees over the years. Some of the popular retirement towns are Knysna and Sedgefield.

Traversing this area can offer you all kinds of adventure activities, from scuba diving, abseiling to fishing. The route is rich with indigenous forests, birdlife, towering mountains, and deep gorges. If you prefer a slower pace of living in small towns, facing the sea, then the Garden Route District is for you. Other benefits of living here include safety, low cost of living, and the absence of traffic and pollution.

Essentials in The Garden Route District:

- **Healthcare:** There are more options of private hospitals in the Western Cape. Here are some of the best choices:
  - Knysna Private Hospital
  - Durbanville Medi Clinic
  - George Medi Clinic
  - Bayview Private Hospital

- **Accessibility:** There are a few airports that serve the Garden Route: Mossel Bay, George Airport, and the Plettenberg

Airport. These small airports connect the city to Cape Town and Johannesburg.

Things You Can Do in The Garden Route District

This top scenic drive in South Africa is famous for its exceptional scenery and fascinating wildlife. The Garden Route is for retirees who seek adrenaline-fueled adventures. Retiring in this part of South Africa will give plenty of opportunities to explore sparkling lagoons, hike through coastal forests, and even bungee jump into a plunging gorge. Anywhere you look, you will be greeted with picturesque towns and an abundance of natural scenery. In the seaside towns of Knysna and Plettenberg Bay, you can enjoy the splendid retreat from city life while exploring its attractions:

- ★ Garden Route National Park
- ★ Garden Route Botanical Garden
- ★ Birds of Eden Bird Sanctuary
- ★ Lakes Area National Park
- ★ Knysna Waterfront
- ★ Featherbed Nature Reserve
- ★ Robberg Nature Reserve
- ★ Keurbooms River Nature Reserve Garden Route Wine Estates
- ★ Storms River Suspension Bridge
- ★ Knysna Elephant Park
- ★ Featherbed Nature Reserve
- ★ Swartberg Pass
- ★ Cango Caves
- ★ Oudtshoorn Ostrich Farms
- ★ Wilderness National Park
- ★ Mossel Bay
- ★ Gondwana Private Game Reserve

Is South Africa LGBT-friendly?

South Africa has a reputation as Africa's most gay-friendly destination for tourists. Cape Town alone has become Africa's de facto 'gay capital.' It is not called a rainbow nation for no reason. LGBT people in the country enjoy the same rights as the non-LGBT community. Changing assigned genders has been legal since 2003, and the LGBT community is allowed to serve openly in the military as well. Same-sex marriages have been permitted since 2006.

Adopting a child for same-sex couples has also been possible since 2002. The LGBT South Africans still struggle with some challenges outside the major cities. Homophobic violence and high rates of HIV infection still exist.

Senior Discounts

If you are a permanent resident in South Africa aged 60 years or older, you can get an older person's grant. This will get you ZAR 1,890 a month, while if you are 75 years and older, you will get ZAR 1,910 a month. It only takes three months to process your application.

There are also various discounts you can enjoy. You can also apply for a senior's card and access public transport concessions and discounts from over 700 establishments.

Living in South Africa: What to Watch Out For

South Africa is not all rainbows. Even if it is a stunning country with a unique history, rich natural resources, and variety there are also disadvantages you have to consider before migrating to the country. Beware of the following:

★ **The crime rate is high.**
Crimes, ranging from petty theft to serious crime, have been steadily increasing in South Africa. The majority of violent crimes come from poor and densely populated neighborhoods so it is best to avoid some areas. For example, in Johannesburg, the criminal hot spots are Joubert Park, Hillbrow, and Berea. In Cape Town, avoid Salt River and Sea Point Mowbray. Make sure that your home is secure at all times and avoid walking around alone. It will also be best to avoid displaying your valuables where criminals can see them.

★ **Racism still exists.**
This is an ongoing problem since the demise of Apartheid. Despite going through all the tribulations over the years, there is still a race divide that you must be mindful of.

★ **The economy remains weak.**
There is a job shortage, especially for foreigners. Without any connections, it may be impossible for you to get hired in South Africa. The money you may earn here may not be worth anywhere else. Plus, there is corruption at every level.

Summary

South Africa may not be the best place for healthcare because of its cost, or not the safest place because of its increasing crime rate. We believe that these can be mitigated, making it worthwhile to give this country a chance. With everything else it offers, particularly the diversity of the people, South Africa has a lot of potential. In the future, we sure hope that it will improve for the better. Here's our overall rating:

Healthcare: ★ ★ ★
Culture: ★ ★ ★ ★
Cost of Living: ★ ★ ★ ★
Housing: ★ ★ ★ ★
Accessibility: ★ ★ ★ ★
Safety: ★ ★ ★

TOTAL STARS: 22 ★

İstanbul, Turkey

Reasons to Retire in Turkey

One of the most visited countries in this part of the world is Turkey. With its accessibility and the flights connecting people from Asia to Europe, Africa, North and South America, the country has become one of the region's main transit hubs. A lot of money has been invested in transportation and tourism so there is no wonder how it became a top-tier destination for travelers.

But how about retiring here? If you stay much longer, you will find how Turkey can be an amazing destination for your golden years, too. The first reason must be considered: its climate. Its strategic location provides a pleasant climate all year round. The winter period is not as cold, while summer is not as hot. Spring and autumn are both beautiful times to explore the country. All these lend to an outdoor lifestyle that promotes healthy living.

The country also has a rich and well-preserved history. Every city features a museum or a UNESCO site and all of it can be reached with an accessible domestic flight away. Turkey also features a variety of landscapes – just look at Cappadocia, where caves were turned into houses and hotels. There are places you can hike through and there are beaches you can swim, sail, snorkel and dive in.

You can explore a westernized type of Muslim culture. Its influences include Central Asian, Arabic, Greek, and many more. This variety also reflects in their amazing choices of food integrated with its restaurant culture.

The Turkish are also warm and nice people who are always ready to help. The cost of living is also low. Even the major city of Istanbul, which gets swarmed with tourists every year, is still relatively cheaper compared to other major cities in Europe.

Why Retire in Turkey:

★ Its weather throughout the year is the best in this part of the world. Winter is not as cold and summer is not as hot.

★ You get the best of both continents: Asia and Europe.

★ The food is amazing!

★ Enjoy the outdoor lifestyle with its varied landscape.

Culture

It is important to keep in mind that you are moving to a Muslim country so you have to be respectful to their traditions and customs. The Muslims have a call of prayer in Arabic five times a day, and the first one starts early in the morning. Living here means getting used to hearing it every day.

Also, some places in Turkey tend to be conservative such as Konya and Rize. Wearing shorts and mini skirts will only get people to stare weirdly. The concept of honor is also embedded in Turkish culture and manifests in their behavior. Despite the cultural pressure, individuals will do everything to protect their personal reputation, or they will feel a deep shame referred to as *yuzsuz*.

Life is approached at an easier pace and you will find the Turkish devoting more time to their personal interactions. That's why older men in towns can be often seen in teahouses sipping drinks and debating over tea all day, while women often visit their neighbors to talk about anything from local to family news.

The country also has a collectivist culture which refers to being loyal to familial and social groups. They keep tight relationships towards their neighbors and community and favors are done for each other whenever it is needed. This might also mean that they protect their own – so finding a Turkish friend and community will be a priority for you once you decide to retire here.

Lastly, if you decide to live outside Istanbul, then be prepared to learn Turkish. In fact, it will bring you more benefits to learn the local language because you can communicate with everyone, keeping your circle big. Otherwise, speaking in English means you can only rely on a guide or socialize with someone who speaks the same language.

Climate

With Turkey's geographical location, it experiences seven distinct geographic weather and climatic regions. For example, its eastern side — where Istanbul, Edirne, and Bursa, along with the Marmara Sea — has temperatures ranging from -16 to 40 degrees Celsius. While the Aegean region, which is characterized by low hills and higher mountains, gets 645 mm of rainfall and temperatures of -8 to 43 degrees Celsius. Nearer the Mediterranean, Turkey's southern shore, temperatures range from -5 to 45 degrees Celsius.

Weather is pretty moderate throughout the country, with its best time being in Spring, which runs from March to mid-June, and autumn that runs from mid-September through October. Summertime, despite the heat, is when people go to the seaside. The temperate winter can be chilly and rainy but, most of the time, the sun is always shining.

Cost of Living

You can live a good quality of life with only AUD 2,055 to spend monthly, even if you move to the popular expat areas or the coastal towns. Turkey offers a good value-for-money not only as a traveler's destination but also to its residents. Living in Istanbul costs more than living in the cities along the Aegean and Mediterranean coasts.

Household bills for a family can be as little as 40 YTL a month. As for transportation, the city's public transport system is extremely cheap, and buses are the main mode of transit. Need a haircut? It will only cost you AUD 8! The cost of entertainment is also very affordable. A fitness club membership is only at AUD 13.70 while a beer at a pub will cost you only AUD 4.11! Here is a quick glance of what a budget in Turkey can look like:

Expenses	Prices
Housing rent (one-bedroom in Ankara)	AUD 301
High-speed internet	AUD 21
Electricity and water	AUD 10.5
Phone with basic data plan	AUD 14
Loaf of white bread	AUD 0.60
A dozen eggs	AUD 2.35
Local beer	AUD 3
Taxi per kilometer	AUD 0.90

Housing

There are a variety of housing options in Turkey. You can find a coastal villa for AUD 1.9 million or an apartment for only AUD 794,600. The country has attracted a large increase in foreign buyers in the cities of Istanbul and Antalya in recent years.

Renting an apartment is much cheaper, as long as you avoid the tourist areas. For instance, you can find a one-bedroom apartment in Antalya for only AUD 685, while in the capital of Ankara, it can cost you 50% cheaper than that.

Retirement homes that offer complete facilities—from nursing to meals and scheduled activities—are also available. The Private Guzelcamli Ada Resthome in Kusadasi is located only a hundred meters from the sea, and is the first private nursing home established in the province. Its staff can speak German, French, Italian, and English.

Healthcare in Turkey

There are two healthcare systems in Turkey: the public and the private system. Unfortunately, you can't access the public healthcare system unless you have spent a year in the country as a resident or if your spouse is somehow a policyholder.

The best option for foreign retirees is going to private hospitals that offer excellent healthcare. Getting a check-up does not have to break the bank. We recommend getting health insurance that can cost as low as AUD 274 a year. Turkey has also made progress in its private healthcare that it is now a common medical tourism destination, especially for cosmetic surgery, dentistry, and fertility treatments.

How to Retire in Turkey (Retirement Visa)?

If you are from the EU, you can enter the country with a visa exemption for 90 days out of every 180 days. If you intend to retire in Turkey, Turkey does not have a retirement visa scheme yet, but they do have a short-term residence permit or the e-ikamet that will allow you to stay for a year or two. It can be renewed and can function as a retirement visa.

The application for an e-ikamet is pretty straightforward. All you need to do is get the permit at the Ministry of the Interior once you arrive in the country. You can only get a long-term residence permit if you have resided in Turkey for a minimum of eight years uninterruptedly and have not received any kind of social relief in the last three years. This also requires a sufficient and regular source of income to prove that you can support yourself, plus valid health insurance.

With the long-term residence permit, you can enjoy the following benefits:

★ Save for social security rights;

★ Any other rights vested in Turkish citizens, except for military service obligation, the right to elect and be elected, holding public office(s);

★ Importing vehicles and other arrangements in the private law.

Work

Most local companies require a good command of the Turkish language so finding work here can be a challenge. Even if you speak Turkish, the laws have made it difficult to apply for a working permit. Unfortunately, job seekers are not welcome in the country – and maybe that's a good thing so you can truly relax in your retirement period.

Tax*

Being a resident in Turkey means you will be subjected to your worldwide income. If you intend to settle in the country or you stay over 183 days in a calendar year, then you will be subject to pay the income tax which is calculated as follow:

Taxable Income	Tax Rate
TRY 1 – TRY 22,000	15%
TRY 22,001 – TRY 49,000	20%
TRY 49,001 – TRY 180,000	27%
TRY 180,001 – TRY 600,000	35%
TRY 600,001 +	40%

* TRY has been retained as default currency for all tax and immigration investment figures in this article. Currency exchange rate TRY1 = AUD0.16.

You also need to pay social security tax of 15% and 5% public health insurance.

If you are a non-resident taxpayer, you will only be subjected to any income you earn from Turkey.

Food

Turkish cuisine is a fusion of Mediterranean, Balkan, Central Asian, Eastern European, and Middle Eastern cuisine. Looking at the Ottomans alone, you will find a variety of culinary traditions that came from Greece, Egypt, and Mesopotamia, to name a few. Turkey's various cultures are reflected in its cuisine.

The cuisine also varies across the country. In Istanbul, Bursa, and Izmir, there is a lighter use of spices. While in the western parts of Turkey, where there is an abundance of olive trees, olive oil is always used in all kinds of cooking.

The usual breakfast often consists of cheese, butter, olives, eggs, cucumber, jam, honey, and sausage. This traditional Turkish dish is called menemen, which will absolutely wake all of your senses up. Homemade food typically starts with soup, salad, meat, and either pilav or pasta. There is an abundance of food in the country and they are reasonably priced. A trip to the market guarantees a feast of plums, apricots, pomegranates, pears, apples, grapes, and many more. Turkey also has a wide range of sweet pastries. In every meal, bread is always abundantly served. Here is the list of food you will have to get used to while living in Turkey:

- **Iskender Kebab** is a popular and delicious meat dish. It is a traditional döner kebab that consists of sliced lamb and tomato sauce, served with traditional bread. It is also topped with yogurt and butter, making it more flavorful.

- **Manti or Turkish** ravioli are little dumplings filled with either lamb or beef. It is topped with three kinds of sauces: caramelized tomato sauce, brown butter sauce, and garlicky yogurt sauce.

- **Mezze** is a small selection of dishes served as appetizers. It often includes yogurt with herbs, hummus, dolmas, kofte, eggplant salad, and white cheese.

- **Baklava** refers to layers of flaky pastry served with nuts and syrup. Originating from the Ottoman Empire, it can now be found in every street corner in the country.

- **Shish Kebab** is common in every local Turkish restaurant. It is grilled chicken, beef, or lamb on skewers served with either rice and fries, and salad.

- **Turkish Apple Tea** can be found in every Turkish café. It is easy to get addicted to its warmth and sweetness. Plus, it is a big part of Turkish hospitality.

- **Gözleme** is your snack-to-go. Similar to a crepe, it is a flatbread made from hand-rolled dough. You can choose from different toppings such as potatoes, meat, vegetables, and cheese.

- **Kumpir** or baked potato is done differently in Turkey. Once it is baked and cut in the middle, it is mixed with a generous portion of butter and kasar cheese. You can also choose from a wide selection of toppings from carrot, olives, sausage, to sweet corn.

- **Kariniyarik** is eggplant stuffed with meat, onion, tomatoes, pepper, and parsley and is often served with pilaf.

- **Pottery Kebab** is meat and vegetables slow-cooked in a sealed pot. In a restaurant, the waiter makes a big deal by bringing out a knife and slicing the top of the pot in front of you. Yes, it is entertaining and not to be missed while in Turkey.

- **Turkish Pizza** or Etli Ekmek, originating from Konya. It is a long, thin piece of bread topped with cheese and meat, cut into small pieces.

- **Turkish Delight** or Lokum, as the locals refer to it, is a mouth-watering combination of pistachios, chopped dates, and nuts. This is the traditional candy that often comes in pink, white, brown, and green.

There is no shortage of international restaurants in Turkey. In the cities of Istanbul, Ankara, and Antalya, restaurants serving fast food and six-course meals are also available.

Recommended Cities in Turkey

Istanbul

Istanbul is the largest city in Turkey and offers a unique culture, amazing nightlife, and shopping options. There is also an abundance of historical attractions you can take your time to explore as you live here, especially given the climate year-round.

Its prime position by the Bosphorus River made it a hub of trade and industry for centuries. If you are not a history lover, there are also other attractions you can enjoy, such as the Princes' Island, which is a ferry ride away.

Istanbul is also a safe city. The crime rate is also low as revealed by the local council, but exercising safety measures and using common sense is always a good recourse. Even if Istanbul is the most expensive city in the country, it is still relatively cheap. You may either shop in the supermarket or at the Grand Bazaar and you will find restaurants and cafes that offer cheap food.

If you don't intend to learn the language, then it will be better to stay in Istanbul as people who live here are more knowledgeable of the language. Getting around is also easy with its efficient public transportation – you can choose from buses, ferries, and trains.

Essentials in Istanbul:

★ **Healthcare:** Istanbul has the highest standard of healthcare in the country. These hospitals have well-trained medical staff with updated equipment. Here are our top choices in Istanbul:
   ★ Acibadem Hospital
   ★ Alman Hastanesi Hospital
   ★ American Hospital Istanbul
   ★ International Hospital

★ **Accessibility:** The Istanbul Airport, which is located on the European side of the country, is the main international airport. The new airport covers 312 destinations including Hong Kong, Delhi, Cairo, New York, and London. It also connects the city to all parts of the country.

Things You Can Do in Istanbul

The lifestyle in Istanbul can be both exotic and familiar. It also offers all the modern comforts and delights, featuring diverse leisure and lifestyle. You may spend your morning getting lost in the Grand Bazaar, Spice Bazaar, or at Beyazit Square flea market. Eating out is the best way to socialize with friends and family, and a lot of the food establishments offer great value. The afternoon can be spent enjoying cultural activities. Concerts, ballets, and operas in the evening, or you can explore the open-air clubs that are filled with either techno music, jazz performances, or belly dancers near the Bosphorus. If you prefer a fitness lifestyle, then you can enjoy the many swimming pools and tennis courts around the city. There are also golf clubs you may join. Here are a few things you can explore while in Istanbul:

★ Hagia Sophia
★ Dolmabahce Palace
★ Sultanahmet District
★ Bosphorus Strait
★ Gulhane Park
★ Galata Tower
★ Emirgan Park
★ Miniaturk
★ Ortakoy
★ Balat
★ Chora Museum
★ Istinye Park
★ Eyup Sultan Mosque
★ Kiz Kulesi
★ Bebek
★ Kapali Carsi

Ankara

Ankara is known to be the younger sister of Istanbul. It is another cosmopolitan with a vibrant atmosphere and intellectual charm. The good thing about this city is it is always overlooked by international travelers so it's less crowded, but you can still find authentic Turkish culture here.

Embassies and all government buildings are here and located near each other so paperwork is generally easier to complete. There is also an amazing array of shopping places and restaurants. Even though it is populated with 5.6 million people, the districts still give you a smaller town vibe. Ankara also boasts beautiful architecture and one of the best examples is the Ziraat Bank Headquarters, which was built by Giulio Mongeri in 1925.

Everywhere you look, there are parks beside skyscrapers, and lush trees line the streets. Because it is a residential and a political city, you will also feel how peaceful and more organized it is. The streets are not overcrowded and even during rush hour, you won't find any excessive car honking.

The best part about living in Ankara is the cost of living. Even with its metropolitan and capital vibe, you can find spacious apartments at a reasonable cost. If you still plan to work, it will be handy to know that the city is a growing hub of innovation so finding work here is easier.

Essentials in Ankara:

- **Healthcare:** Several world-class hospitals can be found in Ankara. The medical staff and doctors are professionally educated in the USA and Europe. Our recommended healthcare institutions include:
  - Liv Hospital Ankara
  - Medicana International Ankara Hospital
  - Ankara Güven Hospital
  - Baskent Universitesi Hastanesi Ankara

- **Accessibility:** The Esenboga International Airport is only 28 kilometres away from the city centre. It connects the city to other parts of Turkey, as well as cities around the world such as Baku, Baghdad, Tehran, Amman, Kiev, Paris, and Doha. Alternatively, Istanbul can be reached in only five hours by bus.

Things You Can Do in Ankara

Ankara has a lot of ways to keep you busy; with over fifty museums and five national orchestras, you can explore something new every week. You can find performances every night in Ankara's opera houses, and in the Turkish State Opera and Ballet where you can watch ballet and opera performances or listen to jazz. Football is also a game that the Turkish take seriously so you can watch and cheer your favorite team in the Turkish Super League season. There are basketball and volleyball games as well. Here are some of the points of interests in the city:

- Museum of Anatolian Civilizations
- Anitkabir
- Citadel Neighborhood
- Erimtan Archaeology and Art Museum
- Ulu's Roman Remnants
- Haci Bayram i-Veli Cami
- Ankara Painting and Sculpture Museum
- Ankara State Opera House
- Gordion
- Gençlik Park
- Eymir Lake

Antalya

The Southern Coast Hub covers a large section of the south coast and Turkey's second most popular destination. It is also the second most popular place for expatriates to live in, given the number of foreign house sales it gets every year. Antalya comprises a large city centre and coastal resorts where you can enjoy an urban lifestyle. If you choose to live in the city centre, you can find a one-bedroom apartment for only AUD 343 in the city centre and have easy access to the best beaches in the country. There is modern and well-developed infrastructure as well.

The city offers great shopping and eating out options, plus an excellent transportation link not only to the rest of Turkey but to places around the world.

Aside from its history and culture, this Turkish Riviera city boasts the glorious Mediterranean coastline that attracts foreigners to live and stay here forever. Once they step into its clean sandy beaches, many people tend to fall in love and decide to come back or stay longer.

Essentials in Antalya:

- **Healthcare:** The city offers many private hospitals and clinics that are known for treating all kinds of conditions; they also specialise in cosmetic surgery. Here are a list of the most important private hospitals in Antalya:
    - Antalya Life Private Hospital
    - Olympos Hospital
    - Medstar Hospital
    - Lara Anatolia Private Hospital

- **Accessibility:** The Antalya Airport is only 10 kilometers from the city. The airport operates daily flights to Moscow, Kiev and Istanbul. More flights are operated during the summer season making it easily accessible to travelers around the world.

Things You Can Do in Antalya

The locals can attest to the heat that Antalya brings during summer. It is almost always summer, with the rainy season lasting no more than three months. There are lots of historical places, historical cities, natural landscapes, waterfalls, caves – the list goes on and on! Antalya is famous for its beaches so almost everyone here goes for a swim, especially during summertime. That means you can expect a beachside lifestyle where you can also pursue all kinds of adventure sports, such as trekking, scuba diving or golf. Here are other places you can fill your time with:

Old Town of Kaleici
- Old Harbor
- Antalya Museum
- Yivli Minare
- Hadrian's Gate
- Roman Fortress
- Aspendos
- Termessos
- Perge
- Olympos and the Chimaera
- Konyaalti Beach
- Karst Springs
- Lara BeachKarain Cave
- Phaselis
- Kocain Magarasi
- Köprülü Canyon National Park

Is Turkey LGBT-friendly?

Being a Muslim country, the LGBT community generally experiences discrimination and harassment, although Turkey is already considered the most tolerant compared to its neighboring Muslim countries.

Same-sex sexual activity has been legal since the Ottoman Empire, while the governing act itself was founded in 1923. It is legal to have sex reassignment surgery, but gay men are not allowed to serve openly in the army or in government service. There is no protection against discrimination as of writing, so if you belong to the LGBT community, you may have to rethink moving to Turkey.

Senior Discounts

For entertainment, discounted prices are available for seniors who are 65 years and older. They can enjoy hotel and flight discounts, and free entry to museums. Since 2014, senior citizens can also access railways, sea lines, and municipality transportation vehicles free of charge or at discounted prices. The government also provides other economic and socio-cultural initiatives so it's good to always ask whenever you purchase anything.

Living in Turkey: What to Watch Out For

Living in Turkey can be the best decision in your life, or the worst if you don't have the right expectation. Like every country in the world, if there are things to look forward to, there are also the negative things you have to watch out for. Some key points to consider:

★ **It is impossible to find a job in Turkey.**
Unless you are an English teacher, it may be difficult for you to find a job in the country. Most jobs would require you to speak the Turkish language. You will require a work permit, which is considered a big commitment for the employer so most companies don't even bother.

★ **The level of English is low.**
A few people are successful in learning and navigating the Turkish language. If learning a new language is not your best pursuit, it is best to stay in a tourism destination or stick to communities where the expatriates live; otherwise, there's always an option of hiring a translator.

★ **Stay away from politics.**
If you want to get to know new friends, it is safe to keep your political views to yourself. The Turks are passionate about their political system so discussions can turn into a messy game. Simply don't join the conversation.

Summary

Turkey is one of the most visited places in the region, but living here is usually met with 'why's' and 'how's'. If people only give it a chance, you will also find it to be a romantic place to spend the rest of your retirement days. Here's our overall rating:

Healthcare: ★★★★
Culture: ★★★★
Cost of Living: ★★★★
Housing: ★★★★★
Accessibility: ★★★★★
Safety: ★★★★

TOTAL STARS: 26 ★

PLANNING YOUR RETIREMENT OVERSEAS

If you've read through this book, you should now have a pretty good idea of which country or countries might be suitable destinations for you as you embark on your retirement adventure. The good news is that that's one important thing you can tick off from your list of things to do in your overseas retirement plan. But there are other equally important matters you need to think about, plan for and do before you take the big leap.

1. Visit before you move

Visiting a new country as a tourist is one thing; living there indefinitely is a totally different matter altogether. Even if you've visited one of the countries featured in this book before and liked or disliked the experience, it doesn't mean that you feel the same way once you start living there as a local. There are many factors that could make your retirement in your new home a happy, blissful experience or the opposite. You'll need to consider factors like your new home country's weather, its culture and overall safety. Try visiting a couple of times, preferably in different seasons. It might be a good idea to visit during off-season for tourists, because this usually means that this is the time when the weather is not the best. If you find that you're happy there even during monsoon season or hot, humid days or dreary winter periods, then that's a good sign that you can really live there. Check if there's an existing Australian or expatriate community already living there – you can connect with them to learn more about life there.

2. Organise your finances

The cost of living in the countries featured in this book is generally much lower, and in some cases significantly lower, compared with Australia. So you could potentially spend less and save more when you retire overseas. But still, make sure your finances are in order so that you can comfortably transition and eventually settle in your new home country. It will be a good idea to organise a new budget for your retirement life, so you can stay on top of your spending and expenses. But remember that the expenses you'll have in retirement could be much different than what you had pre-retirement. Don't forget to consider your health care costs. In certain countries, paying for health care from your own pocket or with private insurance is less expensive than in Australia. It's important not to underestimate your expenses as you now live, and hopefully enjoy, your retirement days. Then calculate how much income you'll be receiving once you stop-working full time. Add up all your guaranteed income, including from your investments, rents, interest on your savings, pension and so on. Compare your total income against your estimated expenses to see if you can cover at the very least your basic living expenses.

3. Get superannuation and tax advice

This subject is so important that we've written a separate article about it. Essentially you'll need to ensure that you receive a proper pension even though you're now living outside Australia. As an expatriate, you can be eligible for an "Outside Australia" pension. But keep in mind that this could be affected by factors like how much time you live overseas, changes to your income, and whether you're also receiving a pension from another country. However, if you are an Australian resident or permanent resident, your superannuation fund should remain under the same rules even if you're living overseas.

Ah taxes! Tax can become very complex now that you're living overseas because now you have to follow the regulations in both Australia and your new home country. Retiring overseas might affect how much tax you pay because different countries have different tax rules for non-citizen expatriates. And even if you're already living overseas, you can still owe taxes back home in Australia, depending on whether you're classified as an Australian or foreign resident. So it's best to get expert help and advice from expert tax consultants as part of your overseas retirement planning. They can help you make sure you avoid penalties for incorrectly reporting your income.

4. Consider visa and residency rules

Immigration, residency and visa laws are different for each country. For each country featured in this book, we've included essential information on how to retire there, what visas you will need to enter and live there, and incentives for retirees. Still it's definitely a good idea to do further research immigration laws in your chosen country to see if you can live there permanently or even work there if you want to.

As of the time of printing of this book, the COVID-19 pandemic still continues to affect many aspects of life, including immigration and visa processes. As of November 2021, Australia's borders are still closed to outgoing and incoming travellers. Assuming this situation persists in 2022, you could apply for a travel exemption because each country has different rules on foreign travellers and quarantine.

5. Check if you can purchase and own property

Last but not least, you need to sort out our living arrangements. We selected many of the countries featured in this book based on how affordable it is to buy a house or apartment there. But even if you could easily afford to buy property in your prospective new home country, check first if you can actually own property there. Some countries do not allow foreign ownership of real estate but do allow long term leases. And even if you can own property in your country of choice, don't be in a hurry to buy. Try renting first in the city or area you're planning to retire to, to see if it has the vibe you're looking for in your retirement. If you like living there, then you can start looking around for a property to buy.

FINANCIAL MATTERS
[pension, superannuation and more]

By now, we're sure you already know that retiring overseas is becoming a more attractive option for more and more Australians. According to some estimates, there were around 90,000 Australian overseas retirees in 2016 and that number is growing yearly. The 22 countries featured in this book are the most preferred destinations not just for Australian retirees but also retirees from other countries.

How does overseas retirement affect your Age Pension? Read these Frequently Asked Questions to find out.

Will you still receive the Age Pension when you're living overseas?

Yes you should still be able to access your Age Pension even if you're already living in another country. This will be paid at the "Outside Australia" rate, which means some of your entitlements could be affected. For a couple, this payment could amount to $34,767 per year and is subject to income, assets and eligibility rules.

Find out more about *payment rules, schedule and rates for people outside Australia* on Services Australia's (Centrelink) website: servicesaustralia.gov.au

Do you need to inform Centrelink that you're moving overseas?

Yes you will need to lodge your claim for the Age Pension locally with Centrelink, unless your new home country has a social security agreement with Australia. If you're already living in your new home country, that means you'll need to come back to Australia first. It's also important to investigate residency requirements in your new home country. Different countries will have different residency requirements.

Find out about rules on *getting the Age Pension outside Australia* and *which countries have an agreement with Australia* and how this could impact your Age Pension payments on Services Australia's (Centrelink) website: servicesaustralia.gov.au

Can you still access Medicare?

Access to affordable and excellent quality health care is one of the most important factors to consider in choosing an overseas retirement destination. We've included a section on this for each country featured in this book. You can of course take out international health insurance, but the cost could be prohibitive.

Medicare is a good, affordable option. And provided you remain an Australian resident for tax purposes, you can have access to government funded medical services in countries that have a reciprocal health care agreement with Australia. Note though that these agreements only cover essential medical treatments and differ across countries.

For more information about *Reciprocal Health Care Agreements, medicine costs, eligibility and receiving medical care when you're in another country,* visit servicesaustralia.gov.au

Can I rent out my home in Australia?

Retiring in another country is a massive decision because it means indefinitely living away from family and friends in Australia. But there are ways for you to experience actually living overseas without giving up pension benefits that you'd be receiving if you live in Australia. As long as you've lived in Australia for at least 35 years, you can live up to 6 months in another country and continue to receive your full pension.

As a result, you could spend 6 months of the year in your new home country and rent out your home in Australia while you're overseas. This helps pay for the expenses of your overseas travel and lets you keep your permanent home in Australia. But it's highly advisable to consult a financial planner or accountant specialising in retirement planning and superannuation to prepare for any tax and Age Pension implications of subletting your home (see number 3 in "Planning Your Retirement Overseas").

Owning a property overseas can help you meet residency requirements in some countries, deciding to buy a house or just rent one in your new home country will depend on your needs and circumstances (see number 5 in "Planning Your Retirement Overseas").

Index

A

About This Book iii

C

Centrelink 322

F

Financial aspects of overseas retirement 322

H

Healthcare 6
 Belize 94
 Cambodia 6
 Colombia 108
 Costa Rica 122
 Croatia 208
 Ecuador 136
 France 222
 Indonesia 20
 Italy 236
 Malaysia 34
 Malta 252
 Mexico 150
 Panama 165
 Peru 178
 Philippines 48
 Portugal 266
 Puerto Rico 192
 South Africa 296
 Spain 280
 Thailand 64
 Turkey 311
 Vietnam 78

I

Introduction, retiring in
 Belize 93

Cambodia 4
Colombia 106
Costa Rica 120
Croatia 206
Ecuador 134
France 220
Indonesia 18
Italy 234
Malaysia 32
Malta 250
Mexico 148
Panama 163
Peru 176
Philippines 46
Portugal 264
Puerto Rico 190
South Africa 294
Spain 278
Thailand 62
Turkey 309
Vietnam 76

L

LGBT environment in 12
 Belize 100
 Cambodia 12
 Colombia 114
 Costa Rica 128
 Croatia 215
 Ecuador 142
 France 229
 Indonesia 26
 Italy 244
 Malaysia 40
 Malta 258
 Mexico 156
 Panama 170
 Peru 184

Philippines 56
Portugal 272
Puerto Rico 198
South Africa 302
Spain 286
Thailand 70
Turkey 316
Vietnam 84

R

Reasons to Retire in Belize 92
 Climate 93
 Cost of Living 94
 Culture 93
 Food 96
 Housing 94
 Senior Discounts 100
 Summary 102
 Tax 95
 Work 95
Reasons to Retire in Cambodia 4
 Climate 5
 Cost of Living 5
 Food 7
 Housing 5
 Senior Discounts 12
 Summary 14
 Tax 7
 Work 7
Reasons to Retire in Colombia 106
 Climate 107
 Cost of Living 107
 Culture 107
 Food 110
 Housing 108
 Senior Discounts 115

INDEX

  Summary 116
  Tax 109
  Work 109
Reasons to Retire in
Costa Rica 120
  Climate 121
  Cost of Living 121
  Culture 121
  Food 123
  Housing 122
  Senior Discounts 128
  Summary 130
  Tax 123
  Work 123
Reasons to Retire in
Croatia 206
  Climate 207
  Cost of Living 207
  Culture 207
  Food 209
  Housing 208
  Senior Discounts 215
  Summary 216
  Tax 209
  Work 209
Reasons to Retire in
Ecuador 134
  Climate 135
  Cost of Living 135
  Culture 135
  Food 138
  Housing 136
  Senior Discounts 143
  Summary 144
  Tax 137
  Work 137
Reasons to Retire in
France 220
  Climate 221
  Cost of Living 221
  Culture 221
  Food 223
  Housing 222

  Senior Discounts 229
  Summary 230
  Tax 223
  Work 223
Reasons to Retire in
Indonesia 18
  Climate 19
  Cost of Living 19
  Culture 19
  Food 22
  Housing 20
  Senior Discounts 26
  Summary 28
  Tax 21
  Work 21
Reasons to Retire in Italy 234
  Climate 235
  Cost of Living 235
  Culture 235
  Food 238
  Housing 236
  Senior Discounts 244
  Summary 246
  Tax 237
  Work 237
Reasons to Retire in
Malaysia 32
  Climate 33
  Cost of Living 33
  Culture 33
  Food 35
  Housing 34
  Senior Discounts 41
  Summary 42
  Tax 35
  Work 34
Reasons to Retire in Malta 250
  Climate 251
  Cost of Living 251
  Culture 251
  Food 254
  Housing 252
  Senior Discounts 259

  Summary 260
  Tax 253
  Work 253
Reasons to Retire in
Mexico 148
  Climate 149
  Cost of Living 149
  Culture 149
  Food 151
  Housing 150
  Senior Discounts 156
  Summary 158
  Tax 151
  Work 151
Reasons to Retire in
Panama 162
  Climate 164
  Cost of Living 164
  Culture 163
  Food 166
  Housing 164
  Senior Discounts 171
  Summary 172
  Tax 166
  Work 166
Reasons to Retire in Peru 176
  Climate 177
  Cost of Living 177
  Culture 177
  Food 179
  Housing 178
  Senior Discounts 184
  Summary 186
  Tax 179
  Work 179
Reasons to Retire in
Portugal 264
  Climate 265
  Cost of Living 265
  Culture 265
  Food 268
  Housing 266
  Senior Discounts 272

Summary 274
Tax 267
Work 267
Reasons to Retire in Puerto Rico 190
 Climate 191
 Cost of Living 191
 Culture 191
 Food 194
 Housing 192
 Senior Discounts 198
 Summary 200
 Tax 193
 Work 193
Reasons to Retire in South Africa 294
 Climate 295
 Cost of Living 295
 Culture 295
 Food 298
 Housing 296
 Senior Discounts 302
 Summary 304
 Tax 297
 Work 297
Reasons to Retire in Spain 278
 Climate 279
 Cost of Living 279
 Culture 279
 Food 281
 Housing 280
 Senior Discounts 287
 Summary 288
 Tax 281
 Work 281
Reasons to Retire in Thailand 62
 Climate 63
 Cost of Living 63
 Culture 63
 Food 65
 Housing 63
 Senior Discounts 70

Summary 72
Tax 65
Work 64
Reasons to Retire in the Philippines 46
 Climate 47
 Cost of Living 47
 Culture 47
 Food 49
 Housing 48
 Senior Discounts 56
 Summary 58
 Tax 49
 Work 49
Reasons to Retire in Turkey 308
 Climate 310
 Cost of Living 310
 Culture 309
 Food 312
 Housing 310
 Senior Discounts 317
 Summary 318
 Tax 311
 Work 311
Reasons to Retire in Vietnam 76, 79
 Climate 77
 Cost of Living 77
 Culture 77
 Senior Discounts 84
 Summary 86
 Tax 78
 Work 78
Recommended Cities in Belize 97
 Ambergris Caye 98
 Cayo District 99
 Placencia 97
Recommended Cities in Cambodia 8
 Kampot 10
 Phnom Penh 9

Siem Reap 8
Sihanoukville 11
Recommended Cities in Colombia 111
 Cartagena 112
 Medellin 111
 Santa Marta 113
Recommended Cities in Costa Rica 125
 Arenal 126
 Central Pacific 127
 The Central Valley 125
Recommended Cities in Croatia 211
 Dubrovnik 213
 Pula 212
 Zadar 214
 Zagreb 211
Recommended Cities in Ecuador 139
 Cuenca 139
 Loja 141
 Quito 140
 Vilcabamba 142
Recommended Cities in France 224
 Bordeaux 227
 Lyon 224
 Montpellier 225
 Sarlat-la-Caneda 227
Recommended Cities in Indonesia 23
 Bali 24
 Lombok 23
 Yogyakarta 25
Recommended Cities in Italy 239
 Abruzzo 239
 Lazio 242
 Puglia 240
 Tuscany 241

INDEX

Recommended Cities in Malaysia 36
  Ipoh 39
  Kota Kinabalu 37
  Kuala Lumpur 36
  Penang 38
Recommended Cities in Malta 255
  Gozo 256
  Sliema 255
  St. Julian 256
Recommended Cities in Mexico 153
  Merida 153
  Puerto Vallarta 155
  San Miguel de Allende 154
Recommended Cities in Panama 167
  Bocas del Toro 167
  Panama City 169
  Pedasi 168
Recommended Cities in Peru 181
  Arequipa 181
  Lima 182
  Trujillo 183
Recommended Cities in Portugal 269
  Coimbra 271
  Porto 270
  The Algarve 269
Recommended Cities in Puerto Rico 195
  Central Mountains 195
  Ponce 197
  West Coast 196
Recommended Cities in South Africa 299
  Cape Town 299
  Stellenbosch 300
  The Garden Route District 301
Recommended Cities in Spain 283
  Bilbao 284
  Costa del Sol 283
  Granada 285
  San Sebastian 286
Recommended Cities in Thailand 66
  Bangkok 66
  Chiang Mai 67
  Phuket 69
Recommended Cities in the Philippines 50, 51
  Cebu 50
  Manila 53
  Palawan 54
  Pampanga 52
Recommended Cities in Turkey 313
  Ankara 314
  Antalya 315
  Istanbul 313
Recommended Cities in Vietnam 80
  Da Nang 81
  Hanoi 80
  Ho Chi Minh 81
  Nha Trang 83
  Vũng Tàu 83
Retirement Planning 320
Retirement Visa 6
  Belize 95
  Cambodia 6
  Colombia 109
  Costa Rica 122
  Croatia 209
  Ecuador 137
  France 222
  Indonesia 20
  Italy 237
  Malaysia 34
  Malta 253
  Mexico 151
  Panama 165
  Peru 178
  Philippines 48
  Portugal 267
  Puerto Rico 193
  South Africa 296
  Spain 280
  Thailand 64
  Turkey 311
  Vietnam 78

S

Superannuation 321, 322, 323

W

What to watch out for 13
  Belize 101
  Cambodia 13
  Colombia 115
  Costa Rica 129
  Croatia 215
  Ecuador 143
  France 229
  Indonesia 27
  Italy 245
  Malaysia 41
  Malta 259
  Mexico 157
  Panama 171
  Peru 185
  Philippines 57
  Portugal 273
  Puerto Rico 199
  South Africa 303
  Spain 287
  Thailand 71
  Turkey 317
  Vietnam 85

About the Real Skinny Guides

The Real Skinny guides are committed to giving you the "skinny" on all things interesting - true information about something that is not known by most people. You can trust the Real Skinny guides to give you only the truth and nothing but the whole truth on topics of interest to you.

Our Writers

Cindy Wong

Cindy pursued her education at the University of Hong Kong while working full-time in her corporate job. Having worked a decade in the travel industry, specializing in the Middle East, Central Asia, and Africa, her work allowed her to travel to over 50 countries, including Antarctica.

Cindy is now a full-time creative entrepreneur. She founded several businesses, including *8Letters Bookstore and Publishing*, aiming to boost the evolving Philippine indie author industry. Aside from offering indie publishing services to professionals and aspiring authors, *8Letters* nurtures a thriving writing community by conducting a monthly LitFest with author launches and writing workshops.

Passion Hustles is another project of hers that helps small businesses thrive by providing website design and web content. Her clients come from all parts of the world. As travel remains in her blood, *Exceptional Wanders* was born, while her latest start-up is *Tita's Lifestyle*, which provides helpful advice and supplies to "titas" in the Philippines. Cindy is also the author of several books, including *31st, Back in Santa Barbara, Embracing Uncertainties, One, Two, Sh*t, The Meatball Club,* and this book. She now resides in Siberia in her pursuit of more adventure and inspiring stories to write.

Jonathan Temporal

Jonathan is a lawyer, university professor and author (his published books are Nephilim, a novel published in 2016 and *WriteTech*, a motivational self-help book published in 2020). One of his big dreams is to start his own publishing house, which he did in 2020 when he started Temporal House in Sydney, Australia. The *Real Skinny Guides* are published by, and Real Skinny books is an imprint of, Temporal House. He is also an Australian immigration lawyer who advises clients on how to move to, live and retire in Australia. His experience in that role, and the fact that he himself is an immigrant to Australia from the Philippines (one of the countries featured in this book) inspired him to publish the first *Real Skinny Guide to the Top 22 Countries to Retire*.

Credits and Acknowledgments

> While the authors and the Real Skinny Guides have taken all reasonable care in preparing this book, we make no warranties about the accuracy or completeness of its contents and, to the maximum extent allowed, disclaim all liability arising from its use.

All rights reserved. No part of this publication may be copied, stored in a retrieval system, or transmitted in any form by any means, electronic, mechanic, recording or otherwise, except brief extracts for the purposes of review, and no part of this publication may be sold or hired, without the written permission of the publisher.

Published by RealSkinny Books (an imprint of Temporal House)
ISBN 978-0-6450587-7-2
First edition - January 2022
(c) Temporal House 2022
Printed in China
Cover, interior design and typesetting by Florencio Ares (aresjun@gmail.com)

Photographs (c) as indicated below

Location / page no.	Credits
Front cover	
Top	Top: Photo by Jeremy Banks on Unsplash
Middle	Photo by Nathan Dumlao on Unsplash
Bottom	Image ID: 90312320 copyright: stockbroker, puchased from 123rf.com
Back cover	
Top	Photo by Chad Montano on Unsplash
Middle	Photo by Taryn Elliott from Pexels
Bottom	Photo by Claudette Bleijenbergon Unsplash
ii	Photo by Rolands Varsbergs on Unsplash
1-2	Photo by Kim Eang Eng on Unsplash
4	Photo by Pou Neang on Unsplash
11	Photo by S. Ratanak on Unsplash
12-13	Photo by Vicky T on Unsplash
15	Photo by Neath So on Unsplash
16-17	Photo by Cassie Gallegos on Unsplash
22	Photo by Janesfairytale on Unsplash
25	Photo by Ern Gan on Unsplash
26	Photo by Anggit Rizkianto on Unsplash
27	Photo by Ruben Hutabarat on Unsplash
29	Photo by Cok Wisnu on Unsplash
30-31	Photo by Marc Wieland on Unsplash
34	Photo by Jeremy tan on Unsplash
39	Photo by Ash Edmonds on Unsplash
43	Photo by Deva Darshan on Unsplash
44-45	Photo by Laurentiu Morariu on Unsplash
46	Photo by Kromatos from Pexels
50	Photo by Alessandra Sio on Unsplash
51	Photo by Bas van Wylick on Unsplash
53	Photo by Gerald Escamos on Unsplash
55	Photo by Kaspars Upmanis on Unsplash
56	Photo by Ej Agumbay from Pexels
57	Photo by Assy Gerez on Unsplash
59	Photo by Avel Chuklanov on Unsplash
60-61	Photo by Syed Ahmad on Unsplash
62	Photo by sippakorn yamkasikorn on Unsplash
70	Photo by Mos Sukjaroenkraisri on Unsplash
71	Photo by Mukiibi John Elijah on Unsplash
73	Photo by Tom Bixler on Unsplash
74-75	Photo by David Emrich on Unsplash
76	Photo by Katherine McCormack on Unsplash
79	Photo by Vy Huynh on Unsplash
82 (left)	Photo by Toomas Tartes on Unsplash
82 (right)	Photo by Nguyen Dang Hoang Nhu on Unsplash
85	Photo by Steffen B. on Unsplash
87	Photo by David Emrich on Unsplash
88	Photo by Dennis Schrader on Unsplash
90-91	Image ID: 93244687 copyright: mathess, puchased from 123rf.com
92	Photo by Meritt Thomas on Unsplash
94	Photo by Meritt Thomas on Unsplash
99	Photo by Nathan Shurr on Unsplash
101	Photo by David Todd McCarty on Unsplash
103	Photo by Meritt Thomas on Unsplash
104	Photo by Saul Mercado on Unsplash
109	Photo by Leandro Loureiro on Unsplash
115	Photo by Daniel Vargas on Unsplash
117	Photo by Ricardo Gomez Angel on Unsplash
118-119	Photo by Adrian Eriksson on Unsplash
120	Photo by Zachary Shea on Unsplash
129	Photo by Tenerife Photographer from Pexels
131	Photo by Ashly Araya on Unsplash
132-133	Photo by Andrés Medina on Unsplash
134	Photo by Andrea Leon on Unsplash
137	Photo by Dayan Quinteros on Unsplash
138	Photo by Andrés Medina on Unsplash
145	Photo by Alexander Schimmeck on Unsplash
146-147	Photo by Roman Lopez on Unsplash
148	Photo by Julieta Julieta on Unsplash
152	Photo by Nadine Primeau on Unsplash
156	Photo by Jezael Melgoza on Unsplash
157	Photo by Roberto Carlos Roman Don on Unsplash
159	Photo by Laurentiu Morariu on Unsplash
160-161	Photo by Julianna Arjes on Unsplash
162	Photo by Ignacio Hernandez on Unsplash
165	Photo by Camilo Pinaud on Unsplash

Page	Credit
173	Photo by Benjamin Achrainer from Pexels
174-175	Photo by Adrian Dascal on Unsplash
176	Photo by Willian Justen de Vasconcellos on Unsplash
179	Photo by Deb Dowd on Unsplash
180	Photo by Pirata Studio Film on Unsplash
181	Photo by Adrian Dascal Film on Unsplash
184 (left)	Photo by Deb Dowd on Unsplash
184 (right)	Photo by Eduardo Flores on Unsplash
185	Photo by Willian Justen de Vasconcellos on Unsplash
187	Photo by Janaya Dasiuk on Unsplash
188-189	Photo by Zixi Zhou on Unsplash
190	Photo by Luis Santiago on Unsplash
193	Photo by Ruoyu Li on Unsplash
197	Photo by Sonder Quest on Unsplash
198 (left)	Photo by Feisdra on Unsplash
198 (right)	Photo by Michael Cox on Unsplash
199	Photo by Sonder Quest on Unsplash
201	Photo by Alex George on Unsplash
202	Photo by Archana Reddy on Unsplash
204-205	Photo by Patricia Jekki on Unsplash
206	Photo by Ivan Ivankovic on Unsplash
210	Photo by Geio Tischler on Unsplash
217	Photo by June 媛君 Liu on Unsplash
218-219	Photo by Paul Rysz on Unsplash
220	Photo by Léonard Cotte on Unsplash
226	Photo by Paul Hanaoka on Unsplash
231	Photo by on Anthony DELANOIX Unsplash
232-233	Photo by Rebe Adelaida on Unsplash
234	Photo by Jakub Kapusnak on Unsplash
235	Photo by Calum Lewis on Unsplash
237	Photo by Damiano Baschiera on Unsplash
241	Photo by Paul Postema on Unsplash
243	Photo by David Köhler on Unsplash
244	Photo by Christopher Czermak on Unsplash
245	Photo by Ruslan Bardash on Unsplash
247	Photo by Igor Oliyarnik on Unsplash
248-249	Photo by CALIN STAN on Unsplash
255	Photo by Mike Nahlii on Unsplash
257	Photo by Nick Fewings on Unsplash
258	Photo by Orimi Protograph on Unsplash
261	Photo by Sara Cardoso on Unsplash
262-263	Photo by Paulo Evangelista on Unsplash
264	Photo by Liam McKay on Unsplash
272	Photo by Lisa from Pexels
273	Photo by Vita Marija Murenaite on Unsplash
275	Photo by Ricardo Resende on Unsplash
276-277	Photo by Igor Oliyarnik on Unsplash
282	Photo by martin becker on Unsplash
285	Photo by Claudette Bleijenberg on Unsplash
287	Photo by San Fermin Pamplona - Navarra on Unsplash
289	Photo by Stéphan Valentin on Unsplash
290	Photo by Taryn Elliott from Pexels
292-293	Photo by Jaman Asad on Unsplash
295	Photo by Phillip Goldsberry on Unsplash
296	Photo by L.Steward Masweneng on Unsplash
297	Photo by STIL on Unsplash
302	Photo by Shashank Kumar on Unsplash
303	Photo by George Brits on Unsplash
305	Photo by Arthur Hickinbotham on Unsplash
306-307	Photo by Andrea Leopardi on Unsplash
308	Photo by svklimkin on Unsplash
309	Photo by Charbel Aoun on Unsplash
311	Photo by Despina Galani on Unsplash
317	Photo by Marvin Meyer on Unsplash
318	Photo by Alex Azabache on Unsplash